Meet Me at the Commons

A Field Guide to the Common Core Standards in Higher Education

Edited by Dorie Combs & Ginni Fair

NEW FORUMS

NEW FORUMS PRESS INC.

Published in the United States of America
by New Forums Press, Inc.1018 S. Lewis St.
Stillwater, OK 74074
www.newforums.com

Copyright © 2015 by New Forums Press, Inc.

All rights reserved. No part of this publication may be reproduced or transmitted in any form or by any means, electronic or mechanical, including photocopy, or any information storage or retrieval system, without permission in writing from the publisher.

Library of Congress Cataloging-in-Publication Data Pending

This book may be ordered in bulk quantities at discount from New Forums Press, Inc., P.O. Box 876, Stillwater, OK 74076 [Federal I.D. No. 73 1123239]. Printed in the United States of America.

ISBN 10: 1-58107-278-3
ISBN 13: 978-1-58107-278-5

Cover design by Katherine Dollar.

Table of Contents

Introduction v

1. Academic Freedom at the Crossroads 1
   Dorie Combs

2. Whose standards are these? A Chronological Glossary of standards in P-12 Education 15
   Richard Day

3. The Power of Collaboration: Faculty Learning Communities as a Vehicle for Professional Development 31
   Faye Deters & Krista Althauser

4. Finding Common Ground in the Core: Getting to know the standards 43
   Ginni Fair

5. Next Generation Science Standards (NGSS), general education and teacher preparation 71
   Rico Tyler, Kerrie McDaniel, Martha M. Day, and Sam Evans

6. It's Going to Get Messy: A Step by side-stepping process to align course Student Learning Outcomes, instructional strategies, and assessment practices with common standards 103
   Ginni Fair

7. So That's the Problem: Why literacy standards matter in general education 147
   Gill Hunter

8. Teacher Education – Standards at a whole new level 167
   Karen Kidwell and Saundra Hamon

9. Assessment and the Common Core 179
   Shannon Gilkey and Cody Davidson

10. Creativity to the Core! How the CCSS can promote
    critical and creative thinking 195
    Dorie Combs

11. What's next? The Promise for our Children's Future 215
    Terry Holliday

About the Authors 231

Introduction

Charlie Sweet and Hal Blythe

As we write this Introduction, America sits one year out from the national election of 2016. One potential Republican candidate, former Florida governor Jeb Bush, has become a political lightning rod because of his defense of the Common Core State Standards (CCSS) inside a party where such support is rare.

The Bush situation is a microcosm of the CCSS problem. In Chapter 2 Richard Day notes how the Obama administration's attempts to link federal Race to the Top (RTTT) grants to a previously voluntary effort birthed political lightning.

That the CCSS is now a political problem is reason alone to read *Meet Me at the Commons*. Every faculty member, both K-12 and higher education, needs to understand the realities of what the standards are, their importance, the myths about them that have grown up, and even the political aura around them in order to make an informed decision. For, against, or neutral, you must know the facts.

The authors of this book guide you down the road to the standards and how implementation of a state-mandated seamless transition between K-12 and higher education was achieved at a university. One detail looms as most important. *Meet Me at the Commons* is not a compilation of detached observations from researchers. The authors have become experts, who underwent this process over a three-year period.

And we can vouch for this authenticity. We were there with them for the journey, sitting on the same Professional Leraning Communities (PLCs) and implementing the CCSS.

But perhaps the ultimate worth of this volume is not its authenticity, but its adaptability. In Kentucky, we had no choice—the state legislature told us to implement this seamless transition. Other states may or may not have a choice, but at least they won't have to trek through the unknown and poorly marked forest.

Want to know how CCSS came about? Read Richard Day's detailed timeline of its genesis in Chapter 2.

Want to learn an effective method of implementing this seamless transition from secondary to post-secondary education? Try Deters and Althauser's explanation in Chapter 3 of how the process of embedded professional learning communities (PLCs) works.

Concerned about how the entire process relates to student learning outcomes, the darling of the assessment forces? Fair warns you in Chapter 6 it's going to get messy, but it can be done.

Worried that adoption of the CCSS will destroy creative and critical thinking? Examine Combs' analysis and recommendations in Chapter 10.

Other chapters explain just how specific-area PLCs, such as those in Teacher Education and the Arts and Sciences, functioned. General education and assessment also receive excellent coverage.

And this book presents the material in the hallmark fashion of New Forums imprints—clear and straight-forward language, solid evidence, and reader-friendly organization.

Whether you are a faculty member or an administrator, the book will provide you with knowledge of the fundamental and powerful concepts orbiting around CCSS. To paraphrase Socrates, the unexamined argument is not worth having.

Chapter 1

Academic Freedom at the Crossroads: Why should faculty support Common Core State Standards?

Dorie Combs

> Right now, the pieces of high school and higher education are not fitting. But the new college- and career-ready standards present an opportunity for states to reexamine and rebuild the connection. To prepare students to succeed in college and beyond, the spirit of these standards—alignment—needs to go to college as well (Tepe, 2014, p.3).

In the summer of 2014 three state university system Chancellors implored higher education to join Higher Education for Higher Standards, a coalition to support the Common Core State Standards (CCSS) (Kirwin, White, & Zimpher, 2014). The chief officers of over 240 colleges and universities from 36 states and eight national higher education professional organizations have since signed on in support of this coalition. The CCSS were initially completed in 2009 and have been adopted by 43 states, the District of Columbia and several territories, but five years later, little impact has been felt in higher education (Common Core State Standards Initiative, 2014).

The road to the Common Core has not been built in a straightforward, progressive direction. Unlike the Oregon Trail, this road wasn't built as the travelers moved toward their destination. Nor has it been built like the first Transcontinental Railroad, starting simultaneously at the beginning and at the end, then meeting in the middle. This road started near the end, though not in collaboration or close communication with those the standards developers were hoping to reach.

The CCSS were born out of widespread concern that high school students were entering college and the workplace woefully unprepared. Nationally, only 20.5% of high school 9th graders graduate from high school and complete a four year degree in six years (NCHEMS, 2014). For ten years, the National Governor's Association, the Council of Chief State School Officers, and Achieve, Inc. led education and content specialists through a process of defining English language arts and mathematics "college and career readiness" knowledge and skills, then "back mapped" these standards all the way to kindergarten.

Now, even with the political upheavals surrounding the CCSS, most states are moving forward on this new Common Core expressway with a great sense that there is an educational El Dorado at the end of the road. Unfortunately, higher education is not creating an exit ramp at their end of the road.

Why align with the Common Core standards?

If the CCSS are to advance college and career readiness, higher education has to be in the loop. Most urgently, teacher preparation programs must ensure that all pre-service teachers have mastered the knowledge and skill set for the grade levels and subjects they will be licensed to teach. But equally as important, all current and prospective teachers must be prepared to teach these new standards, as well. These standards are not about piling on more facts, but developing a student's knowledge and skills to support critical and creative thinking, problem-solving, and analytical skills. While neither the Common Core nor the Next Generation Science Standards (NGSS) specify instructional methods per se, these standards are likely to generate significant shifts in pedagogical practice (Alberti, 2012). For example, in order to move students to analyzing complex texts, teachers are incorporating "close reading" strategies, and teachers of mathematics are putting more emphasis on mathematical practices and problem solving. The goals of aligning content knowledge and pedagogy require substantial change not only in teacher education programs and courses, but also in the content classes, taught primarily in the Colleges of Arts and Sciences.

By the same token, the CCSS should result in changes for all students entering college. "A real P-20 system, one covering preschool through graduate school, would have curriculums that line up. And if the Common Core prepares students better, or even differently, 100-level courses in math, English and language arts should be changed to pick up where high school left off," (Nelson, 2013, para. 58). College courses should facilitate their students' continued learning and readiness for a career and / or further post-baccalaureate success.

The job of college faculty is no longer to weed out the unprepared, immature, or even the irresponsible students, but to meet all students where they are and help them succeed. Our goal is student success and retention – not failure. It is time for college faculty to realize that we are no longer gate keepers who rank our students and then set limits to the number who can advance. We all share responsibility for our students' success. College faculty are part of an academic relay team, carrying students forward, then passing them on to the next member of the team.

All of us, teacher education and content faculty, prepare future teachers in pedagogy as well as content knowledge and skills. Teachers emulate the pedagogy they experienced as college students when they teach. Some of their students come to college, some better prepared than others. A portion of these graduate, start their careers and lives; a small percentage go on to graduate school; others become teachers. Most become parents and encourage their children to be learners. The cycle continues (see Figure 1.1). We reap the academic seeds we sow.

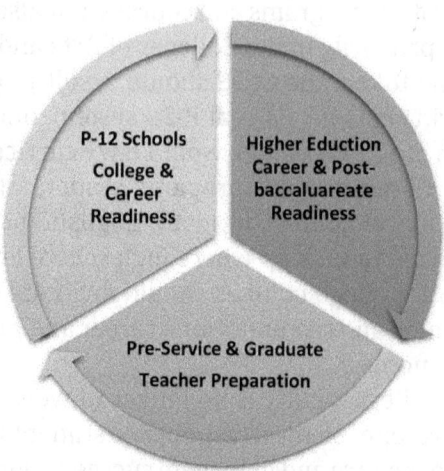

Figure 1.1. The P-20 education cycle describes the connections among the p-12 education system, higher education, and teacher preparation.

Full implementation of the Common Core Standards could significantly alter higher education as we know it. These changes could "Transform dual enrollment programs, placement tests, and remediation. They could force colleges within state systems, and even across states, to agree on what it means to be 'college ready,' and to work alongside K-12 to help students who are unprepared for college before they graduate from high school. In the long run, it could force changes in credit-bearing courses too, to better align with what students are supposed to have mastered by high school graduation," (Nelson, 2013, para. 5).

With higher education administration in support of the CCSS, the pressure to align college courses will soon follow. Accrediting bodies, especially the Council for the Accreditation of Educator Preparation (CAEP), will require that institutions with teacher preparation programs demonstrate that teacher education courses and content courses are aligned to the standards. In some states, education agencies collaborate with higher education governing bod-

Where, then, do we draw the academic freedom line between program accreditation standards and an individual faculty member's knowledge and expertise?

ies or even state legislatures to enforce alignment. Kentucky's Senate Bill 1 of 2009 is one example. This innovative legislation required the Commissioner of Education and the President of the Council on Postsecondary Education to collaborate to revise elementary and secondary standards and align those with postsecondary standards (Kentucky Department of Education, 2009).

Where, then, do we draw the academic freedom line between program accreditation standards and an individual faculty member's knowledge and expertise? To what degree should professional accrediting bodies, government agencies, or even learned societies prescribe the content and skills that should be taught? These are questions that should and do concern higher education faculty. After all, faculty are responsible for developing and communicating the most recent research and knowledge base in their fields of expertise. On the other hand, learned societies and professional organizations represent scholarship and oversee the peer review process in most collegiate programs, especially those leading to professional licensure (i.e., the Association to Advance Collegiate Schools of Business, Commission on Accreditation of Athletic Training Education, Commission on Collegiate Nursing Education, National Association of Schools of Music, and Council for the Accreditation of Educator Preparation).

Public higher education institutions serve at the will of state and local governments, who represent tax-paying citizens. This isn't a straight, hard "line in the sand." Like the path of a river, the line between academic freedom and standards curves in and around the perfect curriculum, adjusting to currents and seasonal pressures. Faculty in public institutions should provide leadership in responding to society's needs while defending scholarship against political and religious pressures, as opposed to promoting particular viewpoints.

> *Like the path of a river, the line between academic freedom and standards curves in and around the perfect curriculum, adjusting to currents and seasonal pressures.*

Why The Common Core State Standards?

Why should we align to the Common Core Standards when some states are now rejecting them? The CCSS represent both a non-partisan political endeavor as well as a collaborative effort to meet the readiness needs for success in postsecondary education and employment. These are "state" standards, as the development was organized by the National Governor's Association and the Council of Chief State School Officers, both of which are non-partisan and include representatives of all U.S. States and territories. Teachers, principals, superintendents, content experts (including higher education faculty), the National Education Association (NEA), the American Federation of Teachers (AFT), the National Council of Teachers of Mathematics (NCTM), and the National Council of Teachers of English (NCTE), among other organizations, participated in the development of the standards. Contrary to what some presume, the CCSS are not mandated by the U.S. Department of Education, but must be adopted (or rescinded) by individual states.

Regardless of the specific standards adopted by a particular state, the ultimate goal of college and career readiness means that the similarities among state P-12 standards are going to be greater than the differences. Each higher education institution should identify its place and ultimate responsibility in the P-20 education cycle, whether that is focused on Common Core State Standards, your own state's "non-Common Core" or a more national or even international focus. Then, it must encourage faculty to collaborate to align and map the standards forward.

> *...standards alignment should be developed from the "bottom up" – by those who will actually implement the changes in curriculum - as opposed to top down.*

The Faculty, who are the content experts, do have legitimate concerns about academic freedom. For this reason, standards alignment should be developed from the "bottom up" – by those who will actually implement the changes in curriculum - as opposed to top down. Faculty would be advised to take charge of the alignment process, or a forced alignment will take charge of the faculty.

Today's students and the future of our economy and our democracy depend on significant reforms both in K-12 education *and* higher education. Working together, schools and colleges can prepare students with the learning they need to meet new challenges and solve unscripted problems in every sphere of their lives—personal, economic, civic, democratic, global, and environmental. (Schneider, as cited in *Association of American Colleges and Universities,* 2014, para. 2)

References

Alberti, S. (2012). Making the shifts. *Educational Leadership. 70*(4). 24-27.

Association of American Colleges and Universities. (2014). AAC&U joins multi-state coalition of higher education leaders mobilizing in support of common core standards. [Press release]. American Association of Colleges and Universities. Retrieved from http://www.aacu.org/press/press-releases/aacu-joins-multi-state-coalition-higher-education-leaders-mobilizing-support

Kirwan, W, White, T., & Zimpher, N. (June 10, 2014). Use the Common Core, use it widely, use it well. *The Chronical of Higher Education.* Retrieved from http://chronicle.com/article/Use-the-Common-Core-Use-It/147007/

Kentucky Department of Education. (2009). Kentucky Senate Bill 1 highlights, KRS 164.020 Section 13. Retrieved from http://education.ky.gov/comm/ul/documents/senate%20bill%201%20highlights.pdf

National Governors Association Center for Best Practices, Council of Chief State School Officers. (2014). Common Core State Standards: Standards in your state. National Governors Association Center for Best Practices, Council of Chief State School Officers: Washington D.C. Retrieved from http://www.corestandards.org/standards-in-your-state/.

NCHEMS (2014). Student pipeline - transition and completion rates from 9th grade to college. Retrieved from http://www.higheredinfo.org/dbrowser/?year=2002&level=nation&mode=data&state=0&submeasure=119

Nelson, L. (2013). The Common Core on campus. *Inside Higher Ed.* Retrieved from https://www.insidehighered.com/news/2013/05/03/common-core-curriculum-k-12-could-have-far-reaching-effects-higher-education

Tepe, L. (2014) Common Core goes to college: Building better connections between high school and higher education. New America Foundation: Washington, D.C. Retrieved from *http://www.newamerica.net/sites/newamerica.net/files/policydocs/CCGTC_7_18_2pm.pdf*

Chapter 2

Whose Standards Are These? A Brief Historical Timeline of the Development of the Common Core State Standards with References to Next General Science Standards, and the C3 Framework for Social Studies.

Richard Day

The elementary and secondary education system was created in the early 1900s to serve a different time when people had different needs. Although the idea of human capital is as old as education itself, the concept of college readiness was hardly a concern when access to college was limited to a relatively few privileged individuals who had the wherewithal to attend. Illiteracy was seen as the state's educational problem. There was no concern that high school graduation rates were too low at a time when very few jobs required knowledge workers. Most students would grow up to work on the farm, in a factory, or in a business. The dominant model of the school was as a sorting machine. If an individual student failed academically he was said to have wasted his opportunity, and the consequences were seen as the student's own fault. But while school failure might relegate a student to a life of manual labor, there were industrial jobs to be had. Indeed, one of the purposes of American high schools from 1920 to the 1940s was an attempt to remove youth from the labor market (Harrison & Klotter, 1997; Spring, 2010). School reform in the early 20th century was largely focused on the development of the American high school (and somewhat separate efforts at vocational education, as with the Smith-Hughes Act of 1917) and were dominated by the prevailing progressive impulse to bring educated elites to the task of improving social conditions in the nation. But by mid-century, nearly every state had compulsory attendance laws, teachers were required to earn a four-year degree, school administration had been removed from patronage-hungry trustees and placed in the hands of professionals, and most young people were earning the coveted high school diploma (Peterson, 1995). But the rise of the Cold War following World War II, and concurrent scientific advancements, brought a new urgency to the task of raising graduation standards. It began with a beep heard around the world.

- **1957: The Soviet Union launched Sputnik**. Despite the fact that the satellite, a 23-inch silver ball with whiskers, was relatively simple, compared to the satellites that would follow, its beeping radio signal quickly galvanized the nation. Not only had the Soviets beat the United States into space, but it became clear that they possessed the technology to launch nuclear bombs. The nation awoke to the need to improve the schools.
- **1958:** In response to the Soviet launch of Sputnik, the Eisenhower administration passed the **National Defense Education Act** which called for higher academic standards.
- **1959:** President Dwight D. Eisenhower suggested that national academic standards were needed (Layton, 2014).
- **1965:** The **Elementary and Secondary Education Act was passed**.
- **1966:** The **Coleman Report**, a massive study officially titled, Equality of Educational Opportunity, was commissioned by the Civil Rights Act of 1964. The 700-page study created shock waves when it found that family background factors had a greater bearing on school performance than did school effects. The report's suggestion that African American students benefitted from non-segregated classrooms served as a catalyst for busing.
- **1968:** In *McInnis v. Shapiro*, **293 F. Supp. 327** (1968), the first fiscal equalization case to make it all the way to the U S Supreme

Court, plaintiffs argued that under the 14th Amendment's equal protection clause, funds should be distributed based on educational need. But they were unable to help the court devise discoverable and manageable standards by which the court could determine when the Constitution is satisfied, and when it is violated. Plaintiffs began looking for a set of judicially manageable standards that could be used to determine whether a state had met its obligation to provide equitable schools for its children (Day, 2003).

- **1973:** The U. S. Supreme Court rejected 14th Amendment arguments altogether in ***San Antonio Independent School District v Rodriguez,* 411 U. S. 1** (1973), creating a new wave of cases based on education clauses in state constitutions (Day, 2003).
- **1983:** President Ronald Reagan's National Commission on Education published its catalytic report, **A Nation at Risk: The Imperative for Educational Reform** (ANAR). The report was a response to the freewheeling reforms of the 1960s and early 1970s (which sought to free the children, challenge authority, and focus on social justice issues) and decried **"a rising tide of mediocrity"** in American high schools (National Commission on Excellence in Education, 1983, para. 1). While the report's statistics were disputed, the nation's attention was galvanized around the idea that American schools were failing and the era of school accountability was born. The Commission made findings in four areas: content, expectations, time, and teaching. In the area of content, the commission recommended an examination of curriculum standards in light of other advanced countries and higher college admission standards. While shocking at the time, the vision of school reform as drawn by ANAR was mild compared to the 21st century vision that would develop around President George W. Bush's No Child Left Behind eighteen years later. ANAR called on states and the nation to craft genuine curriculum standards and strengthen high school graduation standards. "Far from being a revolutionary document, the report was an impassioned plea to make our schools function better in their core mission as academic institutions and to make our education system live up to our nation's ideals" (Ravitch, 2010, pp. 22-26).
- **1985:** In Kentucky, an equally influential contribution to the

policy dialogue had come from the Prichard Committee on Academic Excellence with the publication of ***The Path to a Larger Life: Creating Kentucky's Educational Future.*** The Prichard Committee saw "Education [as] a seamless web running from the earliest years through the highest levels of educational achievement" and called for a more direct connection between secondary and postsecondary education in the form of a set of curriculum standards that anchored a high school diploma to entry-level college standards (Prichard Committee, 1990, p. xiii). Prichard pushed for the publication of school goals, the "identification of the competencies expected of all Kentucky high school graduates," measurement of "the mastery of these competencies," and assuring that a diploma is only awarded "when the student demonstrates that he or she has mastered the desired competencies..." (Prichard Committee, 1990, p. 32).

- **1989:** The **National Center on Education and the Economy** (NCEE) published their highly influential report, **America's choice: High skills or low wages!** which called for a new set of national educational performance standards to be benchmarked to the highest educational standards in the world and met by American students by age 16. Many states began enacting policies recommended by NCEE (National Center on Education and the Economy, 1990).
- **1989: Kentucky** drew national attention when its Supreme Court declared the entire system of schools to be unconstitutional in ***Rose v Council for Better Education***, **790 S. W. 2d 186**, (1989). The Rose court accepted a standards-based rationale for determining whether the state had met its constitutional obligation, and that launched another wave of school reform litigation based on both *equity* and *adequacy* claims as expressed in state constitutions (Day, 2011).
- **1989: President George H. W. Bush invited the nation's governors to an education summit**, where influential AFT President Albert Shanker urged them to begin creating a national system of high standards and rigorous assessments with real consequences. Arkansas Governor Bill Clinton took charge of the governors' effort to draft **national goals for the year 2000,** a major policy shift away from keeping students in school without any real standards of achievement.
- **1990:** In response to the Rose decision, the **Kentucky Gen-**

eral Assembly** passed the nation's most ambitious statewide school reform package, the **Kentucky Education Reform Act of 1990** (KERA) (Day, 2011; Guskey & Oldham, 1997). Arguably, KERA's most powerful feature was the advent of a new kind of high-stakes accountability system based on student achievement outcomes (test scores). The old method of reporting only school-wide means concealed the substandard performance of as much as a third or more of the student population. The new data, disaggregated into subgroup performance, revealed those short-comings and changed the way educators talked about student success. The public reporting of student test score data by subgroups, along with the ranking of schools – a contribution of the news media - proved to be a powerful tool for driving change in this new era of *high-stakes* assessment. The promise of *equality of educational opportunity* that had guided American schools for a century was effectively replaced by a new goal – *equity of student achievement outcomes* (Day & Ewalt, 2014).

- **1993:** Separately, the National Research Council issued a set of **national science standards**, and the American Association for the Advancement of Science published its **Benchmarks for Science Literacy** (U.S. Department of Education, 2010). The Carnegie Corporation of New York and the Institute for Advanced Study published *The Opportunity Equation* calling for a common set of science standards (National Research Council, 2012).

- **1994:** President Bill Clinton's effort to create voluntary national standards fell apart when history standards, which included social justice issues, were attacked by conservative groups as the epitome of left-wing political correctness (in Ravitch, 2010, pp. 16-22). Clinton backed away from national standards and provided funding under his **Goals 2000** program for states to write their own standards, pick their own tests, and be accountable for achievement (Ravitch, 2010).

- **1996:** The **National Governor's Association**, in concert with corporate leaders, created **Achieve, Inc.**, an independent, bipartisan, nonprofit education reform organization based in Washington D. C. that focused its efforts on helping states raise academic standards and graduation requirements, and

strengthen accountability (American Diploma Project, 2011).
- **2001:** Achieve sponsored a **National Education Summit** and joined with the Education Trust, the Thomas B. Fordham Institute, and the National Alliance of Business to launch the **American Diploma Project** (ADP) to identify the *must-have* knowledge and skills most demanded by higher education and employers.
- **2001:** When President George W. Bush signed the bipartisan **No Child Left Behind Act** into law, a new definition of school reform became nationalized, one characterized by accountability (Ravitch, 2010). The Act required states to test every child annually in Grades 3 – 8 in reading and math and report disaggregated test scores. This reauthorization of the Elementary and Secondary Education Act was built upon a standards-based reform whose roots were found in policy responses to *A Nation at Risk* (Kaestle, 2006). Nationally, there was concern over the "vast differences in educational expectations [that] existed across the states" (Conley, 2014, p. 1).
- **2004:** The American Diploma Project (ADP) published, **Ready or not: Creating a high school diploma that counts** which described "specific content and skills in English and mathematics graduates must master by the time they leave high school if they expect to succeed in postsecondary education or high-performance, high-growth jobs." The standards were said to be "considerably more rigorous than [the existing] high school standards" (American Diploma Project, 2007, p. 7).
- **2005:** At the **National Education Summit on high schools** that year, governors from 45 states joined with business leaders and education officials to address a critical problem in American education – that too few students were graduating from high school prepared to meet the demands of college and careers in an increasingly competitive global economy. The result was ADP's creation of a set of benchmarks that were proposed as anchors for other states' high school standards-based assessments and graduation requirements. ADP identified an important convergence around the core knowledge and skills that both colleges and employers – within and beyond ADP states – require (American Diploma Project, 2004). The American Diploma Project set five goals and the criteria against which

participating states were measured to determine if the goal had been met:

1. **Common Standards** – The criteria are met if the standards' writing process is guided by the expectations of the state's postsecondary and business communities, if those communities verify that the resulting standards articulate the knowledge and skills required for success in college and the workplace, and if an external organization verifies the standards' alignment to college- and career-ready expectations (American Diploma Project, 2011).
2. **Graduation Requirements** – High school graduates need to complete a challenging course of study in mathematics that includes the content typically taught through an Algebra II course (or its equivalent) and four years of grade-level English aligned with college- and career-ready standards (American Diploma Project, 2011).
3. **Assessments** – States must have a component of their high school assessment system that measures students' mastery of college- and career-ready content in English and mathematics. The assessment must have credibility with postsecondary institutions and employers such that a certain score indicates readiness (American Diploma Project, 2011).
4. **P-20 Data Systems** – States must have unique student identifiers to track each student through and beyond the K-12 system and must have "overcome all barriers to matching" and have "the capacity to match longitudinal student-level records between K-12 and postsecondary, and matches these records at least annually" (American Diploma Project, 2011, p. 18).
5. **Accountability Systems** – States must value and reward the number of students who earn a college- and career-ready diploma, score college-ready on high school assessments, and enter college without the need for remediation (American Diploma Project, 2011).

- **2006:** ACT's report, **Reading between the lines** argued that there are high costs ($16 billion per year in lost productivity and remediation) associated with students not being ready for college level reading and suggested that students were actually losing momentum during high school, that poor readers struggle, are frequently blocked from advanced work, that low literacy levels prevent mastery of other subjects, and is commonly cited as a reason for dropping out (ACT, 2006). NAEP reading results from 1971-2004 showed average reading scores for 9-year-olds were the highest on record but scores for 13-year-olds had risen only slightly since 1975. Reading scores for 17-year-olds, however, had actually dropped five points between 1992-2004 (Perie, Moran, & Lutkus, 2005).

- **2007:** The **National Center for Educational Statistics (NCES)** issued a report that established the lack of any continuity among the various state accountability systems. Under the provisions of the bipartisan No Child Left Behind Act (NCLB), states were required to report annually the percentages of students achieving proficiency in reading and mathematics for grades 3 through 8. But the law allowed each state to select the tests and set the proficiency standards by which it determines whether the state has met its adequate yearly progress (AYP) goals. The NCES report revealed that proficiency standards varied so much from state to state that comparisons were impossible. Students in states where cut scores for proficiency had been set low appeared to be achieving at remarkable rates. But when the performance in these states was mapped against the estimate of students achieving a "proficient" rating on the National Assessment of Educational Progress (NAEP), there were substantial differences found. The variations could be explained by differences in both content standards and student academic achievement from state to state, as well as from differences in the stringency of the standards adopted by the states. As a result, there was no way to directly compare state proficiency standards in an environment where different tests and standards were used (National Center for Educational Statistics, 2007, p. 482).
- **November 2007:** The **Chief Council of State School Officers (CCSSO) policy forum** discussed the need for one set of shared academic standards.
- **2008:** Achieve report **Benchmarking for success: Ensuring U.S. students receive a world-class education** recommended states upgrade state standards by adopting a common core of internationally benchmarked standards in math and language

arts for grades K-12 to ensure that students are equipped with the necessary knowledge and skills to be globally competitive (National Governors Association, Council of Chief State School Officers, & Achieve Inc., 2008).

- **July 2008:** With the release of **Out of many one: Toward rigorous Common Core Standards from the ground up,** CCSSO Executive Director, Gene Wilhoit, argued that all students should graduate from high school prepared for the demands of postsecondary education, meaningful careers, and effective citizenship, and that a state-led effort is the fastest, most effective way to ensure that more students graduate from high school ready for college and career, a universally accepted goal. "ADP Core has become the common core as a byproduct of the alignment work in each of the states." (Achieve, Inc., Press Release, July31, 2008).
- **Summer 2008:** CCSSO's Executive Director Gene Wilhoit and Student Achievement Partners Co-founder David Coleman convinced philanthropist Bill Gates to spend more than $200 million advancing Common Core. Over the next two years, Gates would fund groups across the political spectrum and by June 2009, CCSS would be adopted by 45 states and the District of Columbia (Layton, 2014).
- **December 2008:** NGA and ADP report urged states to create internationally benchmarked standards.
- **April 2009: NGA & CCSSO Summit in Chicago** called for states to support shared standards.
- **May 2009:** The **CCSS Initiative** development began on the college and career ready standards (National Governors Association Center for Best Practices, Council of Chief State School Officers, 2014).
- **July 2009:** Based on positive responses from the states **Common Core State Standards Writing Panels** began their work.
- **July 2009:** President Barack Obama and Education Secretary Arne Duncan announced $4.35 billion in competitive **Race to the Top** (RTTT) grants. To be eligible, states had to adopt "internationally benchmarked standards and assessments that prepare students for success in college and the work place" (U. S. Department of Education, 2009, para 4). But the support of the Obama administration for this hitherto voluntary national

effort would create confusion as to whether CCSS was a *national* effort or a *federal* effort. When viewed as a federal effort, CCSS became ripe for politicization.

- **September 2009: 48 states (not Texas or Alaska), Washington, D. C., the Virgin Islands and Puerto Rico** were counted as participating in the CCSS effort (National Governors Association, 2009).
- **January, 2010:** Responding to fears that Common Core might squeeze social studies out of the curriculum, an alliance of social studies organizations, including a state collaborative working under the CCSSO called the Social Studies Assessment, Curriculum and Instruction (SSACI), the National Council for the Social Studies, and the Campaign for the Civic Mission of Schools (CMS) began an initiative to focus on the four state standards identified in the No Child Left Behind Act: Civics, Economics, Geography and History. The group expanded to include 15 organizations and formed the **Task Force of Professional Organizations to work with SSACI** (Swann & Griffin, 2013).
- **February 11, 2010: Kentucky adopted CCSS**, the first state to do so.
- **March 2010: First draft of CCSS was officially released**.
- **June 2, 2010:** The standards-development process was completed in approximately one year by Achieve, Inc. (Mathis, 2010). The **Common Core State Standards** (English Language Arts and Math) were finalized on June 2, 2010 (Porter, McMaken, Hwang, & Yang, 2010).
- **July 2010: Kentucky launched Leadership Networks** for teacher, school, and district leaders around the implementation of the Common Core State Standards within the context of highly effective teaching, learning, and assessment practices.
- **September 2. 2010:** Education Secretary Arne Duncan awarded $360 million to two multi-state consortia to develop standardized tests: The **Partnership for Assessment of Readiness for College and Careers (PARCC) and The Smarter Balanced Assessment Consortium (SBAC)** (U. S. Department of Education, 2010)
- **Fall 2010:** Work on state **social studies standards began under the name C3** (Swann & Griffin, 2013).
- **July 1, 2011:** The Carnegie Corporation of New York and the

Institute for Advanced Study published ***A Framework for K-12 Science Education Standards: Practices, Crosscutting Concepts, and Core Ideas,*** the guiding document for **Next Generation Science Standards (NGSS)**.
- **2011:** Achieve began managing the state-led development of the K-12 Next Generation Science Standards.
- **Summer 2011:** The Task Force of Professional Organizations and SSACI hired a writing team to begin work on C3 (Swann & Griffin, 2013).
- **Spring 2012: Kentucky assessed CCSS** in a new accountability system.
- **2013:** Nationally, with bipartisan support for a conservative proposal, and much evidence-based rationale, CCSS seemed to be on track for a relatively easy adoption among the 45 states that remained committed. The thornier issue appeared to be whether a set of national exams based on the CCSS could be agreed to and would be affordable. But backlash against CCSS was surfacing in state legislatures in Alabama, Indiana, Michigan, Missouri, Pennsylvania, Georgia, South Dakota, and Kansas (Ujifusa, 2013).
- **April 9, 2013:** The final **Next Generation Science Standards were released**. The standards required evidence of three-dimensional learning (including practices, crosscutting concepts, and core ideas) and learning progressions outlined with standards at all grade levels, including engineering, and connections with common core standards (NGSS Lead States, 2013).
- **April 2013:** The **Republican National Committee surprised many educators when it passed a resolution bashing the standards**. In a letter to colleagues on the appropriations subcommittee that handles education funding, Sen. Charles Grassley (R, Iowa) calls CCSS an "inappropriate overreach to standardize and control the education of our children" (Strauss, 2013, para. 3). Grassley asked Congress to cut off all future funds for CCSS and its assessments, and "restore state decision-making and accountability with respect to state academic content standards." The letter said in part:
  > While the Common Core State Standards Initiative was initially billed as a voluntary effort between states, federal incentives have clouded the picture. Current federal law makes clear that the U.S. Department of Education may not be

involved in setting specific content standards or determining the content of state assessments. Nevertheless, the selection criteria designed by the U.S. Department of Education for the Race to the Top Program provided that for a state to have any chance to compete for funding, it must commit to adopting a 'common set of K-12 standards' matching the description of the Common Core. The U.S. Department of Education also made adoption of 'college- and career-ready standards' meeting the description of the Common Core a condition to receive a state waiver under the Elementary and Secondary Education Act. Race to the Top funds were also used to fund two consortiums to develop assessments aligned to the Common Core and the Department is now in the process of evaluating these assessments. (Grassley, 2013, para. 2)

- **2013:** Once a public policy issue becomes politicized, it is difficult to accurately predict its future. But a **report from the Center on Education Policy** (CEP) found that, while concern over funding for CCSS implementation was high, state education leaders said that the effort would go forward. In their report, Year 3 of Implementing the Common Core State Standards: State Education Agencies Views on the Federal Role, CEP found that the majority of the 40 states responding to the survey, said that it is unlikely that their state would reverse, limit, or change its decision to adopt CCSS this year or next. Few state education leaders said that overcoming resistance to CCSS was a major challenge in their state (Renter, 2013).
- **September 17, 2013** (Constitution Day): The **C3 Framework was published online** by the National Council for the Social Studies.
- **June 2014:** By this time **43 States, the Department of Defense and several U. S. territories had adopted CCSS in ELA/literacy and Math** (CCSS Initiative, 2014).

References

ACT. (2006). Reading between the lines: What the ACT reveals about college readiness in reading. Iowa City: ACT. Retrieved from http://www.google.com/url?sa=t&rct=j&q=&esrc=s&source=web&cd=1&ved=0CCwQFjAA&url=http%3A%2F%2Fwww.act.org%2Fresearch%2Fpolicymakers%2Fpdf%2Freading_report.pdf&ei=Usv3UfqLDLOh4APg9IGQAw&usg=AFQjCNH9ZA-6pr1WyoZFC8dnHfEO9yGAvQ&sig2=OglCONUcQExenxKFYDiRMA&bvm=bv.49967636,d.dmg&cad=rja

American Diploma Project. (2004). Ready or not: creating a high school diploma that counts. Washington: Achieve, Inc. Retrieved from http://www.achieve.org/ReadyorNot

American Diploma Project. (2007). Aligned expectations?: A closer look at college admissions and placement tests. Washington: Achieve, Inc. Retrieved from http://www.achieve.org/AlignedExpectations

American Diploma Project. (2011). Closing the expectations gap 2011: Sixth annual 50-state progress report on the alignment of high school policies with the demands on college and careers. Washington: Achieve, Inc. Retrieved from http://www.achieve.org/ClosingtheExpectationsGap2011

Conley, D. T. (2014). Common Core State Standards: Insight into their development and purpose. Council of Chief State School Officers. Retrieved from http://www.ccsso.org/Resources/Publications/The_Common_Core_State_Standards_Insight_into_Their_Development_and_Purpose.html

Day, R. E. (2003). Each child, every child: The story of the Council for Better Education, equity and adequacy in Kentucky's schools (Doctoral dissertation). Kentucky: *Council for Better Education*. Retrieved from http://kycbe.com/downloads/webDissertation.pdf

Day, R. E. (2011). Bert Combs and the Council for Better Education: Catalysts for school reform. *The Register of the Kentucky Historical Society, 109*(1), 27-62. (Available at: http://works.bepress.com/richard_day/4) Accessed July 29, 2013.

Day, R. E. & Ewalt, J. G. (2013). Education reform in Kentucky: Just what the court ordered, in J.C. Clinger and M.W. Hail, *Kentucky government, politics, and policy*. Lexington: University Press of Kentucky.

Grassley, C. (2013). Letter to Sen. Tom Harkin and Sen. Jerry Moran, United States Senate, Senate Appropriations Committee. Retrieved from http://www.scribd.com/doc/136967446/Senator-Grassley-Letter-to-Defund-Common-Core

Guskey, T. R. & Oldham, B. R. (1997). Despite the best intentions: Inconsistencies among components in Kentucky's systemic reform. *Educational Policy, 11*(4), 426-442.

Harrison, L. H. & Klotter, J. C. (1997). *A new history of Kentucky*. Lexington, KY: The University Press of Kentucky.

Kaestle, C. (2006). Forward. *Politics, ideology, and education: Federal policy during the Clinton and Bush administrations*. New York, NY: Teachers College Press.

Layton, L. (2014). Common standards for nation's schools a longtime goal. *The Washington Post*. Retrieved from http://www.washingtonpost.com/local/education/common-standards-for-nations-schools-a-longtime-goal/2014/06/09/cbe7e9ec-edb1-11e3-92b8-52344c12e8a1_story.html

Layton, L. (2014). How Bill Gates pulled off the swift common core revolution. *The Washington Post*. Retrieved from http://www.washingtonpost.com/politics/how-bill-gates-pulled-off-the-swift-common-core-revolution/2014/06/07/a830e32e-ec34-11e3-9f5c-9075d5508f0a_story.html

Mathis, W.J. (2010). The "Common Core" standards initiative: An effective reform tool? *Great Lakes Center for Education Research and Practice*. Retrieved from http://www.manateelearn.com/pluginfile.php/2204/mod_resource/content/1/PB-NatStans-Mathis.pdf

McInnus v. Sharpiro, 293 F. Supp. 327 (1968).

National Center on Education and Economy. (1990). *America's choice: High skills or low wages*. Rochester, NY: National Center on Education and the Economy.

National Center for Educational Statistics. (2007). Mapping 2005 state proficiency standards on the NARP scales: Research and development report. Institute of Educational Services, 482.

National Commission on Excellence in Education. (1983). *A nation at risk: The imperative for educational reform*. Washington, DC: U.S. Department of Education.

National Governors Association. (2009). Forty-nine states and territories join Common Core Standards initiative. Retrieved from http://www.nga.org/cms/home/newsroom/news-releases/page_2009/col2-content/main-content-list/title_forty-nine-states-and-territories-join-common-core-standards-initiative.html

National Governors Association, Council of Chief State School Officers, & Achieve Inc. (2008). Benchmarking for success: Ensuring U.S. students receive a world-class education. Washington, DC: National Governors Association. Retrieved from http://www.edweek.org/media/benchmakring%20for%20success%20dec%202008%20final.pdf

National Governors Association Center for Best Practices, Council of Chief State School Officers. (2014). Complete timeline. Retrieved from http://www.corestandards.org/about-the-standards/development-process/

National Research Council. (2012). *A framework for K-12 science education: Practices, crosscutting concepts, and core ideas*. Washington D. C.: The National Academies Press. Retrieved from http://www.nap.edu/openbook.php?record_id=13165&page=R1

NGSS Lead States. (2013) *Next Generation Science Standards: For states, by states*. Washington, DC: The National Academies Press.

No Child Left Behind Act of 2001, P.L. 107-110, 20 U.S.C. § 6319 (2002).

Peterson, P. E. (1995). The new politics of choice. In D. Ravitch & M.A. Vinovskis (Eds.), *Learning from the past: What history teaches us about school reform*. Baltimore, MD: Johns Hopkins University Press, 226-227.

Porter, A., McMaken, J., Hwang, J. & Yang, R. (April 2010). Common Core Standards: The new U.S. intended curriculum. *Educational Researcher. 40*(3), 103-116. Retrieved from http://edr.sagepub.com/content/40/3/103.short

Prichard Committee for Academic Excellence. (1990). *The path to a larger life: Creating Kentucky's educational future* (2nd Ed.). Lexington: University Press of Kentucky. Retrieved from http://books.google.com/books?id=aEB8RxhktC8C&pg=PR3&source=gbs_selected_pages&cad=3#v=onepage&q&f=false)

Ravitch, D. (2010). *The death and life of the great American school system: How testing and choice are undermining education*. Basic Books: New York.

Rentner, D. S. (2013). Year 3 of implementing the Common Core State Standards: State education agencies' views on the federal role. Washington, D. C.: Center on Education policy. Retrieved from http://www.cep-dc.org/displayDocument.cfm?DocumentID=420

Robelen, E. W. (July 13, 2010). Panel moves toward Next Generation Science Standards. *Education Week.*

Rose v. Council for Better Education, 790 S. W. 2d 186. (1989).

Spring, J. (2010). *American education.* New York, NY: McGraw Hill.

Strauss, V. (2013). Common Core Standards attacked by Republicans. *Washington Post, The Answer Sheet blog.* Retrieved from http://www.washingtonpost.com/blogs/answer-sheet/wp/2013/04/19/common-core-standards-attacked-by-republicans/

Swan, K. & Griffin, S. (2013). Beating the odds: The college, career, and civic life (C3) framework for social studies state standards. *Social Education*, 77(6), 317-321.

Ujifusa, A. (March 14, 2013). Exit strategy: State lawmakers consider dropping Common Core. *Education Week.*

U. S. Department of Education. (2009). Race to the Top Fund. Retrieved from http://www2.ed.gov/programs/racetothetop/phase1-resources.html#announcements

U. S. Department of Education. (2009). Press release: President Obama, U.S. Secretary of Education Duncan announce national competition to advance school reform. Washington D. C.: U.S. Department of Education. Retrieved from http://www.whitehouse.gov/the_press_office/President-Obama-US-Secretary-of-Education-Duncan-announce-National-Competition-to-advance-school-reform

U. S. Department of Education. (2010). Press release: U. S. Secretary of Education Duncan announces winners of competition to improve student assessments. Washington D. C.: U. S. Department of Education. Retrieved from http://www.ed.gov/news/press-releases/us-secretary-education-duncan-announces-winners-competition-improve-student-asse

Chapter 3

The Power of Collaboration: Faculty Learning Communities as a Vehicle for Professional Development

Krista Althauser and Faye Deters

Charged with the mandate to align key university courses in general education and teacher preparation to the K-12 Kentucky Core Academic Standards, those leading the charge at Eastern Kentucky University (EKU) chose to utilize the structure of Professional Learning Communities (PLCs) to undertake this work. PLC models had been commonly used across the campus for several years for faculty professional development, research, and problem-solving; therefore, faculty members were accustomed to working within this format (Fair, Sweet, Blythe, Combs, & Phillips, 2013). The content areas that were targeted, as well as the facilitators who would represent each, were selected by the Executive Committee of the Curriculum Alignment for Retention and Transition at Eastern (CARTE) initiative. The CARTE Executive Committee was comprised of the two directors of the University's Teaching and Learning Center (TLC) and two faculty from the College of Education. The facilitators chosen to lead each of the five content areas, English, natural science, math, social science, and teacher preparation, made up the overarching PLC or "Super PLC". The Super PLC met with the Executive Committee regularly to examine and discuss the operation and progress of the content PLCs. The facilitators of the Teacher Preparation PLC, the authors, were members of the overarching PLC, or "Super" PLC.

PLC Model

The PLC model employed for the CARTE initiative at EKU was derived from two existing models of learning communities used by faculty within the university and with P-12 partners. The Cox Faculty Learning Community (FLC) model (Cox, 2004) was frequently used by the TLC to promote faculty professional development and research. Cox defines a Faculty Learning Community (FLC) as

> ...A cross-disciplinary faculty and staff group of six to fifteen members...who engage in an active, collaborative, yearlong program with a curriculum about enhancing teaching and learning and with frequent seminars and activities that provide learning, development, the scholarship of teaching, and community building (Cox, 2004, p.8).

FLCs employed by the TLC at EKU frequently examined research about innovations in teaching and learning, applied strategies from the research in individual courses, and discussed the results of implementation on teaching effectiveness and student learning. Focus features of the FLC model included improving student learning through inquiry and research, analyzing assessment data as a starting point, achieving a desired result, and engaging in a collaborative, faculty-led approach.

The additional model of PLCs used within the university reflected the model described by DuFour, DuFour, Eaker, and Many (2006) that was being utilized by faculty in the College of Education with P-12 partners. In defining a Professional Learning Community (PLC), DuFour et al. presented the following:

> A professional learning community is a group of educators committed to working collaboratively in ongoing processes of collective inquiry and action research in order to achieve better results for the students they serve. PLCs operate under the assumption that the key to improved learning for students is continuous, job-embedded learning for educators (p.3).

These PLCs were focused on ensuring high levels of learning for all students, building a collaborative culture among teachers, and achieving the continuous improvement results being sought. The cycle of continuous improvement consists of gathering evidence of the current levels of student learning, developing strategies to build on strengths and address weaknesses in the learning, implementing the strategies, analyzing the impact on learning, and applying the knowledge gained to the next cycle.

While several differences exist between the two models, the major differences that perpetuated a blending of the two were the initial impetus for forming the PLCs and the use of scholarship within them. While the DuFour model of PLCs typically originated with the identification of an area of concern in K-12 student achievement data, the Cox model of PLCs generally began with a common interest in research about innovations within higher education. Therefore, whereas scholarship was typically a starting point for the PLCs utilized by the TLC, scholarship was typically used in the K-12 PLCs later in the continuous improvement cycle to determine strategies and ideas to increase student achievement. A key feature included in each PLC model is the emphasis on the professional development of the faculty participants that results from engagement in the PLC. The Executive Committee determined the need to synthesize the best elements of both models in forming the PLCs charged with aligning the curriculum to the Kentucky Core Academic Standards (Fair et al., 2013).

Purpose of the PLC

The proposed outcomes and focus of the resulting PLCs in the five content areas were primarily identical: a) to align syllabi for common core courses taken by teacher education candidates to the College and Career Readiness and Kentucky Core Academic Standards (KCAS) and b) to illustrate how the standards were reflected within the student learning outcomes in those courses. The Super PLC agreed upon which courses in each content area would be the focus of the alignment efforts and invited faculty to participate. Each PLC consisted of a dozen faculty members.

Prior to the content PLCs undertaking their charges, the Executive Committee planned and provided a professional development opportunity for all members of each content PLC. Members of the

Executive Committee as well as some of the Super PLC members developed and presented sessions that engaged the members of each PLC in learning about KY's Senate Bill 1 mandate, College and Career Readiness, the KCAS, professional learning communities, and formative and summative assessments. Additional professional development opportunities were planned and provided as the PLCs undertook their work, and issues or areas of concern were identified by facilitators and subsequently discussed at the Super PLC meetings.

Overarching Assertion

There is growing consensus that the most promising strategy for sustained, substantive school improvement is developing the capacity of school personnel to function as a professional learning community. Research on effective professional development identifies several key features that must be present (Darling-Hammond, Wei, Andrea, Richardson, & Orphanos, 2009). Effective professional development includes the following features: a) a focus on improving student learning; b) ongoing, continuous, and incremental improvements over time; and c) reliance on investigation, interaction, research, and hands-on practice. These particular components were evident in the Teacher Preparation PLC and thereby provided a model of a professional development for the faculty participants.

Planning is the KEY

A famous quote by Hunter S. Thompson (2015) illustrates a key consideration in planning any event, "Anything worth doing is worth doing right." Most would agree that establishing a professional learning community to address the improvement of student achievement, is a worthwhile endeavor (DuFour, 2004). Planning is the key if a PLC is to serve as a positive force to initiate change in instruction and assessment to promote student achievement.

Planning is the key if a PLC is to serve as a positive force to initiate change in instruction and assessment to promote student achievement.

Emily Post, with her expertise for party planning, can provide insight for designing a PLC. One must admit, Emily knew how to throw a well-organized party! Her parties were perhaps a little more structured than most partygoers today would enjoy, but they were always well planned. According to Emily Post, there are six ways to be both a good host and a good guest at a party. These ideas can be translated to the design and planning of an effective PLC. In the following paragraphs, the planning ideas of Emily Post (1922) will be compared to the PLC model utilized in the Teacher Preparation PLC. The planning responsibilities of the host (PLC facilitator) are discussed first, followed by the responsibilities of the guests (PLC participants).

The Host Prepares for the Party

According to Post (1922), the first key for any event to be successful is to "invite clearly." An invitation to participate in a PLC must include necessary information about a PLC and how it differs from a committee. Too many administrators and faculty confuse committee meetings for PLCs (DuFour, 2004). A committee has a predetermined purpose, is directed by a chair, makes decisions using the majority vote, follows Robert's Rules of Order, and focuses on task oriented jobs to accomplish the same goal. A PLC is open-ended and discovery oriented, has a facilitator, makes decisions by consensus, and is innovative and reflective. In addition, the participants own the process and the subject/content of focus. Giving the participants responsibility allows them to identify opportunities to work together to improve assessment and instruction. Making the purpose and process clear for participants enables them to accomplish the work of the PLC.

Faculty who taught the key courses targeted for alignment as well as other faculty whose expertise and experiences could inform the work of the PLC were invited to participate in the Teacher Preparation PLC. Faculty from several departments within the College of Education comprised the resulting learning community. As a result, the efforts represented both vertical and horizontal program alignment, ensuring that candidates were prepared with the appropriate content to enable them to teach the KCAS.

Another responsibility for the party planner, and the facilitator alike, is to "plan well" (Post, 1922). Most professionals have attended meetings that were not well planned or not planned at all. In these instances, participants' opinions of the meeting are generally negative and most likely viewed it as a waste of time.

Regardless of the good intent, it is doubtful that anyone had an interest in returning for a second meeting. Ben Franklin (2015) describes this best in one of his famous quotes: "By failing to plan, you are planning to fail."

The Teacher Education PLC members were largely familiar with the KCAS and the process of aligning curriculum in teacher preparation courses to standards, therefore, the PLC members decided to focus their efforts on utilizing the notion of assessment for learning in examining the achievement of students in the targeted courses. The Teacher Preparation PLC chose to begin by examining the work of Stiggins, Arter, Chappuis, and Chappuis (2009) in *Classroom Assessment for Student Learning: Doing It Right – Using It Well* as the starting point for their work. Subsequently, additional research was examined as points of discussion that surfaced during the PLC meetings led to inquiry into related scholarship. The Teacher Education PLC met once monthly at an agreed upon day and time and followed a common structure for each meeting. The facilitators would arrange the meeting space, provide materials needed, and guide the meetings. PLC members agreed to prepare for the next meeting by completing the reading or actions and prepare notes or materials for sharing during the next meeting.

After the clear invitation has been issued and the event is well planned, it is time to gather for the party or meet as a learning community. This is when the host or facilitator faces the most challenging responsibilities, which are to "remain calm" and "be flexible and gracious." Anyone who has had the opportunity to work with teachers or faculty realizes that it is not always an easy endeavor. The teaching profession inherently draws people who exhibit passion for teaching and learning. At times this can create spirited debates or intense environments where civility may be difficult to maintain. Each individual member has his or her own ideas and agendas; therefore, the facilitator needs to graciously provide the opportunity for the participants to share their ideas and thoughts. Furthermore, when the discussion enters

> *The teaching profession inherently draws people who exhibit passion for teaching and learning. At times this can create spirited debates or intense environments where civility may be difficult to maintain.*

unplanned territory, the facilitator must be flexible and allow the dialogue to unfold. This must be done while observing an important planning rule, "start on time – end on time."

In beginning each meeting of the Teacher Preparation PLC, one of the facilitators would go over the agenda for the day and then lead the discussion on a topic, problem, or question determined by the PLC at the previous meeting. In leading these discussions, the facilitators ensured that each faculty participant had the opportunity to share his or her ideas, experiences, or concerns. The PLC members would provide suggestions or recommendations for action based upon the discussion. Subgroups were formed to work on aligning the syllabi for targeted courses and progress made by each subgroup since the last meeting was shared. Finally, near the end of the meeting, the PLC would determine next steps and persons responsible as well as materials or readings that would guide the next meeting.

For the PLC to produce positive changes, participants need to meet on a consistent basis and be actively engaged. To ensure active participation, the participants must "feel welcome" and that their contributions are important to the learning community. To ensure this, the facilitator should acknowledge all participants by "expressing appreciation" for their attendance and the expertise they contribute. As the PLC evolves, the participants will take on these roles of supporting each other, promoting collaboration.

The Teacher Preparation PLC as described here reflects the purposes of both the Dufour (2004) and Cox (2004) models. Tenets of the DuFour model reflected in the PLC process encompass the following: faculty accepted learning as the fundamental purpose of their school; faculty were willing to examine all practices in light of their impact on learning; faculty assessed effectiveness on the basis of results rather than intentions; individuals, teams, and the school sought relevant evidence and information and used that information to promote continuous improvement. The Cox (2004) model is reflected through the lens of the teacher educators' focus on enhancing teaching and learning through the examination of scholarly work that directed frequent activities, resulting in learning and community building.

Planning Responsibilities of the PLC Participant

Even though planning is usually considered the responsibility of the host or the facilitator, the participants also hold planning responsibilities. These responsibilities play a crucial role in the success of the PLC. The first and foremost key responsibility of the participant is to notify the facilitator whether or not he or she will be attending. It is difficult for the facilitator to plan for a PLC when she has no idea who or how many participants will be in attendance. The likelihood is that the meeting will be spent playing musical chairs or waiting for mystery people to arrive. As a result, valuable time is lost and little is accomplished.

In movies, books, and television shows the concept of time is always relevant. For example, in the movie, Star Trek VI: The Undiscovered Country, the audience hears an actor say, "As you know, time is of essence," indicating the importance of using time wisely. Whereas in the movie, *Alice in Wonderland*, the rabbit is always late and has very little time left to accomplish the tasks he set out to do. In reference to the PLC, it is the participant's responsibility to be on time to achieve completion of the purpose identified for the time scheduled.

There is a phrase that is commonly used when leading a group of people to achieve a common goal – "The group is only as good as its members." The message conveyed is the need for everyone to step up and be a willing participant. Each participant should offer to provide his or her expertise or assistance when possible. For a PLC to create positive change, the participants must accept responsibility for shared leadership.

One of the most common regrets of partygoers attending a party is overindulgence of food, beverage, or both. The results can be painful and embarrassing afterwards. In a PLC setting, overindulgence of verbiage can also be painful and embarrassing, leaving others frustrated and unable to think on their own. It is the participants' responsibility to control the amount of verbiage each contributes. After all, many opinions and ideas on how to fix the ship are desirable and in the worst case scenario where nothing works, everyone sinks with the same collaborative plan.

Collaboration

"On the plus side it's something for your PLC to chew on."

Note: From Mark Anderson Cartoon #6562. On the plus side it's something for your PLC to chew on. Reprinted with permission. www.Andersontoons.com.

The best educational experiences are offered in schools that adopt the practice of gathering quantitative and qualitative data to better understand the effectiveness of their instructional practices on student achievement and sharing with others what they have learned (Pfeffer & Sutton, 2006). The Teacher Preparation PLC discovered an effective way to convey newly found information on improving student learning was by organizing a professional learning community (PLCs) to cultivate a collaborative culture within the college (DuFour, DuFour, Eaker & Many, 2010). Once the PLC was organized, the first critical decision for the Teacher Preparation PLC to make was what to focus the collaborative efforts on initially.

The Teacher Preparation PLC chose to collaborate on aligning syllabi for the teacher preparation courses to the K-12 KCAS and identifying formative assessment strategies. As explained in an earlier section, this decision was based on the mandate for alignment. The overarching goal was for all instructors to form a collaborative culture to improve learning for our teacher education candidates on implementation of the KCAS and assessment strategies. The members of the Teacher Preparation PLC recognized that their levels of working knowledge related to the new state standards as well as formative assessment strategies differed among individuals. This inconsistency was identified as the first area of focus. The Teacher Preparation PLC realized the crucial importance of becoming a unified group of instructors who modeled the process of implementing curriculum, instruction, and assessment, as well as supported the development of a shared purpose for student learning and collective responsibility to achieve it (Newmann & Wehlage, 1995). Hence, the PLC recognized the critical need for all instructors to communicate a unified vision and message concerning the teaching and assessment of the KCAS.

According to DuFour, DuFour, Eaker, & Many (2010), teachers who accept learning as the fundamental purpose of the school should focus their collective effort around four critical questions: 1) What do we want each student to learn and where are they now? 2) How will we know when each student has learned it and how will we get them there? 3) What do we do for those who struggle? 4) What do we do for those who already know it? The PLC Cycle, shown below (see Figure 3.1), served as the compass that directed the discussions on two focal topics the Teacher Preparation PLC addressed, the KCAS and formative assessment.

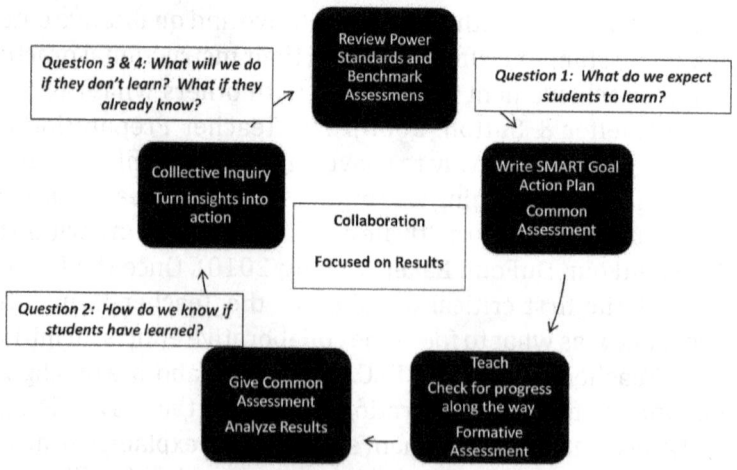

Figure 3.1. The PLC cycle provides guidance for the Professional Learning Community discussions.
(Retrieved from http://whittyplcguy.blogspot.com/2013/07/teacher-autonomy-experimentation-in-plc.html).

The two topics of focus for the Teacher Preparation PLC were the KCAS (math and English language arts) and formative assessment strategies. The Teacher Preparation PLC gathered information on what the teacher education candidates knew about the KCAS and formative assessment strategies. The information was then shared among the members of the PLC. The discussion gave much needed insight as to what our teacher education candidates had been previously taught and their level of understanding.

Over the next few months, the PLC meetings continued to focus on the KCAS standards and formative assessment strategies, with the discussion becoming more in-depth, gathering input on what our teacher education candidates need to understand and be able to proficiently demonstrate in practice once they are placed in a classroom for clinical experiences, student teaching, and as teachers in their own future classrooms. Once the group had a firm understanding of the teacher education candidates' current location on the learning continuum and the additional knowledge they needed before exiting the program, the PLC's focus then centered on instruction. To address various teaching ideas, the PLC participants shared and modeled a variety of instructional activities for teaching KCAS and formative assessment strategies. Depending on how the instructional activities were designed, either or both the KCAS standards and assessment strategies were shared independently or simultaneously.

The final discussion focused on how to formatively assess the teacher education candidates to determine the working knowledge level each had on the KCAS and formative assessment. This proved to be the most challenging for the Teacher Preparation PLC members. The conversation triggered much debate on the topic of assessment and differentiation strategies. Each faculty member had his or her own opinions and ideas on what formative assessment and differentiation strategies should look like in the classroom and passionately defended his or her personal practices. In the end, the group realized they were all sharing similar practices and ideas; the confusion was with the explanation of how the strategies were being implemented and the terminology used. This is one problem the PLC realized that required immediate attention. Even though most of the members were teaching the same or similar concepts, they were not making the connections clear between the various courses, thereby confusing the teacher education candidates and creating a mindset among students that "No one has ever taught this to me before." In many cases, the solution was to use a common language and to make connections among courses explicit. As demonstrated by the Teacher Preparation PLC, professional learning communities can help lead the way to ending the practice of solo teaching in our isolated classrooms and lead to sharing our personal knowledge into a collectively built, widely shared, and cohesive professional knowledge base to build common ground among the courses taught (Fulton, Yoon, & Lee, 2005).

Seven Keys to Effective Teams

Many plans we make in life start with good intentions to create positive change in a somewhat chaotic situation. Unfortunately, there are incidents where the urgency placed behind these good intentions to propel them to create positive change loses its power and effectiveness. One might say this is the result of poor planning, lack of interest, or misguided intentions; but whatever the reason, an opportunity to collaborate with colleagues has been missed. DuFour et al. (2010) devised the "seven keys to effective teams" to provide guidance on developing effective PLC teams that retain the power to create change. These seven keys unlock the mystery of how to retain the strong force created through collaboration in an effective PLC.

> *Many plans we make in life start with good intentions to create positive change in a somewhat chaotic situation. Unfortunately, there are incidents where the urgency placed behind these good intentions to propel them to create positive change loses its power and effectiveness.*

Cox (2004) provided similar guidance for Faculty Learning Communities (FLC), and referred to them as Multidisciplinary and Community Elements. As shown in the chart below (see Figure 3.2) the keys and the elements may be worded differently but both have very similar connotations. For the purpose of this PLC, we meshed the two models together and pulled the components that best fit the purpose of the Teacher Education PLC.

Figure 3.2. Comparison of the essential elements of Professional Learning Communities (DuFour et al., 2010) and Faculty Learning Communities (Cox, 2004).

Professional Learning Communities (PLC) Seven Keys to Effective Teams (DuFour et al., 2010)	Faculty Learning Communities (FLC) Multidisciplinary and Community Elements (Cox, 2004)
Embed collaboration in routine practices of the school with the focus on learning	Meet consistently for a period of at least six months
Schedule time for collaboration into the school day and school calendar	Meet at a designated time and in an environment conducive to learning
Focus team on critical questions	Engage in studying complex problems
Make products of collaboration explicit	Treat individual projects the same way. with the group contributing suggestions
Establish team norms to guide collaboration	Employ the Kolb (1984) experiential learning cycle
Pursue specific and measurable team performance goals	Operate by consensus, not majority Develops empathy among members Energizes and empowers participants Holistic in approach.
Provide teams with frequent access to relevant information	Have voluntary membership and establishes a timely schedule to share information and report progress on working toward completion.

Assessment for Learning & of Learning in Our Courses

For PLCs to serve as a platform for faculty professional development there must be some resulting impact on the faculty's teaching practices. For those faculty engaged in the Teacher Preparation PLC, the focus on assessment *for* learning and assessment *of* learning should have resulted in each faculty member examining his or her own assessment practices and potentially changing those practices to better reflect the information learned from the research and discussion that guided the PLC. Beyond examining their own assessment practices, faculty implemented strategies they had learned about and then shared their experiences with the PLC. Further, the syllabi for the redesigned courses reflected these newly adopted assessment practices.

For example, an examination of one of the undergraduate courses targeted for redesign to align with the new KCAS standards,

ELE 491 Mathematics in Elementary Grades P-5, revealed evidence that the Teacher Preparation PLC's focus on assessment practices impacted the course significantly as demonstrated through several key features. The required course text list revealed the addition of a new text focused on assessment, *How to Assess While You Teach Math* (Islas, 2011). Student learning outcomes were revised to include specific and explicit focus on demonstrating knowledge of the KCAS for Mathematics and how to teach, learn, and assess learning of these standards. The course outline included a new focus on formative assessment strategies during the "Integrated Mathematics Assessment" unit. Existing units indicated the relevant KCAS domains that aligned to each. As might be expected, given the PLC's focus on formative and summative assessment, the evaluation methods for the course revealed the most notable revisions. Assessment tools were clearly indicated, connected to each of the student learning outcomes, and were denoted as assessment for learning or assessment of learning. Further, summative assessments comprised the largest percentage of the candidates' final grades, while formative assessments comprised a very small percentage.

While it would be expected that evidence of a PLC member's professional growth would be present in the examination of a product specifically targeted for redesign and submitted as part of the CARTE initiative, another indicator that professional growth has occurred would be if evidence existed in courses that were not specifically targeted for redesign. As faculty participated in the Teacher Preparation PLC, discussions increasingly revealed that members were rethinking their own assessment practices and applying strategies to existing courses they were teaching that were not part of the CARTE initiative.

One example can be illustrated through the examination of an online graduate course taught by a faculty member in the PLC, EME 874 Language Arts in the Curriculum. While the required text for the course did not change and the revisions to the syllabus primarily increased clarity in student learning outcomes and revisions to the evaluation methods, the most significant revisions were evident in the modules that comprised the instruction and assessment for the course. The first component that revealed significant revision was the addition of clearly stated student learning targets in each module introduction that were aligned to each learner outcome, worded as "I can" statements, and connected to the assessment method used to assess each target. The second notable revision was the inclusion of a student self-assessment component related to the learning outcomes for the course at the onset with goal setting and also self-assessment opportunities in each module that were specific to the learning targets for the module. Further, formative assessments were designed to provide detailed feedback and comprised a small percentage of the candidate's grade. Finally, formative assessments reflected a focus on a limited number of learning targets that built skill and expertise on components of the summative assessment, with multiple opportunities for feedback along the way prior to the summative assessment experience.

> *As faculty participated in the Teacher Preparation PLC, discussions increasingly revealed that members were rethinking their own assessment practices and applying strategies to existing courses they were teaching that were not part of the CARTE initiative.*

The revisions made by Teacher Preparation PLC faculty to these courses are indicative of the types of changes to assessment practices reportedly being made by many of the participants. This indicates that, in these instances, participation in the PLC served as a vehicle for professional growth with direct impact on improving teaching practice, and consequently, student achievement.

The Results of the Teacher Preparation PLC

The participants of the Teacher Preparation PLC recognized that the quality of a post-secondary education cannot exceed the quality of its teachers. The only way to improve outcomes is to improve instruction (Barber, Chijioke, & Mourshed, 2010). As a result of implementing the professional learning community process to support professional development through teacher collaboration, positive changes were made to the alignment of the syllabi to KCAS and formative assessment strategies were not only found in the updated syllabi but were also demonstrated during instruction. The faculty realized that the potential for improvements was an accessible outcome with their focused efforts pinpointed on specific educational components that could improve their instruction and provide positive changes in learning. In the classrooms that implemented the changes, faculty appeared more energized with their instruction, and the students more engaged with learning. Overall, the Teacher Preparation PLC initiated a stronger, more positive influence on teaching than most stand-alone, one-shot-now, Professional Development in which the faculty had participated in the past.

References

Barber, M., Chijioke, C., & Mourshed, M. (2010). How the world's most improved school systems keep getting better. Retrieved on January 8, 2010. Retrieved from http://mckinseyonsociety.com/downloads/reports/Education/How-the-Worlds-Most-Improved-School-Systems-Keep-Getting-Better_Download-version_Final.pdf

Cox, M. (2004, Spring). Introduction to faculty learning communities. *New Directions for Teaching and Learning, 97.*

Darling-Hammond, L., Wei, R., Andrea, A., Richardson, N., & Orphanos, S. (2009). *Professional learning in the learning profession: A status report on teacher development in the United States and abroad.* Oxford, OH: National Staff Development Council.

DuFour, R. (2004, May). What is a "professional learning community?" *Educational Leadership,* 6-11.

DuFour, R., DuFour, R., Eaker, R., & Many, T. (2010). *Learning by doing: A handbook for professional learning communities at work* (2nd ed.). Bloomington, IN: Solution Tree Press.

Fair, G., Sweet, C., Blythe, H., Combs, D., & Phillips, B. (2013). Incorporating Common Core Standards with professional learning communities. *Learning Communities Journal, 5,* 1-25.

Franklin, Benjamin (n.d.).Notable Quotes.com. Retrieved from http://www.notablequotes.com/f/franklin_benjamin.html.

Fulton, K., Yoon, I., & Lee, C. (2005). *Induction into learning communities.* Washington, DC: National Commission on Teaching and America's Future.

Islas, D. (2011). *How to assess while you teach math: Formative assessment practices and lessons, grades K-2: A multimedia professional learning resource.* Math Solutions: Sausalito, CA.

Newmann, F., & Wehlage, G. (1995). *Successful school restructuring: A report to the public and educators by the center for restructuring schools.* Madison, WI: University of Wisconsin.

Pfeffer, J. & Sutton, R. (2006). Hard facts, dangerous half-truths and total nonsense: Profiting from evidence-based management. Boston: Harvard Business School Press. In R. DuFour, R., DuFour, R. Eaker, & T. Many, (2010). *Learning by doing: A handbook for professional learning communities at work* (2nd ed.). Bloomington, IN: Solution Tree Press.

Post, E. (1922). Party etiquette tips for hosts and guests. Retrieved from http://www.emilypost.com/social-life/hosts-and-guests/466-party-etiquette-tips-for-hosts-and-guests

Stiggins, R., Arter, J., Chappuis, J., & Chappuis, S. (2009). *Classroom assessment for student learning: Doing it right—using it well.* Boston, MA: Pearson.

Thompson, H. (n.d.). BrainyQuote.com. Retrieved from http://www.brainyquote.com/quotes/authors/h/hunter_s_thompson.html

Chapter 4

Finding Common Ground in the Core: Getting to know the standards

Ginni Fair

Standards-based reform efforts are not especially new. The release of *A Nation at Risk* (National Commission on Excellence in Education, 1983) publicized the shortcomings in U.S. education and warned of future economic consequences if changes weren't made. One of those recommendations was that standards based instruction be implemented. "Although some states had accountability systems in place at the time, many states initiated or updated accountability policies and procedures during the 1980s and 1990s with the goal of elevating student achievement in core subjects (e.g., mathematics, language arts)" (Dingman, Teusher, Newton, & Kasmer, 2013, p. 541).

When No Child Left Behind, which mandated the reporting of student proficiency scores, was passed in 2001, standards-based instruction and assessment garnered new attention. But the proficiency scores reported by states indicated that the criteria for proficiency - and the standards upon which those criteria were based –varied widely; not only that, but student performance on the National Assessment of Educational Progress (NAEP) remained dismal. Tepe reports that "in 2005, for example, 87 percent of Tennessee's fourth graders tested proficient on their state mathematics test, while just 28 percent were proficient on NAEP" (2014, p. 3).

This lack of standardization was one impetus for the Common Core State Standards initiative. Another was the growing recognition that a college education is, as Haycock (2010) explains, "the best, if not the only, chance [low income and students of color] have to enter the American mainstream" (p. 15). Trying to clarify what successful college students truly need to know and be able to do, research from such organizations as the Benchmarks of the American Diploma Project, Achieve, and ACT, to name a few, revealed that core demands for colleges and careers were much more consistent than K-12 standards had been (Haycock, 2010; King, 2011).

Still another catalyst for the initiative was the partnership of the National Governors Association (NGA) and the Council of Chief State School Officers (CCSSO) to organize a state-led effort and develop preparedness standards for college and career in English/language arts and mathematics. This work began in 2009, and multiple drafts were vetted and concerns summarized at various points in the process. The coalition finalized these Common Core State Standards (CCSS) in 2010, and states began voluntarily adopting the standards. As of the date of this publication, 43 states, the District of Columbia, four territories, and the Department of Defense Education Activity have adopted the Common Core (NGA Center & CCSSO, 2014). McLaughlin and Overturf (2012) explain why states have been motivated to support the adoption of these standards: "First, adopting a 'common set of standards' was a requirement for states applying for federal Race to the Top funds. A second, less influential factor was that, although they have adopted the CCSS, individual states may modify them by adding up to 15% of new content" (p. 154).

The NGA and CCSSO expressed several goals in developing the Common Core. Because of the ineffective, albeit well-intentioned, standards-based mistakes of the past, the organizers of *this* movement wanted to learn from past oversights. In other words, they wanted the Common Core standards to be

- fewer, clearer, and higher, to best drive effective policy and practice;
- aligned with college and work expectations, so that all students are prepared for success upon graduating from high school;
- inclusive of rigorous content and applications of knowl-

edge through higher-order skills, so that all students are prepared for the 21st century;
- internationally benchmarked, so that all students are prepared for succeeding in our global economy and society; and
- research and evidence-based (NGA Center & CCSSO, 2010a).

In addition, Jones and King (2012) note that while the CCSS allow for state, national, and global benchmarking, they also "provide actionable guidance for teachers, help them connect student learning from one grade to the next, and build essential skills" (p. 39). Students who have mastered the CCSS are expected to be prepared for entry-level, credit-bearing English and mathematics courses without requiring remediation. Benchmark assessment, therefore, is important in this process as well. The assessment process should provide timely feedback to parents, students, teachers, and higher education faculty so that interventions can address any deficiencies while the opportunities still exist, especially in high school classrooms. Some, such as Tepe (2014), even argue that "a college ready designation on the state-adopted Common Core standards – aligned PARCC assessment should be sufficient to meet state minimum eligibility criteria for unconditional admission to the state's public universities" (p. 10). Many states are, in fact, working to establish such a policy for higher education admission.

> *The assessment process should provide timely feedback to parents, students, teachers, and higher education faculty so that interventions can address any deficiencies while the opportunities still exist...*

Ultimately, the creators of the CCSS realize that adoption – even compliance – with the standards is insufficient. The standards define basic learning outcomes for college and career readiness but do not provide a curriculum or recommend instructional approaches. In addition, the standards themselves reflect several paradigm shifts. Jaeger (2014) identifies a few of these:
- Research should be used to build as well as present knowledge.
- Students need to read more nonfiction.
- Reading should help build students' core background knowledge.

- Students need to utilize their research and reading as evidence for discussions and writing.

In addition, in E/LA specifically, educators have noted the new attention on "close reading" and on comprehension as a "base skill" upon which the rigor of the standards is built. Dingman et al. (2013) identified some key shifts in mathematics as well. There are:

> (1) changes in grade level(s) at which some mathematical content is taught, (2) changes in the number of grade levels in which particular mathematical topics appear, (3) changes in emphasis (increased/decreased) on particular mathematical topics, and (4) changes in the nature and level of reasoning expectations (p. 554-555).

Limitations of the Standards

Not all educators are pleased with the content of the standards, however, and some raise thought-provoking questions and concerns:

- Robbins (2013) discusses the impact of the standards on the very nature of education: "Expanding on—and perhaps warping—the belief of iconic Progressive educator John Dewey in 'teaching through occupations,' the heirs to Progressive thought decided that education should be reshaped to be utilitarian: designed to produce not more complete people, but more useful people. So we have here two related but separate strains of thought—educating the workforce and shaping students to accept particular ideas and beliefs" (p. 10). He goes on to explain: "Common Core represents a convergence of the two. This is especially apparent in the English language arts (ELA) standards.... The objections to Common Core are many, including the unconstitutionality of nationalizing education, the use of political coercion to ensure state adoption, the illegality of imposing the national curriculum that the standards will inevitably entail, and the loss of local and parental control over children's education" (p. 12). Keep in mind that the standards technically are not nationally *required*. States do have the option to adopt them or not. However, Race to the Top funds have been tied to the implementation of the Common Core standards.

- Burns (2012) cautions educators about using the Common Core standards as a complete curriculum, noting that some of the purposes and applications of the standards may contradict what is best for literacy development. He explains that the standards'
  > autonomous model, the corporate interests it reflects along with its P21 counterparts, the impulse toward standardization, and the subordination of professional knowledge all put the lie to, for example, Kentucky's quotation of John Dewey in its Model Curriculum Framework: 'If we teach today's students as we did yesterday's, we are robbing them of tomorrow' (2012, p. 49). Yesterday, we taught students using the autonomous model of literacy to prepare them for economic competition and used corporate-sponsored accountability systems to evaluate success. That failed. Today we are doing the same (p.96).
- Main (2012) cites several researchers in listing his concerns about the math standards, specifically:
  > Milgram (2010) condemns the Common Core Standards noting that there are 'many serious flaws" (p. 3). He claims that he was not able to certify that the Common Core Mathematics Standards are benchmarked at the same 74 level as standards of other high achieving countries (Milgram, 2010). The Trends in International Mathematics and Science Study (TIMSS) demonstrate that on eighth grade math and science tests, eight of the 10 top scoring countries had national standards, but so did 9 of the 10 lowest scoring countries in math (Kohn 2010). McCluskey (2010) points out that on the most recent TIMSS to include high school seniors, done in 1995, the United States finished poorly in the combined math and science literacy scale, fourth from the last. The three nations it outperformed all had national standards, but 3 out of the 5 top performing countries did not have national standards, including the top performer (McCluskey 2010). Another study found no correlation between the rigor of a particular state's standards and its National Association for Educational Progress (NAEP) scores (Whitehurst 2009) (p. 74-75).
- Other educators had concerns about some of the language and terminology used within the standards. Haycock, in

2010, had questions in the literacy standards. She wondered what "complex" text really looked like; she wondered what qualities of an argument make it "effective;" she questioned how teachers would differentiate between "approaching" a standard and "meeting" it. She believed that the samples were helpful but that more work would be needed for teachers to understand them deeply (p. 18). She asserted, too, that "standards are just a starting point. They'll need to be accompanied by curricula, the redesign of high-school courses, and the development of other teaching tools. And, of course, we'll need common assessments to go with those common standards" (p. 19). The work that Haycock suggests has been done... and is being done in many states. Educators at the P-12 level – at least in Kentucky - are generally accustomed to this process of implementation in standards-based instruction, though many may not be proficient or even comfortable still with the process.

- Conley & Gaston (2013) note that some of the limitations of the standards are intentional, too: "By intent, they do *not* do several things. Calling out these points is not the same as finding fault with the standards as they exist, but to identify additional areas that, if addressed, will strengthen the implementation of the standards" (p. 27). "Standards are not a curriculum, nor does it tell HOW to teach, they are complex, multilevel, and dense... it's a learning progression, and not much is said about how well students must do to be considered proficient" (p. 27).

Other educators may find fault with a perceived lack of creative thinking, a "too much, too fast" approach, a linked emphasis on standardized assessment, or a loss of emphasis on literature. As the CCSS creators assert, however, the standards are not meant to define the entire curriculum of any spe-

> *...the standards are not meant to define the entire curriculum of any specific grade level or class; they define the minimum skill set necessary for college and career readiness.*

cific grade level or class; they define the minimum skill set necessary for college and career readiness. While limitations of the standards are clear, they do provide a useful starting point for conversations among stakeholders, not only about what students must know and be able to do for college and career, but also for how curricula, assessment, and instruction can be aligned... at the P-12 and higher education levels.

Organization of the Standards

For a deep understanding of the CCSS, one must study both the content and the organization of the standards. The English/language arts (ELA) and the mathematics standards share several characteristics in their organizational structure but are different in a few important ways as well. First, as Conley & Gaston (2013) describe, "each begins with a unifying set of concepts designed to be integrated into and demonstrated through the context of specific content. In mathematics, these are the Standards for Mathematical Practice. In ELA, they are the Anchor Standards" (p. 1).

The Mathematical Practices are derived from important recommendations about *process* from the National Council for Teachers of Mathematics and those related to *mathematical proficiency* as specified in the National Research Council's report, "Adding it Up" (NGA Center & CCSSO, 2010b.) The standards for mathematical practice, then, are these:

CCSS.MATH.PRACTICE.MP1: *Make sense of problems and persevere in solving them.* Math students are expected to identify the problem, analyze factors that influence possible solutions, conjecture, plan, monitor, and evaluate.

CCSS.MATH.PRACTICE.MP2: *Reason abstractly and quantitatively.* "[Mathematically proficient students] bring two complementary abilities to bear on problems involving quantitative relationships: the ability to *decontextualize* – to abstract a given situation and represent it symbolically and manipulate the representing symbols as if they have a life of their own, without necessarily attending to their referents – and the ability to *contextualize*, to pause as needed during the manipulation process in order to probe into the referents for the symbols involved" (NGA Center & CCSO, 2010. para. 3).

CCSS.MATH.PRACTICE.MP3: *Construct viable arguments and critique the reasoning of others.* Not only should proficient math students be able to construct their own arguments, but they can recognize assumptions, use counterexamples, and justify or refute conclusions.

CCSS.MATH.PRACTICE.MP4: *Model with mathematics.* This involves application of math concepts, relationships, and technologies to solve problems in the "real world" and to consistently re-evaluate those applications to improve upon or confirm their usefulness.

CCSS.MATH.PRACTICE.MP5: *Use appropriate tools strategically.* Various technology and implements serve math problem solvers well; proficient math students are not only aware of these tools, but they strategically access such resources to help them solve problems or to deepen their understanding.

CCSS.MATH.PRACTICE.MP6: *Attend to precision.* Accurate, careful, and efficient, proficient math students calculate with precision and communicate their findings with similar explicitness.

CCSS.MATH.PRACTICE.MP7: *Look for and make use of structure.* Patterns and structures are critical to mathematical proficiency, and students need to recognize the significance of such patterns in order to solve problems.

CCSS.MATH.PRACTICE.MP8: *Look for and express regularity in repeated reasoning.* Because mathematically proficient students notice patterns, they can apply both "general methods" and "shortcuts." Such reasoning processes develop math students' automaticity but must be tempered with their continued assessment of results. (© Copyright 2010 National Governors Association Center for Best Practices and Council of Chief State School Officers. All rights reserved.)

These mathematical *practice* standards, "describe ways in which developing student practitioners of the discipline of mathematics increasingly ought to engage with the subject matter as they grow in mathematical maturity and expertise throughout the elementary, middle, and high school years" (NGA Center & CCSSO, 2010b, para. 10), whereas the mathematical *content* standards are a "balanced combination of procedure and understanding" (para. 11). Those mathematical content standards will be reviewed in more detail a little later.

In ELA, the "unifying set of concepts" are known as Anchor Standards. These are the optimal standards that students must master in order to be college and career ready in ELA. Figure 4.1 indicates the anchor standards for the four strands: reading, writing, speaking/listening, and language (NGA Center & CCSSO, 2010c).

Figure 4.1. Common Core Standards: College and Career Anchor Standards for English Language Arts

Anchor Standards for the **READING** strand	Anchor Standards for the **WRITING** strand	Anchor Standards for the **SPEAKING** and **LISTENING** strand	Anchor Standards for the **LANGUAGE** strand
CCSS.ELA-Literacy.CCRA.R.1 Read closely to determine what the text says explicitly and to make logical inferences from it; cite specific textual evidence when writing or speaking to support conclusions drawn from the text.	CCSS.ELA-Literacy.CCRA.W.1 Write arguments to support claims in an analysis of substantive topics or texts using valid reasoning and relevant and sufficient evidence.	CCSS.ELA-Literacy.CCRA.SL.1 Prepare for and participate effectively in a range of conversations and collaborations with diverse partners, building on others' ideas and expressing their own clearly and persuasively.	CCSS.ELA-Literacy.CCRA.L.1 Demonstrate command of the conventions of standard English grammar and usage when writing or speaking.
CCSS.ELA-Literacy.CCRA.R.2 Determine central ideas or themes of a text and analyze their development; summarize the key supporting details and ideas.	CCSS.ELA-Literacy.CCRA.W.2 Write informative/explanatory texts to examine and convey complex ideas and information clearly and accurately through the effective selection, organization, and analysis of content.	CCSS.ELA-Literacy.CCRA.SL.2 Integrate and evaluate information presented in diverse media and formats, including visually, quantitatively, and orally.	CCSS.ELA-Literacy.CCRA.L.2 Demonstrate command of the conventions of standard English capitalization, punctuation, and spelling when writing.

CCSS.ELA-Literacy.CCRA.R.3 Analyze how and why individuals, events, or ideas develop and interact over the course of a text.	CCSS.ELA-Literacy.CCRA.W.3 Write narratives to develop real or imagined experiences or events using effective technique, well-chosen details and well-structured event sequences.	CCSS.ELA-Literacy.CCRA.SL.3 Evaluate a speaker's point of view, reasoning, and use of evidence and rhetoric.	CCSS.ELA-Literacy.CCRA.L.3 Apply knowledge of language to understand how language functions in different contexts, to make effective choices for meaning or style, and to comprehend more fully when reading or listening.
CCSS.ELA-Literacy.CCRA.R.4 Interpret words and phrases as they are used in a text, including determining technical, connotative, and figurative meanings, and analyze how specific word choices shape meaning or tone.	CCSS.ELA-Literacy.CCRA.W.4 Produce clear and coherent writing in which the development, organization, and style are appropriate to task, purpose, and audience.	CCSS.ELA-Literacy.CCRA.SL.4 Present information, findings, and supporting evidence such that listeners can follow the line of reasoning and the organization, development, and style are appropriate to task, purpose, and audience.	CCSS.ELA-Literacy.CCRA.L.4 Determine or clarify the meaning of unknown and multiple-meaning words and phrases by using context clues, analyzing meaningful word parts, and consulting general and specialized reference materials, as appropriate.
CCSS.ELA-Literacy.CCRA.R.5 Analyze the structure of texts, including how specific sentences, paragraphs, and larger portions of the text (e.g., a section, chapter, scene, or stanza) relate to each other and the whole.	CCSS.ELA-Literacy.CCRA.W.5 Develop and strengthen writing as needed by planning, revising, editing, rewriting, or trying a new approach.	CCSS.ELA-Literacy.CCRA.SL.5 Make strategic use of digital media and visual displays of data to express information and enhance understanding of presentations.	CCSS.ELA-Literacy.CCRA.L.5 Demonstrate understanding of figurative language, word relationships, and nuances in word meanings.

CCSS.ELA-Literacy.CCRA.R.6 Assess how point of view or purpose shapes the content and style of a text.	CCSS.ELA-Literacy.CCRA.W.6 Use technology, including the Internet, to produce and publish writing and to interact and collaborate with others.	CCSS.ELA-Literacy.CCRA.SL.6 Adapt speech to a variety of contexts and communicative tasks, demonstrating command of formal English when indicated or appropriate.	CCSS.ELA-Literacy.CCRA.L.6 Acquire and use accurately a range of general academic and domain-specific words and phrases sufficient for reading, writing, speaking, and listening at the college and career readiness level; demonstrate independence in gathering vocabulary knowledge when encountering an unknown term important to comprehension or expression.
CCSS.ELA-Literacy.CCRA.R.7 Integrate and evaluate content presented in diverse media and formats, including visually and quantitatively, as well as in words.	CCSS.ELA-Literacy.CCRA.W.7 Conduct short as well as more sustained research projects based on focused questions, demonstrating understanding of the subject under investigation.		
CCSS.ELA-Literacy.CCRA.R.8 Delineate and evaluate the argument and specific claims In a text, Including the validity of the reasoning as well as the relevance and sufficiency of the evidence.	CCSS.ELA-Literacy.CCRA.W.8 Gather relevant information from multiple print and digital sources, assess the credibility and accuracy of each source, and integrate the information while avoiding plagiarism		

CCSS.ELA-Literacy.CCRA.R.9 Analyze how two or more texts address similar themes or topics in order to build knowledge or to compare the approaches the authors take.	CCSS.ELA-Literacy.CCRA.W.9 Draw evidence from literary or informational texts to support analysis, reflection, and research.		
CCSS.ELA-Literacy.CCRA.R.10 Read and comprehend complex literary and informational texts independently and proficiently.	CCSS.ELA-Literacy.CCRA.W.10 Write routinely over extended time frames (time for research, reflection, and revision) and shorter time frames (a single sitting or a day or two) for a range of tasks, purposes, and audiences.		

Figure 4.1. College and Career Anchor Standards for the four strands: reading, writing, speaking/listening, and language. These are the unifying concepts that represent what all students should be able to do to be college and career ready after completing high school.
© Copyright 2010 National Governors Association Center for Best Practices and Council of Chief State School Officers. All rights reserved.

One can see, by carefully reading through the Anchor Standards and the Standards for Mathematical Practice, that the emphasis is not on rote memorization or even basic conceptual understandings. Instead, students' learning must be demonstrable and requires application. Success is defined by the actual *learning* that takes place. The standards for both mathematics and ELA are designed for progression, so that students incrementally master skills and demonstrate competencies to ultimately achieve college and career readiness. The standards point to this understanding: learning is not a simply grade-by-grade, isolated mastery of skills; rather, learning progresses and builds, and educators can use that intentional progression to identify and target the embedded skills that must be mastered along the way. This is why Conley and Gaston (2013) remind their readers that "[the standards] embody the assumption that success in the 21st century requires much more than content knowledge alone. As today's young people enter postsecondary education and pursue career paths, they will need to draw from and apply literacy and numeracy knowledge and skills across a much wider range of new situations and for more varied purposes than was required of those entering college and the workplace even a generation or two ago" (p. 27). While

> ...students' learning must be demonstrable and requires application. Success is defined by the actual learning that takes place.

the similarities in purpose and general format are clear, educators do need to study the structure and content of the individual content areas to develop a deep understanding of each's content.

Math

The K-8 standards and the high school mathematics standards are slightly different in the way they are organized. First, the K-8 standards are broadly organized by *domains*. These represent the larger groups of related standards. These vary slightly from grade level to grade level. In Kindergarten, for example, domains include the following: "Counting and Cardinality," "Operations and Algebraic Thinking," "Number and Operations in Base Ten," "Measurement and Data," and "Geometry," whereas the 6th grade domains include the following: "Ratios and Proportional Relationships," "The Number System," "Expressions and Equations," "Geometry," and "Statistics & Probability." These variations represent the different emphasis areas of content mastery that are developmentally appropriate for each grade and that help students progress incrementally.

Within each domain are clusters, which summarize groups of related standards. Refer to Figure 4.2 to see an example from 2nd grade that designates how the clusters and standards are represented. The high school mathematics standards also utilize domains, clusters, and standards; however, the high school standards are divided into conceptual ideas as opposed to grade levels. The various high school concepts include the following: "Number and Quantity," "Algebra," "Functions," "Modeling," "Geometry," and "Statistics and Probability." While the CCSS do not require a specific sequence for these high school concepts, they do specify the mathematics that high school students should master in order to be college and career ready.

Figure 4.2. An Example of 2nd grade "Cluster" within the Mathematics Standards Under "Operations and Algebraic Thinking"

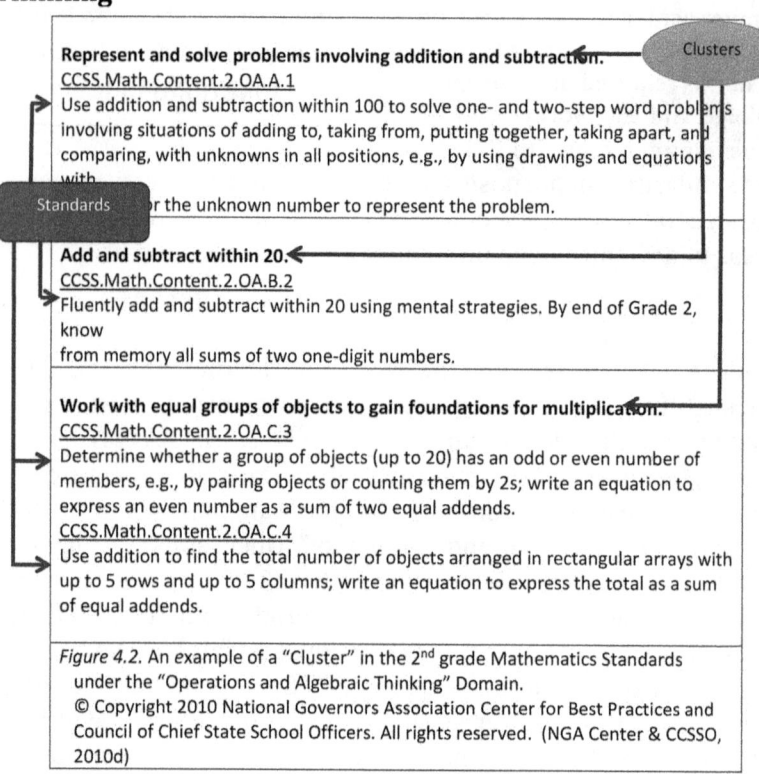

Figure 4.2. An example of a "Cluster" in the 2nd grade Mathematics Standards under the "Operations and Algebraic Thinking" Domain.
© Copyright 2010 National Governors Association Center for Best Practices and Council of Chief State School Officers. All rights reserved. (NGA Center & CCSSO, 2010d)

Dingman et al. (2013) note some specific differences in the comparison of CCSS for Math to pre-CCSS math state standards. The four key changes, specifically in the K-8 mathematics curriculum, include the following:

- There are changes in some grade levels when some mathematical curriculum is to be taught/learned. For example, multiplication and division of basic facts, and fractions are to be taught in earlier grades. Other topics, on the other hand, have been moved to later grades. According to Dingman et al. (2013), "this includes multiplication and division of whole numbers as well as standards that require students to formulate statistical questions" (p. 556). In addition, "One of the biggest movements to a later grade level is probability, where topics that once spanned grades K–8 in the State Standards Analysis are expected only at grade 7 in CCSSM" (p. 556). Main (2012) points out that while NCTM ultimately endorses the final CCSS for mathematics, they, too, expressed concerns about "a few serious placement issues about the learning progressions being overambitious and beyond the bounds of what is known from research" (p. 73).

- Also, there are changes in how many grade levels include some mathematical topics. Dingman et al. (2013) explain:
  > In some cases mathematical topics will typically be given expanded coverage in CCSSM. For example, addition and subtraction with whole numbers on average spanned three grade levels of coverage in the State Standards Analysis. However, CCSSM provides attention to this topic across five grade levels. Similarly, standards for division of whole numbers cross four grade levels in CCSSM, up from an average of two grade levels in the State Standards Analysis. Conversely, in some states certain topics will see decreased coverage in CCSSM when compared with the State Standards Analysis. This includes fraction addition and subtraction, where 32 of 42 states provided three or more grade levels of coverage to this topic, yet CCSSM includes this topic in two grade levels. Additionally, the probabilities that began in early grade levels and spanned multiple grades in many states will be reduced in CCSSM, with coverage only at grade 7 (p. 556).

- Third, there is increased and/or decreased emphasis on some mathematical concepts. For example, algebraic concepts receive more attention in 6-8 instead of being split between the K-5 and 6-8 grade bands. Alternately, some states indicate a decreased emphasis in such concepts as measurement and statistics: "For example, in the State Standards Analysis, 58% of all statistics standards were in grades K–5; however, in CCSSM, this number drops to approximately 33%, as the emphasis for statistics is shifted away from the elementary grades and to-

> *The authors of the CCSS acknowledge the concerns that may arise with the scope and sequence of mathematical concepts within the standards.*

ward the middle grades" (p. 557).
- Finally, there are differences in the "nature and level of reasoning expectations" (p. 556). Dingman et al. (2013) cite one example as changed emphasis on geometric thinking and another as a greater percentage of standards that require students to "evaluate statistical processes" (p. 558).

Some of these changes feel rather dramatic, perhaps, to parents and educators. The authors of the CCSS acknowledge the concerns that may arise with the scope and sequence of mathematical concepts within the standards. They note that students' progression within the standards depends upon their previous learning but also realize the following: "Ideally then, each standard in this document might have been phrased in the form, 'Students who already know A should next come to learn B.' But at present this approach is unrealistic—not least because existing education research cannot specify all such learning pathways. Of necessity therefore, grade placements for specific topics have been made on the basis of state and international comparisons and the collective experience and collective professional judgment of educators, researchers and mathematicians" (NGA Center & CCSSO, 2010e, para. 5).

English/Language Arts

The English/language arts standards have similar components within their structure as their math counterparts but may look very different at an initial reading. First of all, the standards themselves are broken into different sections: There is a K-5 section, a 6-12 section, and a 6-12 content area literacy (i.e., history/social studies, science, and technical subjects) section. The K-5 and 6-12 sections have Reading, Writing, Speaking and Listening, and Language strands, whereas the content literacy section has only Reading and Writing strands. Each grade level standard aligns specifically to those anchor standards for college and career readiness that were identified in Figure 4.1. See Figure 4.3 below to view the organization of the E/LA standards (NGA Center & CCSS0, 2010c). Again, note the link to the anchor standards, the strand, the clusters, and the standards themselves.

Figure 4.3. Common Core State Standards for English Language Arts 7th grade, Speaking and Listening

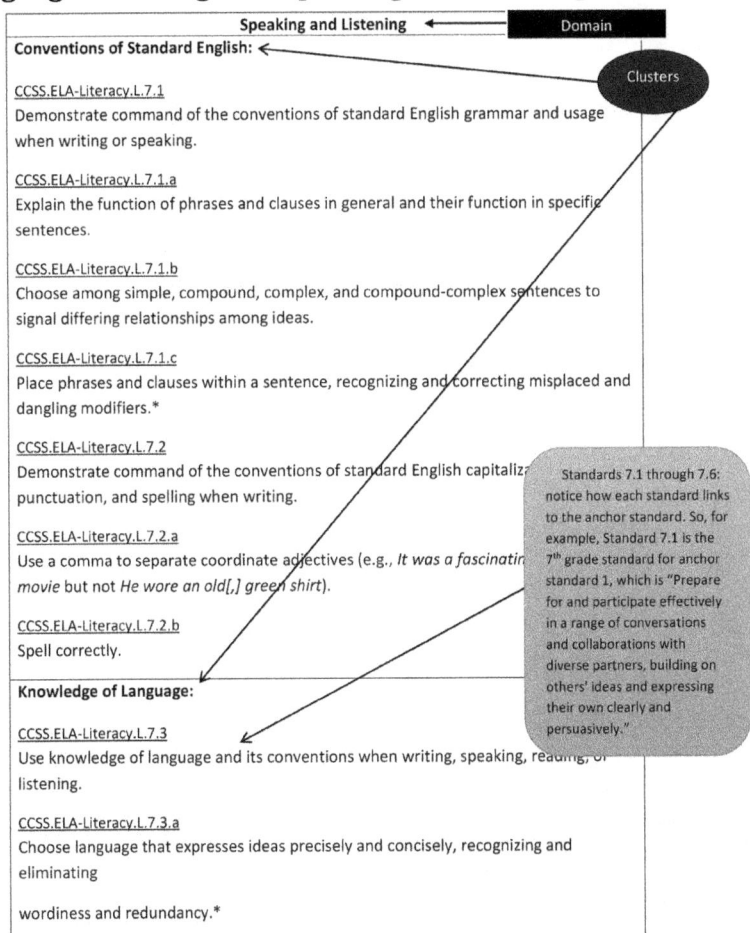

Vocabulary Acquisition and Use:

CCSS.ELA-Literacy.L.7.4
Determine or clarify the meaning of unknown and multiple-meaning words and phrases based on *grade 7 reading and content*, choosing flexibly from a range of strategies.

CCSS.ELA-Literacy.L.7.4.a
Use context (e.g., the overall meaning of a sentence or paragraph; a word's position or function in a sentence) as a clue to the meaning of a word or phrase.

CCSS.ELA-Literacy.L.7.4.b
Use common, grade-appropriate Greek/Latin affixes & roots as clues to the meaning of a word (e.g., *belligerent, bellicose, rebel*).

CCSS.ELA-Literacy.L.7.4.c
Consult general and specialized reference materials (e.g., dictionaries, glossaries, thesauruses), both print and digital, to find the pronunciation of a word or determine or clarify its precise meaning or its part of speech.

CCSS.ELA-Literacy.L.7.4.d
Verify the preliminary determination of the meaning of a word or phrase (e.g., by checking inferred meaning in context or in a dictionary).

CCSS.ELA-Literacy.L.7.5
Demonstrate understanding of figurative language, word relationships, and nuances in word meanings.

CCSS.ELA-Literacy.L.7.5.a
Interpret figures of speech (e.g., literary, biblical, and mythological allusions) in context.

CCSS.ELA-Literacy.L.7.5.b
Use the relationship between particular words (e.g., synonym/antonym, analogy) to better understand each of the words.

CCSS.ELA-Literacy.L.7.5.c
Distinguish among the connotations (associations) of words with similar denotations (definitions) (e.g., *refined, respectful, polite, diplomatic, condescending*).

CCSS.ELA-Literacy.L.7.6
Acquire and use accurately grade-appropriate general academic and domain-specific words and phrases; gather vocabulary knowledge when considering a word or phrase important to comprehension or expression.

Figure 4.3. Common Core State Standards for English Language Arts 7th grade, Speaking and Listening indicating the organization of domains, clusters and alignment with anchor standards.
© Copyright 2010 National Governors Association Center for Best Practices and Council of Chief State School Officers. All rights reserved

As with the math standards, educators notice some distinct characteristics of these new standards. First of all, comprehension is a base skill upon which deeper understanding and application must be built. McLaughlin and Overturf (2012) explain that "research purports that comprehension is a multifaceted process that typically involves strategies such as activating relevant background knowledge, monitoring, visualizing, self-questioning, inferring, summarizing, and evaluating" (p. 159). However, *strategies* – both learning and instructional – are not the focus of the standards: student *learning* defines each standard. Educators should not assume that because comprehension strategy "language" is not clearly defined within the standards that such instructional approaches should not be engaged. In fact, the CCSS authors insist that their intent was *not* to dictate strategy use but rather to emphasize what students should know and be able to do. *How teachers facilitate students' progress depends upon the instructors' strategic use of instruction and resources.*

> *...the CCSS authors insist that their intent was not to dictate strategy use but rather to emphasize what students should know and be able to do.*

In addition, phrases like "text complexity" and "close reading" have sparked conversations and prompted new scholarship. Standard 10, within the Reading strand, states that students should read within each grade level's "text complexity band;" this text complexity band is described and defended in more detail in one of the appendices that accompanies the E/LA common core standards, Appendix A (NGA & CCSSO, 2010f). This document reviews research that reveals how K-12 students are reading less complex texts, are certainly not reading complex texts independently, and that students who are incapable of reading complex texts are ill-prepared for demands of higher education. The document goes on to explain how educators can identify and choose appropriately complex texts. In fact, three components of a text's usefulness ought to be considered:

- Quantitative measures, such as Lexile scores, can help educators determine appropriate texts. Figure 4.4 depicts the recommendations from the CCSS (NGA Center & CCSSO, 2010f).

Figure 4.4. Text Complexity Grade Bands (in Lexiles)

Text Complexity Grade Band in the Standards	Old Lexile Ranges	Lexile Ranges Aligned to CCR expectations
K-1	n/a	n/a
2-3	450-725	450-790
4-5	645-845	779-980
6-8	860-1010	955-1155
9-10	960-1115	1080-1305
11-CCR	1070-1220	1215-1355

Figure 4.4. Text Complexity Grade Bands as depicted in Lexile Scores. The CCR revised the former Lexile Grade Bands to increase text complexity, especially for middle and high school grades.
© Copyright 2010 National Governors Association Center for Best Practices and Council of Chief State School Officers. All rights reserved.

- Qualitative measures include the following factors:
    - levels of meaning (for literary texts) or purpose (for informational texts);
    - structure (i.e., conventional, explicit structures are less complex, for example, than nonconventional or subtle text structures);
    - language conventionality and clarity; and
    - knowledge demands (assumptions of extensive background knowledge indicate higher, more complex knowledge demands) (NGA Center & CCSSO, 2010f).
- Text and reader characteristics also impact the choices that an educator must make. How will the text be used? What scaffolding will be in place? What are the specific needs of the readers themselves? All of these questions must be considered as part of the "text and reader characteristics" component in order to carefully meet the expectation for textual complexity that the standards require.

"Close" reading has also emerged as a practice that is necessary; this facilitates students' mastery of standards that require them to base their speaking and writing on textual evidence.

The Common Core emphasizes using evidence from texts to present careful analyses, well-defended claims, and clear information. Rather than asking students questions they can answer solely from their prior knowledge and experience, the standards call for students to answer questions that depend on their having read the texts with care. The reading standards focus on students' ability to read carefully and grasp information, arguments, ideas, and details based on evidence in the text. Students should be able to answer a range of *text-dependent* questions, whose answers require inferences based on careful attention to the text (NGA Center, 2010g, para. 7-8).

> *Rather than asking students questions they can answer solely from their prior knowledge and experience, the standards call for students to answer questions that depend on their having read the texts with care.*

Close reading, according to Hinchman and Moore (2013), can be used for varied purposes, from making sense of text, to transforming text based upon readers' experiences, to discerning one's position according to social markers, for example. Such purposes, of course, drive educators' choices and teaching of text. Close reading as an instructional technique includes the following components: reading AND rereading, annotating, summarizing (based upon text dependent questions), monitoring or self-explaining, and "after reading" that requires students' use of text (e.g., determining relevance of text) (Frey & Fisher, 2013; Hinchman & Moore, 2013). Again, all of this focus on text helps students *use* text as evidence in their speaking and writing; this combats the late trend of having students express only opinions or lower-level interpretations of text.

> *Because informational text is increasingly more prevalent as students progress to career or college, the new standards emphasize the need for inclusion of such informational texts.*

A final element of the ELA standards worth noting is the emphasis on nonfiction. Because informational text is increasingly more prevalent as students progress to career or college, the new standards emphasize the need for inclusion of such informational texts. In K-5 and 6-12 standards there are 10 standards each for literature and for informational text, indicating the expectation for equal attention to both. By 6-12, standards (which include content area literacy standards for history and social studies, and science and other technical texts) indicate that literary nonfiction (e.g., biographies, science/social studies texts that are narrative, etc.) should be utilized as well. The authors promote the following breakdown of informational to literary texts at different grade levels, based upon the 2009 National Assessment of Education Progress (NAEP) Reading Framework: By grade 4, 50% of reading instruction should be literary and 50%, informational; by grade 8, 45% should be literary and 55%, informational; by grade 12, the distribution should be 30% literary and 70% informational (NGA Center & CCSSO, 2010h).

A Thorough Examination of the Standards

In order for educators to deepen their understanding of the Common Core standards, however, they must be familiar with more than just the overall structure and shifts within the standards. Here are a few steps to help you really dig into the standards. First of all, read them! Read the anchor standards carefully, perhaps even circling key skills or emphasized terms within them. It is also really helpful to do this reading with a small group of colleagues so that you can discuss any questions or observations about the language and learning embedded within the standards. Next conduct a "horizontal" reading of one grade level at a time. In other words, across the grade, look at the standards relevant for that level. For 5th grade ELA, this would include looking at, for example, the "Literature," "Foundational Skills," "Informational Text," "Writing," "Speaking and Listening," and "Language" components. Then "vertically" investigate the 4th and 6th grade components as well. This deep look at a few grade levels provides an interesting overview of the expectations for those grade levels. Compare the language of those standards to the anchor standards; again, small group discussions around these activities provide powerful insight and analysis. Finally, do a "vertical" analysis of a few standards over several grade levels. Notice how the rigor of the standard changes and how intentional students must be in their skill development. Consider Figure 4.5 as an example of a vertical analysis of standard 3 from the speaking and listening strand.

Figure 4.5 An Example of Vertical Alignment: Speaking and Listening, Standard 3

Anchor Standard: CCSS.ELA-Literacy.CCRA.SL.3 **Evaluate a speaker's point of view, reasoning, and use of evidence and rhetoric.**	
Kindergarten	Ask and answer questions in order to seek help, get information, or clarify something that is not understood.
1st grade	Ask and answer questions about what a speaker says in order to gather additional information or clarify something that is not understood.
2nd grade	Ask and answer questions about what a speaker says in order to clarify comprehension, gather additional information, or deepen understanding of a topic or issue.
3rd grade	Ask and answer questions about information from a speaker, offering appropriate elaboration and detail.
4th grade	Identify the reasons and evidence a speaker provides to support particular points.
5th grade	Summarize the points a speaker makes and explain how each claim is supported by reasons and evidence.
6th grade	Delineate a speaker's argument and specific claims, distinguishing claims that are supported by reasons and evidence from claims that are not.
7th grade	Delineate a speaker's argument and specific claims, evaluating the soundness of the reasoning and the relevance and sufficiency of the evidence.
8th grade	Delineate a speaker's argument and specific claims, evaluating the soundness of the reasoning and relevance and sufficiency of the evidence and identifying when irrelevant evidence is introduced.
9th-10th grade	Evaluate a speaker's point of view, reasoning, and use of evidence and rhetoric, identifying any fallacious reasoning or exaggerated or distorted evidence.
11th-12th grade	Evaluate a speaker's point of view, reasoning, and use of evidence and rhetoric, assessing the stance, premises, links among ideas, word choice, points of emphasis, and tone used.

Figure 4.5 An Example of Vertical Alignment: Speaking and Listening, Standard 3, showing the progression of one Anchor Standard from Kindergarten through 11th-12th grade.
© Copyright 2010 National Governors Association Center for Best Practices and Council of Chief State School Officers. All rights reserved.

Impact of the Standards on Higher Education

Higher education faculty need not heave a huge sigh and sit back, however, expecting all of their students' remediation and developmental needs to disappear (though, over time, hopefully these will decline). Nor should faculty believe that the Common

Core standards will not and should not impact their own classroom practice. In fact, the Common Core standards imply that students' readiness skill set must empower them for college *and* career. And certainly upcoming *education students* must be fully aware of how they can teach, assess, and utilize the standards themselves. Besides those obvious connections, the standards (and particularly the ELA anchor standards) provide relevant learning goals for higher education students across all disciplines as well: as texts and content increases in rigor, the same competencies in reading, writing, speaking, listening, and language are expected of students... so why not have conversations within faculty groups about their applicability to course design and instructional practice in college/university classrooms? Perhaps higher education faculty, however, are at a loss as to how to begin such a journey. Tepe reports the following:

> A recent survey conducted by the Center on Education Policy (CEP) indicated that of the 40 responding states, 35 reported that their postsecondary institutions are involved in preparing students in teacher preparation programs to teach the Common Core standards. Of those responding states, only 24 are planning to revise teacher preparation curriculum to reflect the new standards; just 17 indicated they are planning to make the entry requirements for the teacher preparation program more rigorous; and merely 12 reported they were revising course requirements for a teaching degree to require more courses in subject matter content. Even these survey results should be interpreted with caution. It is easy enough for a state education agency to answer affirmatively to a broad question about future plans. The real test will come with substantive changes to teaching practice at the departmental level within institutions, changes that, as with developmental course instruction, many states have no experience with or mechanisms for adjudicating. (2014, p. 22-23)

And Conley and Gaston (2013) acknowledge the perceived impact of the Common Core standards at the higher education level as well, citing a 2011 study done by the Educational Policy Improvement Center (EPIC):

> The study found that most of the nearly 2,000 instructors in 25 different areas, including both general education and more career-oriented courses, stated that the vast majority of the CCSS were

applicable to their courses and important for success in those courses. While the exact profile of standards needed for success in each of the 25 areas varied, the CCSS overall were found to provide solid foundation upon which to undertake postsecondary studies. An overwhelming majority of respondents (96 percent) agreed with the statement that the standards reflect a level of cognitive demand sufficient for students who meet the standards to be prepared to succeed in their course. (p. 2)

And while the P-12 educational backdrop may help facilitate more skilled and strategic readers, writers, speakers, listeners, and mathematicians, higher education faculty may want to think carefully about what role they can play in the further development of the students who cross their doorways.

Some scholars (Robbins, 2013) do worry that a shift in emphasis from teaching objective knowledge (e.g., specific literary works) to subjective thinking skills is much more tenuous and therefore less powerful in preparing students for higher education, but Conley and Gaston (2013) assert that postsecondary faculty have a much different view than secondary educators of what they want students to know and be able to do. In fact, "differences exist regarding the quantity of work that students are expected to produce, the pace at which they are expected to work, and the cognitive challenge levels the work must meet" (p. 28). This is another reason why higher education faculty must work in tandem with secondary teachers. In Kentucky specifically, this work has occurred in many different ways: through Kentucky Leadership Networks (Kentucky Department of Education, 2014), through specific university-district partnerships, and through cooperative partnerships across the state.

An amalgamation of recommendations from King (2011) and Jones and King (2012) provides the following recommendations for how higher education can support the work of the Common Core Standards:

1. Higher education institutions must align key policies for the transition from high school to college, which may include, for example, a recommended college -prep curriculum.
2. Higher education stakeholders must assist in the development of K-12 assessments and aligning college placement policies with those assessments. Not only can colleges and universities use such assessments to determine develop-

mental or placement needs, but students/teachers can also use data from such assessments to provide resources and additional instruction along the way. Students, parents, and educators are all thereby informed throughout the students' educational careers about the skills, competencies, and possible deficiencies that may arise.
3. Higher education faculty must collaborate with K-12 educators to create "seamless transitions between sectors, and to reassess their own curricula for adult, developmental, and general education in light of these new common state benchmarks" (King, 2011, p. 4). This includes aligning entry-level, credit bearing college/university courses with the Common Core standards as well.
4. Finally, higher education faculty must re-consider their curricula and professional development for educator preparation.

Concluding Thoughts

Because, as Merisotis (2013) asserts in a Lumina Foundation report, Americans are "highly mobile," a national approach to K-postsecondary standards allows for success at all levels. They argue that "If our citizens are no longer defined by local geography, our educational standards can't be either" (p. ii). And while teachers in P-12 education have the benefit of professional development and guidance in their reading, understanding, and application of the Common Core standards, higher education faculty may have to seek out their own opportunities to better understand and utilize them. The standards *do* have their limitations – some of which are intentional, – but they have been widely adopted and therefore must not be ignored. If higher education is to partner effectively with P-12 schools to meet the college and career readiness parameters set forth within the standards, discussions and analyses of the standards within higher education institutions must be

> *And while teachers in P-12 education have the benefit of professional development and guidance in their reading, understanding, and application of the Common Core standards, higher education faculty may have to seek out their own opportunities to better understand and utilize them.*

promoted and guided. In Chaper 6, we will explain just how we did that at Eastern Kentucky University.

References

Burns, L.D. (2012). Standards, policy paradoxes, and the new literacy studies: A call to professional political action. *Journal of Adolescent & Adult Literacy, 56*(2), 93-97. doi:10.1002/JAAL.00108

Conley, D.T. & Gaston, P.L. (2013). A path to alignment: Connecting K-12 and higher education via the Common Core and the degree qualifications profile. Retrieved from http://www.luminafoundation.org/publications/DQP/A_path_to_alignment.pdf

Dingman, S., Teuscher, D., Newton, J.A., & Kasmer, L. (2013). Common mathematics standards in the United States: A comparison of K-8 state and common core standards. *The Elementary School Journal, 113*(4), 541 – 564.

Frey, N. & Fisher, D. (2013). Close reading. *Principal Leadership,* 57-59.

Haycock, K. (2010). Building common college-ready standards. *Change,* 14-19.

Hinchman, K. A., & Moore, D.W. (2013). Close reading: A cautionary interpretation. *Journal of Adolescent & Adult Literacy, 56*(6), 441-450. doi:10.1002/JAAL.163

Jaeger, P. (2014). Hear ye, hear ye: A dozen messages from the New York Common Core crier. *Knowledge Quest, 42*(3), 52-57.

Jones, A.G., & King, J.E. (2012). The Common Core Standards: A vital tool for higher education. *Change,* 37-43.

Kentucky Department of Education (2014). Kentucky Core Academic Standards. Retrieved from http://education.ky.gov/curriculum/docs/Pages/Kentucky-Core-Academic-Standards---NEW.aspx

King, J.E. (2011). Implementing the Common Core standards: An action agenda for higher education. *American Council on Education.* Retrieved from http://www.acenet.edu/news-room/Documents/Implementing-the-Common-Core-State-Standards-2011.pdf

Main, L.F. (2012). Too much too soon? Common Core math standards in the early years. *Early Childhood Education, 40,* 73-77.

Mccracken, B.J. (2014). Common core from the outside looking in. *Knowledge Quest, 42*(3), 8-9.

McLaughlin, M. and Overturf, B. (2012). The Common Core: Insights into the K-5 standards. *The Reading Teacher, 66*(2), 153-164. DOI:10.1002/TRTR.01115

Merisotis, J. (2013). Two promising tools for reshaping the system. In *A path to alignment: Connecting K-12 and higher education via the Common Core and the Degree Qualifications Profile* by Conley, D.T. & Gaston, P.L. Lumina Foundation. Retrieved from http://www.luminafoundation.org/publications/DQP/A_path_to_alignment.pdf

National Commission on Excellence in Education. (1983). *A Nation at Risk.* http://www2.ed.gov/pubs/NatAtRisk/title.html

National Governors Association Center for Best Practices & Council of Chief State School Officers. (2014). About the standards: Development process. About the standards. Council of Chief State School Officers, Washington D.C. Retrieved from http://www.corestandards.org/about-the-standards/development-process/

National Governors Association Center for Best Practices & Council of Chief State School Officers. (2010a). Common core state standards initiative standard setting criteria. Retrieved from http://www.corestandards.org/assets/Criteria.pdf

National Governors Association Center for Best Practices & Council of Chief State School Officers. (2010b). *Common Core State Standards for Mathematics.* Washington, DC: Authors. Retrieved from http://www.corestandards.org/Math/Practice/

National Governors Association Center for Best Practices & Council of Chief State School Officers. (2010c). *Common Core State Standards for English language arts and literacy in history/social studies, science, and technical subjects.* Washington, DC: Authors. Retrieved from http://www.corestandards.org/ELA-Literacy/

National Governors Association Center for Best Practices & Council of Chief State School Officers. (2010d). *Common Core State Standards for Mathematics.* Washington, DC: Authors. Retrieved from http://www.corestandards.org/Math/

National Governors Association Center for Best Practices & Council of Chief State School Officers. (2010e). *Common Core State Standards for Mathematics.* Washington, DC: Authors. Retrieved from http://www.corestandards.org/Math/Content/introduction/how-to-read-the-grade-level-standards/

National Governors Association Center for Best Practices & Council of Chief State School Officers. (2010f). Appendix A. Council of Chief State School Officers, Washington D.C. Retrieved from http://www.corestandards.org/assets/Appendix_A.pdf

National Governors Association Center for Best Practices & Council of Chief State School Officers. (2010g). Key shifts in English language arts. Council of Chief State School Officers, Washington D.C. Retrieved from http://www.corestandards.org/other-resources/key-shifts-in-english-language-arts/

National Governors Association Center for Best Practices & Council of Chief State School Officers. (2010h). Key design considerations. Council of Chief State School Officers, Washington D.C. Retrieved from http://www.corestandards.org/ELA-Literacy/introduction/key-design-consideration/)

Robbins, J. (2013). Uncommonly bad. *Academic Questions, 26.* 8-19. DOI 10.1007/s12129-013-9336-9

Tepe, L. (2014) Common Core goes to college: Building better connections between high school and higher education. New America Foundation: Washington, D.C. Retrieved from http://www.newamerica.net/sites/newamerica.net/files/policydocs/CCGTC_7_18_2pm.pdf

Chapter 5

Next Generation Science Standards (NGSS) and Teacher Preparation

Rico Tyler, Kerrie McDaniel, Martha M. Day, and Sam Evans

Brief History of Science Standards

The last twenty-five years have produced a bountiful harvest of K-12 science curriculum atlases, benchmarks, frameworks, and standards. Science for All Americans (1989) was the first in a series of science curriculum documents that include Benchmarks for Science Literacy (1993), National Science Education Standards (1996) and finally, The Atlas of Science Literacy (2001). The influence of these documents can easily be seen in the current Next Generation Science Standards (NGSS).

Common to all of these documents is the desire to go beyond merely creating sequenced lists of important constants, formulas, laws, and theories to include standards which address the important skills, practices and insights that define how science and engineering is actually practiced. The first chapter of *Science for All Americans* is titled "The Nature of Science" with categories for "The Scientific World View," "Scientific Inquiry" and "The Scientific Enterprise." Chapter 11 is titled "Common Themes" and covers systems, models, scale, constancy and change (Ahlgen & Rutherford, 1991). The introduction to the *National Science Education Standards* states the four goals that underlie the standards are to educate students who are able to:
- experience the richness and excitement of knowing about and understanding the natural world;
- use appropriate scientific processes and principles in making personal decisions;

- engage intelligently in public discourse and debate about matters of scientific and technological concern; and
- increase their economic productivity through the use of the knowledge, understanding, and skills of the scientifically literate person in their careers (NRC, 1996).

Five of the eight standards created to support these goals are outside specific subject area classifications:
- unifying concepts and processes in science;
- science as inquiry;
- physical science;
- life science;
- earth and space science;
- science and technology;
- science in personal and social perspectives; and
- history and nature of science.

This distinction is notable because it establishes the need to teach the process and behavior skills associated with scientific work along with the content knowledge required to understand scientific principles.

The Next Generation Science Standards (NGSS)

The Next Generation Science Standards were developed based on *A Framework for K-12 Science Education* released in 2012 by the National Academies National Research Council (NGSS Lead States, 2013). The goal of the framework was to establish a vision for the sufficient knowledge and understanding in science and engineering that high school graduates need so that they can engage in discussions that relate to science, are careful consumers of scientific and technical information, and possess foundation knowledge sufficient such that they may enter the career of their choice (National Research Council, 2012, p.1). A large number of states have adopted the Common Core Standards in mathematics (43 states) and English/language arts

This type of instruction allows students to form connections among the various scientific disciplines.

(44 states) (ASCD, 2014). The Common Core movement created a rich environment for states that adopted Common Core Standards to also adopt common standards in K-12 science education.

Three Dimensions of the NGSS

The framework introduced a three-dimensional organization that has become a defining feature of the NGSS. The three dimensions are scientific and engineering practices; crosscutting concepts that unify the study of science; and disciplinary core ideas in physical science, life science, engineering, and earth and space sciences (NRC, 2012). The framework's vision is for students to explore core ideas from the scientific disciplines by actively engaging in scientific and engineering practices. This type of instruction allows students to form connections among the various scientific disciplines, thus developing understanding of the crosscutting concepts that abound in science (NRC, 2012).

Scientific and engineering practices include the methods scientists and engineers use to achieve their ends (NRC, 2012). These practices include the following:
- asking questions (science) and defining problems (engineering);
- developing and using models;
- planning and carrying out investigations;
- analyzing and interpreting data;
- using mathematics, information and computer technology, and computational thinking;
- constructing explanations (science) and designing solutions (engineering);
- engaging in argument from evidence;
- obtaining, evaluating, and communicating information (NRC, 2012, p.42).

Crosscutting concepts outline important ideas that cross traditional disciplinary boundaries and have explanatory value across science and engineering (NRC, 2012). These practices include
- patterns;
- cause and effect;
- scale, proportion, and quantity;
- systems and system models;

- energy and matter;
- structure and function;
- stability and change (NRC, 2012, p.84).

The last dimension, disciplinary core ideas, is divided into physical science, life science, engineering and earth and space sciences.

Physical Sciences
PS 1: Matter and its interactions
PS 2: Motion and stability: Forces and interactions
PS 3: Energy
PS 4: Waves and their applications in technologies for information transfer (NRC, 2012, p.105)

Life Sciences
LS 1: From molecules to organisms: Structures and processes
LS 2: Ecosystems: Interactions, energy, and dynamics
LS 3: Heredity: Inheritance and variation of traits
LS 4: Biological Evolution: Unity and diversity (NRC, 2012, p.142)

Earth and Space Sciences
ESS 1: Earth's place in the universe
ESS 2: Earth's systems
ESS 3: Earth and human activity (NRC, 2012, p.171)

Engineering, Technology, and the Applications of Science
ETS 1: Engineering design
ETS 2: Links among engineering, technology, science, and society (NRC, 2012, p.203)

Standards documents created before the NGSS tended to establish content objectives at different grade levels. Inquiry, the nature and history of science, technology, and social perspectives were separate and independent from the content standards (NRC, 1996). While this type of layout allows for easy scaffolding of content expectations between grade levels, it leaves room for mundane, paper-pencil instruction that is not an accurate representation of how science works. In contrast, the NGSS, designed around a three dimension framework of Disciplinary Core Ideas (the content), Engineering and Science Processes (how science and engineering is done) and the Cross-cutting Concepts (the silver threads that tie all disciplines of science together) allowed the authors to create for grades P-12 a set of assessable performance expectations. Each performance expectation combines core disciplinary ideas, science and engineering processes, and cross-cutting concepts (NGSS Lead States, 2013). The expectations are based on doing science rather than just memorizing facts. This structure encourages science to be learned by performing observations, experiments, asking questions, and solving problems- acts which involve actually doing science.

> *This structure encourages science to be learned by performing observations, experiments, asking questions, and solving problems- acts which involve actually doing science.*

Implications for Higher Education

The implementation of the Next Generation Science Standards requires all science teachers, regardless of experience, to engage students in real scientific inquiries that cultivate a deep understanding of science content and process (Davis, Petish, & Smithey, 2006; Darling-Hammond, 2006; Mislevy & Duran, 2014). Furthermore, the teacher is expected to facilitate the success of all students and assess the accomplishment of learning outcomes that integrate science content, science processes, engineering practices, cross-cutting concepts, literacy, and math. Within these extraordinary expectations lie specific obstacles that the teacher must overcome. It is the responsibility of the university to recognize the challenges that new teachers will face in implementing the NGSS and provide support in their undergraduate preparation that will help them successfully enact reform (Henderson, Finkelstein, & Beach, 2010). At the university level, the NGSS challenge us in two main ways: a) preparation of future teachers to implement the NGSS, and b) extending the experiences implemented in K-12 through the NGSS into the college curriculum for undergraduate education.

Next Generation Science Standards and Teacher Preparation Programs

Introduction

The adoption and implementation of the Next Generation Science Standards will necessitate changes in educator preparation and the nature of teacher candidate interactions with P-12 students in classroom settings and learning environments outside the classroom. To fully cover all three NGSS dimensions, teacher candidates will need to master ways to provide greater opportunities for their students to be actively engaged in the learning process with a focus on critical and creative thinking, problem solving, observation, and data analysis with reduced emphasis on memorization of the content. These strategies will not only require a transformation of education in the P-12 setting but also in educator preparation programs in higher education.

If we perused education in historical perspective, would we observe that teachers and schools in which they work look much different from what we would find today? This same question could be asked of educator preparation programs and attributed to the following quote taken from a journal written by Cyrus Peirce in the 1800's. In fact, it sounds very similar to what is occurring in educator preparation programs today.

> Twice every day the Principal of the Normal School goes into the model school for general observation and direction, spending from one half hour to one hour each visit. In these visits, I either sit and watch the general operations of the school, or listen attentively to a particular teacher and her class, or [teach] a class myself, and let the teacher be the listener and observer. After the exercises have closed, I comment upon what I have seen and heard before the teachers, telling them what I deem good, and what faulty, either in their doctrine or their practice, their theory or their manner.... In these several ways, I attempt to combine, as well as I can, theory and practice, precept and example. (as cited in Goldstein, 2014, p. 25)

The quote relates to practice in what was considered an outstanding Normal School and is one that is probably emulated in many educator preparation programs today. Unfortunately, educator preparation programs are under heavy criticism today for accepting academically weak students into the programs and graduating individuals who lack sufficient content knowledge. Further, programs are often unable to adequately prepare P-12 students for the demands of the workplace or entry into postsecondary education. Students in the United States are falling behind similar groups of peers in many other countries (Ripley, 2013; Tucker, 2011; Wagner, 2008), with achievement gaps existing among various cultural groups in American schools. These achievement gaps are posing questions as to whether American students are achieving at their fullest potential (Dwyer, 2007) with long term ramifications on our economy (Friedman, 2005; Friedman & Mandelbaum, 2011). Schools are a reflection of society and the community in which they are located, and the school climate can only change through a rigorous, standards-based, intentional education provided by highly trained teachers who have a deep understanding of their content discipline and a strong pedagogical framework to guide their practice.

For these changes to occur, we must transform our system of education to include how we prepare educators for the classroom and the environment in which they work (Sahlberg, 2011). Teachers must be prepared to positively impact learning for all students, and findings from numerous studies indicate that the teacher is the number one variable impacting student learning (Metlife Inc., 2013; Rice, 2003; Sanders, 1998; Sanders & Rivers, 1996). The ability of teachers to successfully implement the NGSS will require a deep knowledge of the disciplines in the field of science, and one educator preparation program in the Southeastern part of the United States is already exploring the option of requiring all elementary education majors to complete, at a minimum, a minor in the broad field of science as part of a five year program of study leading to a master's degree upon successful completion of the program of study. Candidates would be engaged in clinical experience at the beginning of their program of study, and content specialists and pedagogical faculty members would mentor teacher candidates along with master teachers in a teaching school model, similar in concept to a teaching hospital. Teacher candidates would be designing and implementing differentiated learning experiences built on an analysis of student data and aligned with NGSS in settings characterized by diversity.

High School Teacher Preparation

The Next Generation Science Standards call for a deeper understanding of content than before their inception and require mastery of content that can provide rich experiential opportunities for learners. Secondary teachers are the most prepared of all levels for delving deeper into subject matter content. Teacher preparation for secondary teachers typically involves earning a four year, undergraduate degree in the subject area they are going to teach and a major, minor or certificate in educational practices. Secondary science pre-service teachers typically take a content-rich set of courses with laboratory courses that provide exposure to hands-on learning and the scientific method in a STEM discipline. On the surface, it looks like universities are doing what is necessary to prepare science teachers to easily implement NGSS. However, the question arises as to the efficacy of current college teaching practices in preparing future science teachers. The main issue universities need to consider concerning the NGSS are whether the content provided adequately prepares pre-service teachers for implementing the NGSS in their classrooms. Within this overarching issue are the following questions:

- Is the content of the NGSS covered?
- Is the depth of coverage adequate?
- Do pre-service teachers develop an understanding of pedagogical content knowledge?
- Are science processes, engineering practices, and cross-cutting standards addressed?

Undergraduate pre-service secondary teachers take core courses in their academic major and then choose electives to deepen their understanding and complete their required course hours. It is often assumed that this practice produces teachers who have adequately experienced the information needed to teach high school science. Some studies show that teachers who have completed traditional programs may not be sufficiently prepared to teach their content (McKeachie, Pintrich, Lin, Smith, & Sharma, 1990). Teachers with gaps in their content knowledge were less likely to do lab activities and engage students in inquiry than those with strong content knowledge (Koldner et al., 2003; Organization for Economic Cooperation and Development, 2009; Volkmann & Anderson, 1998). Providing an undergraduate curriculum that successfully prepares teachers is necessary if teachers are to be able to implement NGSS into their teaching practice. It is important that universities *align their curriculum* in core science courses to insure that the topics prescribed in the content standards are actually covered sufficiently (Duncan & Hmelo-Silver, 2009). This involves looking at the content that is specified by the NGSS and comparing it with the content covered in undergraduate college classes. If gaps are present, then adjustments need to be made to insure adequate coverage of content. In addition to what content is taught, evaluation of how the courses are taught is important as well. Are these large lecture sections? Is there explanation of scientific inquiry? Moreover, is science process woven throughout the course as an integral method of teaching content? Awareness of what content future teachers are required to teach and how they are to teach it is the first step in making sure they are prepared.

> Awareness of what content future teachers are required to teach and how they are to teach it is the first step in making sure they are prepared.

In addition to subject matter content is the idea of Pedagogical Content Knowledge, (PCK) (Shulman, 1987). This is the notion that in addition to just knowing the content, the teacher should have an idea of how to effectively teach the content to students. This includes knowing best practices, problems that can be used to help with student learning, and addressing com-

> Preparation of teachers to seamlessly teach content through science process and engineering practices requires universities to model scientific process and engineering practices in content courses.

mon misconceptions (Hanuscin & Lee, 2010). For the NGSS, PCK would include integrating science process as a best practice. The NGSS are concerned with students learning science through doing science rather than doing worksheets about science facts. They do not use scientific process as a topic that is covered during week 1, but as a way of performing science in all areas of content throughout the school year. In addition, integrating the Cross-cutting Concepts into science instruction requires an understanding of connections between the disciplines of science. Studies have found that pre-service high school science teachers do not have a comprehension of the connections between classes and disciplines, making it unlikely that they will be able to translate these connections to their own students. (Gess-Newsome & Lederman, 1993; Lederman, 1994).

Preparation of teachers to seamlessly teach content through science process and engineering practices requires universities to *model* scientific process and engineering practices in content courses. Teachers teach the way they were taught (McNally, 2006). Teachers who were taught through mostly lecture spend more time lecturing than other teachers (Darling-Hammond & Bransford, 2005). Although there has been a recent shift in pedagogy at the collegiate level towards classes that are more student-centered, traditional classrooms that transfer information by didactic lectures are common in STEM college level classes (McKeachie et al., 1990; Schwartz & Lederman, 2002; Nelson, 2008; Nicol & Macfarlane, 2006). Most college STEM professors lack formal training in pedagogical practices and lack PCK (Jang, 2008; Jang, 2011; Lenze & Dinham, 1994; Brown & Tanner, 2012; National Research Council (NRC), 1996). Pedagogical change by college STEM faculty is slow and hard (Henderson & Beach, 2011). Resistance to altering traditional teaching include vast amounts of content that are expected to be covered in a short time, lack of preparation time for teaching by the Instructor, large class sizes, lack of training and greater emphasis on research than teaching in many universities (Henderson, Finkelstein, & Beach, 2010).

Developing college professors with effective PCK is necessary to producing future teachers who can effectively implement NGSS. The PCK of the college professor is one of the most important factors in producing PCK in teachers (NRC, 1996). Universities should reward excellent teaching at the college level that models best practice and integrates the three aspects of the NGSS. Emphasis and rewards for teaching should be equal to those in successes in research (Lederman, 1992). It is the responsibility of the university to insure that pre-service teachers are in classes that model scientific process so that they can instigate this type of learning into their classroom, meeting the expectations of the NGSS.

From a practical point of view, modeling best practices and integrating science processes and engineering practices in college STEM classes can be enhanced by motivating students to think critically and solve problems that they find relevant (Ertmer, Schlosser, Clase, & Adedokun, 2014). One example of a pedagogy that lends itself to integration of content with engineering practices is problem-based learning. Problem-based learning is one method to promote high order thinking, problem-solving and content mastery (Ertmer & Simons, 2006). The skills applied in problem-based learning naturally use engineering practices as defined in the NGSS. While not every lesson lends itself to this type of pedagogy, college professors could teach some content with problem-based learning, modeling best practices for integrating NGSS. Technology offers simple support for college professors looking for ways to analyze data, perform simulations (like engineers), and search for facts that bolster content (Kim et al., 2011).

Middle School Teacher Preparation

Preparing pre-service middle school teachers to implement the NGSS shares some of the same challenges with preparing high school teachers. Other features are unique to middle school teacher preparation. While secondary science teachers usually major in a single STEM content area, pre-service middle school teachers need to take a wider range of science courses. The need for content breadth constantly competes with content depth. In some cases, middle school teachers do not feel like they have a "home" academic department so they lack a firm connection to content faculty both during and after their formal academic training. They are "jacks of all trades (sciences), masters of none." The NGSS require a deeper understanding of fewer topics. Middle school teachers are expected to have the background necessary to provide learning through science processes and engineering practices and make connections with other courses and disciplines. Yet, 100 and 200 level science courses are not designed to address this need. Often these lower level courses are taught in large, lecture settings where little hands-on learning or scientific process is modeled (Mazur, 2009; Cross, 1990). Just as with secondary teachers, middle school teachers teach the way they were taught (Darling-Hammond & Bransford, 2005). Ineffective didactic lectures can find their way into the middle school classroom such that many middle school students lose their interest in science (Ertmer et al., 2014). Poor science experiences in middle school result in reduced performance in science in high school (ACT, 2008; Finkelstein & Fong, 2008; Tassell et al., 2012). It is imperative that middle school teachers are prepared to implement the NGSS and understand the content knowledge and PCK contained within them. The stakes are high. Achievement in 8th grade has been found to be one of the best predictors of college and career readiness for students who graduate from high school (ACT, 2008). Universities need to step up to the plate and make sure that future middle school science teachers embrace the NGSS and implement them with aplomb.

Elementary Teacher Preparation

Pre-service elementary teachers offer the greatest challenge to adequately preparing teachers to teach science content using the NGSS. The elementary education college curriculum requires few science courses. The science classes that are prescribed usually fulfill general education requirements and are low level classes often taught in large, lecture sections that are designed to educate the masses rather than prepare teachers to do science inquiry with their students. Pre-service elementary teachers report to have had a negative experience in college science classes (Young & Kellog, 1993). As a result, elementary science teachers lack content knowledge and confidence in teaching science concepts (Crawford, 2000; Keys & Bryan, 2000). The general consensus in the literature is that these teachers have an unsophisticated grasp of science content and have a multitude of misconceptions about science concepts (Davis et al., 2006). There is a strong association between a teacher's confidence to teach science and the use of inquiry in the elementary classroom (Murphy, Neil, & Beggs, 2007; Supovitz & Turner, 2000). Whereas inquiry is just one part of the NGSS, it is integral to the implementa-

> *There needs to be an understanding that excellent teaching at the university level is time-consuming and demanding and adjust workloads and reward scales to reflect this.*

tion of science process as a way of learning science. Universities must be familiar with content and PCK that elementary teachers must possess before entering the classroom in order to adequately implement the NGSS. In many cases, tough choices about curricular issues need to be made in favor of more science content, especially science content that is taught with PCK, in lieu of reducing total credit hours to graduate.

Summary of Implications in Preparing Future Teachers

If educational reform is going to happen in the area of science education as presented in the NGSS, then all entities must play an active role. Public school administrators need to champion the NGSS, and teachers must take the time and make the effort to implement them properly. Universities must ensure that teachers at all levels understand the NGSS and are prepared to implement them in the classroom. There needs to be an understanding that excellent teaching at the university level is time-consuming and demanding and adjust workloads and reward scales to reflect this.

Universities need to do the following:
- recruit and develop a "talent pool" of science faculty who are familiar with the NGSS and have had extensive experiences with K-12 schools and teachers. This group should also demonstrate a history of collaboration with teacher education faculty;
- support and reward faculty who create and teach classes that model best practices of the NGSS in their content classes;
- be cognizant of class size and workload for those faculty modeling best practice for NGSS;
- align curriculum in core content classes with topics taught in the NGSS;
- ensure that science processes and engineering practices are used as best practices to teach science content in core classes;

- emphasize relationships between science disciplines and other courses (cross-cutting standards) so that students are aware of these connections;
- create courses where NGSS are explained and modeled;
- support curricular changes for elementary teachers that deepen both science content knowledge and pedagogical content knowledge; and
- encourage and support an extensive long-term program of content specific K-12 professional development. Such a program would support new K-12 teachers, inform experienced K-12 teachers and be an initiation and training ground for new higher education faculty.

The Next Generation Science Standards in Higher Education: Examples from a Regional University

Introduction

The ideas and concerns presented in the previous section are abstractions. Different universities, with their associated colleges and departments, will respond to NGSS according to their current situation, priorities, existing polices, needs, strengths, and constituent concerns. The authors, faculty members at Western Kentucky University, a regional state university with an enrollment of approximately 21,000 students, have all been involved with different NGSS related university level initiatives. The following paragraphs describe several examples. They range from large, externally funded, multi-million dollar complete program revisions to new courses and an example of a proposed change that has not yet been translated into actual coursework. None offer a panacea to the challenges posed by the NGSS. They are shared as examples of the range of responses a college, department or group of interested faculty might attempt in an effort to address the needs of science teachers in successful NGSS implementation.

UTeach Model Replication

The recruitment, training, and preparation of high quality teachers in the STEM disciplines are critical to the successful implementation of standards-based education reform. A 2010 report by the National Academies of Science and Engineering, *Rising above the Gathering Storm,* identified UTeach as an innovative program with the potential to significantly address STEM teacher shortages (National Academy of Sciences, 2007). UTeach is a secondary and middle grades STEM teacher preparation program developed and implemented in 1997 by the University of Texas at Austin. The program concentrates on the development of STEM teachers who are highly competent in their areas of content expertise with early and frequent clinical field experiences in their teacher preparation programs. Students are taught, mentored, and coached by content professors, education pedagogy professors, and master teachers. The model promotes teacher retention through strong teacher induction support and ongoing teacher professional development.

In 2006, the University of Texas at Austin established the UTeach Institute to support national replication of the UTeach model. In the fall of 2008, 13 universities across the United States began implementing the UTeach model through grant support from the National Mathematics and Science Initiative. Western Kentucky University (WKU) implemented a replication program called SKyTeach, as part of the UTeach Institute's inaugural replication cohort. Currently, 44 universities across the nation are replicating the UTeach model of STEM teacher preparation. UTeach replication programs similar to SKyTeach are operated in an innovative management structure that facilitates communication among all stakeholders in the program. At WKU, STEM teachers are jointly trained in a partnership between the College of Education and Behavioral Sciences and Ogden College of Science and Engineering with leadership provided by a Co-Director representing each college. This partnership between colleges enables the program to implement curricula in both the content areas and professional education coursework that best meets the needs of pre-service teachers. Students earn both a professional education degree in science and mathematics education (SMED), and a content area degree in middle grades mathematics, middle grades science, biology, chemistry, physics, earth and space science or secondary mathematics in a four-year teacher preparation program. In addition to the content area coursework required to complete content area training in the respective teaching disciplines, SMED coursework is delivered in the sequence outlined in

Figure 5.1. Most of the 34 hour sequence is designed to address the specific needs of science and mathematics teachers. MGE/SEC 490 Student Teaching and SMED 489 Student Teaching Seminar are exclusively for science and mathematics teachers.

Figure 5.1. The WKU SKyTeach program coursework in Science and Mathematics Education

SKyTeach Course	Content Summary	Clinical Field Hours
SMED 101 Step One *Intro to Inquiry-Based Approaches/ Teaching* 1 credit hour	Introduction to theory and practice necessary to design and deliver high quality inquiry-based math and science instruction. Students explore and practice the guided inquiry process, create lesson plans and implement them during visits to elementary classrooms.	30
SMED 102 Step Two *Introduction to Inquiry-Based Lesson Design* 2 credit hours	Further exploration of inquiry-based learning experiences, developing skills designing, teaching, analyzing, and assessing inquiry-based math and science lessons. Students design lesson plans and implement them during visits to middle school classrooms.	30
SMED 310 Knowing and Learning 3 credit hours	Introduction to theories and principles of cognition and learning with emphasis on knowing and learning in math and science. Introduction to research on learning, memory, individual development, motivation and intelligence. Applications of learning theory will be explicitly tied to design of lesson plans, instruction and assessment.	20
SMED 320 Classroom Interactions 3 credit hours	Designed to expand students' abilities to understand how learning theories are applied in instructional settings as students develop, implement and evaluate activities and strategies for teaching diverse students equitably.	40
SPED 330 Introduction to Exceptional Education: Diversity in Learning 3 credit hours	Characteristics of exceptionality, special education programs, schools, and community resources and research relative to exceptionality. Field experiences in public schools and/or other appropriate settings away from campus are required in this course.	15

SMED 340 Perspectives on Science and Mathematics 3 credit hours	Introduction to the historical, social, and philosophical implications of math and science through investigations of pivotal experiments and findings. Includes integrated laboratory experiences that replicate significant discoveries.	20
SMED 360 Research Methods 3 credit hours	Laboratory-based introduction to the tools and techniques used by scientists and mathematicians to further an understanding of the natural world and application of this knowledge to math and science education. Students will design and carry out laboratory investigations, and present written and oral reports of results.	20
SMED 470 Project-Based Learning 3 credit hours	Methods, techniques, and technologies used to implement and assess problem based investigations in math and science classrooms.	40
SMED 489 Student Teaching Seminar 3 credit hours	Provides a bridge between the theory and practice of math and science teaching. Methods, techniques, technologies and issues pertinent to math and science instruction in middle grade and secondary classrooms.	n/a
MGE/SEC 490 Student Teaching 10 credit hours	Supervised assignment in approved school setting. Must complete a minimum of sixteen weeks in one or two placements depending on certification requirements.	16 week student teaching experience

Figure 7.1. The SKyTeach program coursework in Science and Mathematics Education shows how curricula in both the content areas and professional education are integrated into coursework that best meets the needs of pre-service teachers.

Students learn how to deliver STEM content to students using the 5E inquiry model of teaching developed by Biological Sciences Curriculum Study, (BSCS) in 1987, (Bybee et al., 2006). The 5E model of instruction has five phases: engagement, exploration, explanation, elaboration, and evaluation. During the engagement phases, the teacher assesses students' prior knowledge through a short activity that promotes thinking along the central theme of the lesson. In the exploration phase, students conduct an initial investigation to generate new ideas about the lesson topic. The explanation phase provides the learners with opportunities to explain their understanding of the topic. In elaboration, the teacher challenges the students' conceptual understanding of the topic. Evaluation occurs throughout the 5E learning cycle and serves a two-fold purpose of allowing students to gauge their own understanding while the teacher evaluates progress towards mastery of the lesson objectives. Under the tutelage of master teachers, students teach 5E inquiry based lessons to local area elementary, middle, and high school students during their first semester in the program, and they continue to gain valuable teaching experience throughout the program. The program's master teachers are master's degree level content area specialists in a STEM discipline. Each master teacher has an extensive track record of successful classroom teaching in a STEM discipline with a minimum of five years of middle or secondary teaching experience. The master teachers foster relationships with local area schools to facilitate student clinical teaching experiences and also supervise student work in clinical experiences. In addition to the expertise offered by the master teachers, students enrolled in the SKyTeach program have access to a STEM teacher work and supply room for the purposes of lesson development and preparation.

As described earlier in this chapter, the NGSS include three dimensions: scientific and engineering practices; crosscutting concepts that unify the study of science; and, disciplinary core ideas of physical sciences, life sciences, earth and space sciences (NRC, 2012). SKyTeach pre-service teachers develop content disciplinary ideas in their respective major area courses. Therefore, SMED coursework is devoted to developing pre-service teachers' skills in the NGSS scientific and engineering practices and crosscutting concepts in a clinical model of teaching. Since the students complete 215 clinical field hours in their SMED coursework, there are ample opportunities for students to develop, practice, and apply pedagogy that encompasses NGSS standards. Students complete focused activities in each of the SMED courses that specifically address the NGSS concepts and practices within each course. The application of cross-cutting concepts is slowly developed over the course of pre-service teachers' PCK development within program progression in the coursework. The NGSS concepts and practices applied in each of the SMED courses are listed in Figure 5.2.

Figure 5.2. NGSS Integration in SKyTeach Courses

Science and Mathematics Education Course	Course activity	NGSS Scientific and Engineering Practices	NGSS Crosscutting Concepts
SMED 101 Step One *Intro to Inquiry-Based Approaches/ Teaching*	5E model lesson 5E teaching cycle (elementary)	1,3,4,5,6,7,8	Skill development during lesson planning
SMED 102 Step Two *Introduction to Inquiry-Based Lesson Design*	5E teaching cycle (middle school) Focused inquiry observation	1,3,4,5,6,7,8	Skill development during lesson planning
SMED 310 Knowing and Learning	5E lesson plan Inquiry Teaching Reflection	1,3,4,5,6,7,8	Skill development during lesson planning
SMED 320 Classroom Interactions	Video analysis project Equity issues in education	1,2,3,4,5,6,7,8	Skill development during lesson planning
SPED 330 Introduction to Exceptional Education: Diversity in Learning	Practical observations in special education	n/a	n/a
SMED 340 Perspectives on Science and Mathematics	Using history to improve mathematics and science instruction STEM teacher professional development	1,2,3,4,5,6,7,8	1,2,3,4,6,7
SMED 360 Research Methods	Inquiry presentation	1,2,3,4,5,6,7,8	1,2,4,7
SMED 470 Project-Based Learning	Project-based unit plan Voice of the customer clinical interview	1,2,3,4,5,6,7,8	3,5,6,7
SMED 489 Student Teaching Seminar	Teacher work sample	1,3,4,5,6,8	1,2
MGE/SEC 490 Student Teaching	Teaching Practicum	n/a	n/a

Figure 7.2. NGSS Integration in SKyTeach Courses shows the courses in which specific NGSS Science and Engineering Practices and Cross-cutting Concepts are integrated across the pre-service teacher preparation coursework.

All of the SMED courses emphasize STEM disciplines and help students strengthen their pedagogical content knowledge. These skills are developed through specific, sequential exercises that occur throughout the teacher training program. Further, the exercises are prescribed in a gradual release format. The professors and master teachers first model the techniques and then students are asked to reflect on their observations of the model lesson. Next, students are asked to conduct focused observations of veteran teachers in a field placement using classroom observation protocol instruments. Students then deliver master teacher prepared lessons in a clinical setting after they practice teaching the inquiry lesson to their peers with feedback and critique from the master teacher. Finally, students work in teams to develop their own inquiry based lessons and practice teaching the lesson with the master teacher in preparation for full delivery in a clinical setting. Students learn how to apply scientific and engineering practices during their early SMED coursework during the acquisition of lesson planning skills. Cross-cutting concepts are applied in more advanced SMED courses since the more sophisticated lessons implemented in later coursework are more conducive to the application of cross-curricular STEM instruction. This model of skill development allows the pre-service teachers to slowly internalize the desired skill acquisition in a setting designed to provide a continuous feedback loop for maximum teaching effectiveness.

Revising the Middle School Teacher Preparation Program: Biology 303

Understanding that middle school teachers have unique needs to becoming prepared science teachers, WKU developed an undergraduate middle school teaching major with several courses specifically aimed at science content combined with PCK. One of these courses directly targets preparing pre-service teachers to implement the NGSS. This course, Life Science for Middle School Science Majors (Biology 303) is housed in the Ogden College of Science and Engineering in the Department of Biology and is taught by a STEM faculty member with an understanding of pedagogy. The course is designed to delve deeper into the life science content specified by the NGSS and offer practical discussions, activities, and inquiries into how the topics could be taught. Because this major reaches students attending regional campuses, the format of the course was set up as online learning. Although this seems to be counter-intuitive to hands-on, inquiry learning, the course is rich with hands-on activities that are used to teach core concepts. Each topic begins with a look at the NGSS so that future teachers understand the integration of science process/engineering practice with cross-cutting concepts and student outcome expectations. Short, Tegrity-lecture, capture software generated "mini-lectures" review the main ideas of the biological concepts outlined in the content standards and the PCK is demonstrated through hands-on activities, experiments, discussions and assignments. Pictures of students doing the activities are required as part of the assessment. In addition to working with the content of each standard using science processes and/or engineering practices, each content standard must be written as a lesson or unit and graded at the end of the semester. Activities performed in class may be included but are not required. Misconceptions are addressed and formative assessment is given during the semester. In fact, a colleague teaching an education course was surprised when he asked his class for examples of college professors providing formative assessment, and students responded with examples from an online course (Biology 303)! Examples of clarifying NGSS include an email from a student asking about the "catalase experiment." The professor's response was that it was not a catalase experiment, but that they were using the catalase experiment as a way to understand how proteins/enzymes work. Within this activity, the cross-cutting concept of form and function (the shape of the enzyme dictates its function) is inherent. NGSS can be as simple as a change in perception about science teaching. It is not a set of activities or experiments that have to be checked off but a repertoire of experiences that engage learners to understand content. This is the concept behind the inception of Biology 303.

SMED 300-Middle Grades Science Skills and Methods and SMED 400-Applying Middle Grade Science across Disciplines

In the fall of 2008, faculty from Western Kentucky University College of Education and Behavior Sciences and Ogden College of Science and Engineering were awarded an NSF grant to conduct a

2-year study of the mathematics and science teaching practices of middle grades teachers in Western Kentucky. As a part of this study, 25 STEM/ED (science, technology, engineering, math and education) faculty from six postsecondary partner institutions made site visits to 30 Western Kentucky middle schools. Two hundred, seventy-two mathematics and science teachers were observed in the classroom and interviewed (Tassell et al., 2012). Some of the important findings of the study included the following:

- Only a few mathematics and science teachers found one or more real-world examples within the content covered.
- In just a few science classrooms, students were engaged in investigations at higher levels, with most completing pre-planned activities requiring little or no analysis.
- Classroom observations indicated instruction is teacher-led and centered on mastery of factual information or reviewing content.
- Teachers and students have disparate views on whether presented math/science content or activities relate to their daily lives as well as the frequency of teacher lecture in science vs. inquiry-based instruction (Tassell et al., 2012).

Observers also reported extremely low frequency of observation of students developing and using science skills such as observing, measuring, classifying, inferring, predicting, communicating results, designing experiments, conducting experiments, interpreting data, and forming conclusions (Tassell et al., 2012).

As these data were collected, SKyTeach faculty observed that middle grades science pre-service teachers were typically performing one letter grade below their secondary pre-service teaching peers in SMED 360 (Research Methods). SMED 360 is a course intended to develop students' skills in science research practices. A consensus developed among SKyTeach faculty that these observations indicated a curricular deficiency in the middle grades science teacher preparation program. Many of the science courses taken by middle grade science teachers are also general education courses. Taken as a group, these courses were not explicitly designed to teach science and engineering practices at the level needed by middle grade science teachers. To help address this issue, SKyTeach created two new science content courses specifically to address the pedagogical needs of pre-service middle grades science teachers.

The first of these courses is SMED 300-Middle Grades Science Skills and Methods. This course addresses the range of NGSS science and engineering practices. The second course, SMED 400-Applying Middle Grade Science across Disciplines, uses a project-based approach designed around real-world applications and examples to teach crosscutting concepts such as patterns, cause and effect, scale and proportion, systems, and energy. Both courses are taught by SKyTeach master teachers and have proven very successful in developing PCK competencies and NGSS process and skill competencies with pre-service middle grades science teachers. Inspired by the example of Biology 303, both SMED 300 and SMED 400 have been adapted for interactive video delivery at regional campus sites, with each site having a master teacher to co-teach the course and facilitate clinical field experiences in local area schools.

An Idea Still in Development: Revising the Elementary Science Sequence

As discussed in the previous section on elementary teacher preparation, elementary pre-teachers are traditionally prepared as generalists in content. Therefore, the teacher candidates only take science content coursework that satisfies general education requirements. Since these courses are selected from a range of options, there is currently no mechanism in place to ensure that specific content across the entire range of NGSS in life sciences, physical sciences and earth and space sciences are addressed within elementary teacher preparation programs in science. Further, the majority of elementary education majors are required to take only one 3-credit hour course in elementary science teaching methods. A single semester, 3-credit hour course lends only a scant amount of time for instructors to develop pre-service teachers' pedagogical content knowledge in scientific and engineering practices and cross cutting concepts outlined in the NGSS. Additionally, the clinical field hours assigned to the elementary science teaching methods course are

Researchers have found that teachers who lack sufficient scientific content knowledge are limited in their ability to identify and correct students' misconceptions regarding scientific content.

combined with other elementary content area methods courses in a block style, clinical format, thus creating clinical experiences that are generalized in nature rather than providing focused clinical experiences in teaching scientific practices.

Researchers have found that teachers who lack sufficient scientific content knowledge are limited in their ability to identify and correct students' misconceptions regarding scientific content (Davis, 2004; Jarvis, Pell, & McKeon, 2003; Shallcross, Spink, Stephenson, & Warwick, 2002). Shulman (1986) asserts that pedagogical content knowledge includes an understanding of what makes the learning of specific content topics simple or challenging, along with the typical conceptions and misconceptions that students of various backgrounds and ages generally possess. Thus, to develop the ability to teach science content effectively, a teacher must possess both scientific and pedagogical content knowledge. In order to accomplish this, science teacher preparation programs at the elementary level must redesign coursework to address the unique needs of the elementary teacher in developing a content knowledge base across scientific disciplines in life, physical, and earth and space sciences, which cannot be accomplished through the typical general education requirements that exist in undergraduate curricula.

A proposed solution is to shift the elementary teacher preparation program to a three course sequence that addresses both the scientific content and pedagogical content needs required for successful teaching in elementary grades science. The traditional elementary education science coursework entails a 4-credit hour biology course and a 3-credit hour elementary science methods course that includes 30 clinical field hours. Figure 5.3 shows the usual science course sequence WKU elementary majors complete.

Figure 5.3. Typical Elementary Education Science Coursework

Course Title	Credit Hours	Clinical Field Hours
General Biology	4	0
Elementary Science Methods	3	30
General Education Science Elective	3-4	0

Figure 5.3. Typical Elementary Education Science Coursework and related field requirements that WKU elementary science majors complete.

This format does not ensure any specific content in earth and space science and the physical sciences. Further, the topics addressed in the general biology coursework are not aligned with content outlined in the NGSS for grades K-8. In fact, pre-service elementary teachers report that they see little relationship between laboratory science courses in traditional college science laboratories and what they need to know in order to develop elementary level, hands-on science activities (Schoon & Boone, 1998). Four years ago, a faculty committee was formed to study the issue and make recommendations. The group included faculty representation from biology, chemistry, geology, physics, and teacher education. The group proposed that a more appropriate approach to elementary teacher preparation in science is to implement a three-course sequence of science content and science teaching methods that is aligned with the NGSS in content and skill development. Figure 5.4 outlines the proposed coursework for a more comprehensive science sequence. This sequence ensures, in each discipline, basic NGSS content coverage.

Figure 5.4. Proposed Comprehensive Elementary Education Science Sequence

Course Title	Credit Hours	Clinical Field Hours
Life Sciences for Elementary Teachers	3	15
Earth and Space Science for Elementary Teachers	3	15
Physical Sciences for Elementary Teachers	3	15
Figure 5.4. Proposed Comprehensive Elementary Education Science Sequence with credit hours and related field experience requirements.		

In the proposed model, elementary education science coursework would be co-taught by content area professors in the respective disciplines of life, physical, and earth and space science and a master teacher with extensive science teaching experience in a K-8 classroom. The professor and master teacher would jointly plan and deliver content that is specifically aligned with the NGSS in a manner that is appropriate for elementary teachers. The professor would act as the principal in charge of ensuring that the pre-service teachers develop appropriate scientific content knowledge and the master teacher would facilitate the development of pedagogical content knowledge. This model affords elementary pre-service teachers the opportunity to develop sufficient content knowledge across scientific disciplines and allows them to cultivate pedagogical content knowledge that is age appropriate to their future students. The proposed model would also provide a rich opportunity to study and compare elementary teacher self-efficacy in science content and the development of science content and process skills across the traditional and proposed teacher preparation models.

While the committee recommendation was well received and the committee began preliminary curriculum design and textbook selection, the proposal has not yet been adopted. The difficulty of finding "room" in an already crowded course sequence and finding enough faculty to staff the courses has, so far, kept this proposal from becoming implemented in the elementary pre-service teacher program of studies.

Summary

The Next Generation Science Standards are an exciting development towards ensuring scientific literacy for all Americans. The success of these standards will depend in large part on how well in-service teachers understand and are prepared to teach these standards (NRC, 2012, p. 257). Pre-service teachers too often bring to the university a mindset that teaching is mostly about lists, facts, and rules (Hattie, 2009). This is a misconception their university experiences can either encourage or change. This makes it especially important that science departments, as well as teacher education programs, encourage, support and reward faculty who work toward understanding the NGSS, model best practices based on the NGSS, and support K-12 teachers as they work to bring NGSS standards into their classrooms.

References

ACT. (2008). *The forgotten middle: Ensuring that all students are on target for college and career readiness before high school.* Iowa City, IA: ACT.

Adams, P.E., & Krockover, G.H. (1997). Beginning science teacher cognition and its origins in the pre-service secondary science teacher. *Journal of Research in Science Teaching, 349*(6), 633-653.

Ahlgen, A. & Rutherford, J. (1991). *Science for All Americans.* New York, NY: Oxford University Press.

American Association for the Advancement of Science. (2001). *Atlas of Science Literacy.* New York, NY: Oxford University Press.

American Association for the Advancement of Science. (1993). *Benchmarks for Science Literacy.* New York, NY: Oxford University Press.

Anderson, W. (2011). Changing the culture of science education at research universities. *Science, 331,* 152-153.

Andrews, T.M., Leonard, M.J., Colgrove, C.A., & Kalinowski, S.T. (2011). Active learning not associated with student learning in a random sample of college biology courses. *Life Sciences Education, 10,* 394-405.

Association of Supervision and Curriculum Development. Common Core State Standards adoption by state. Retrieved from http://www.ascd.org/common-core-state-standards/common-core-state-standards-adoption-map.aspx

Britton, E., McCarthy, Ringstaff, C., & Allen, R. (2012). Addressing challenges faced by early career mathematics and science teachers: A knowledge synthesis. Retrieved from http://www.mspkmd.net/papers.

Brown, S., & Tanner, K. (2012). Barriers to faculty pedagogical change: Lack of training, time, incentives, and... tensions with professional identity? *Life Science Education, 11,* 339-346.

Bybee, R., Taylor, J., Gardner, A., Van Scotter, Powell, J., Westbrook, A., & Landes, N. (2006). The BCBS 5E instructional model: Origins and effectiveness. A report prepared for the Office of Science Education National Institutes of Health. Retrieved from http://science.education.nih.gov/houseofreps.nsf/b82d55fa138783c2852572c9004f5566/$FILE/Appendix%20D.pdf

Crawford, B. (2000). Embracing the essence of inquiry: New roles for science teachers. *Journal of Research in Science Teaching, 37,* 916-937.

Cross, K.P. (1990). Teaching to improve learning. *Journal of Excellence in College Teaching, 1*(1), 9-22.

Darling-Hammond, L., & Bransford, J. (2005). *Preparing Teachers for a changing world. What teachers should learn and be able to do.* San Francisco, CA: Jossey-Bass.

Darling-Hammond, L. (2006). Constructing 21st-century teacher education. *Journal of Teacher Education, 57*(3), 300-314.

Davis, A., Petish, D., & Smithey, J. (2006). Challenges new science teachers face. *Review of Educational Research, 76*(4), 607-651.

Davis, E. (2004). Knowledge integration in science teaching: Analysing teachers' knowledge development. *Research in Science Education, 34*(1), 21-53.

Duncan, R. & Hmelo-Silver, C. (2009). Learning progressions: Aligning curriculum, instruction and assessment. *Journal of Research in Science Teaching, 46*(6), 606-609.

Dwyer, C. A. (Ed). (2007). *America's challenge: Effective teachers for at-risk schools and students.* Washington, DC: National Comprehensive Center for Teacher Quality.

Ertmer, P., & Simons, K. (2006). Jumping the implementation hurdle: Supporting PBL in K-12 classrooms. *eInterdisciplinary Journal of Problem Based Learning, 1*(1), 41-56, Retrieved from http://dx.doi.org/10.771/1541-5015.1005.

Ertmer, P., Schlosser, S., Clase, K., & Adedokun, O. (2014). The grand challenge: Helping teachers learn/teach cutting edge science via a PNL approach. *Interdisciplinary Journal of Problem-based Learning, 8*(1). http://dx.doi.org/10.771/1541-5015.1407.

Finkelstein, N.D., & Fong A.B. (2008). Course taking patterns and preparation for post-secondary. (Issues and Answer Report –REL 2008- No. 035). Washington D.C.: U.S. Department of Education, Institute of Educational Sciences, National Center for Educational and Regional Assistance, Regional Educational Library West.

Friedman, T. L. (2005). *The world is flat: A brief history of the twenty-first century.* New York, NY: Farrar, Straus and Giroux.

Friedman, T. L., & Mandelbaum, M. (2011). *That use to be us: How America fell behind in the world it invented and how we can come back.* New York, NY: Farrar, Straus and Giroux.

Gess-Newsome, J., & Lederman, N.G. (1993). Pre-service biology teachers' knowledge structures as a function of professional teacher education: A year-long assessment. *Science Education, 77*(1), 25-45.

Goldstein, D. (2014). *The teacher wars: A history of America's most embattled profession.* NY, New York: Doubleday.

Hattie, J. (2009). *Visible learning. A Synthesis of over 800 meta-analyses relating to achievement.* New York, NY: Routledge.

Hanuscin, D. & Lee, M. (2010). Elementary teachers' pedagogical content knowledge for teaching the nature of science. *Science Education, 95*(1), 145-167.

Henderson, C., & Beach, A. (2011). Facilitating change in undergraduate STEM instructional practices: An analytic review of the literature. *Journal of Research in Science Teaching, 48,* 952-984.

Henderson, C., Finkelstein, N., & Beach, A. (2010). Beyond dissemination in college science teaching: An introduction to four core change strategies. *Journal of College Science Teaching, 39*(5), 18-25.

Jang, S. (2011). Assessing college students' perceptions of a case teacher's pedagogical content knowledge using a newly developed instrument. *Higher Education, 61,* 663-678.

Jang, S. (2008). The effects of integrating technology, observation and writing into a teacher education methods course. *Computers and Education, 50*(3), 853-865.

Jarvis, T., Pell, A., & McKeon, F. (2003). Changes in primary teachers' science knowledge and understanding during a two year in-service programme. *Research in Science & Technological Education, 21*(1), 17-42.

Keys, C.W., & Bryan, L.A. (2000). Co-constructing inquiry-based science with teachers: Essential research for lasting reform. *Journal of Research in Science Teaching, 38*, 631-645.

Kim, M.C., Ertmer, P.A., Fang, J., Kim, W., Tomory, A., & Freemyer, S. (2011). Challenges of facilitating technology-enhanced inquiry among high school students: A multiple case study. Paper presented at the annual convention of the American Educational Research Association, New Orleans, LA.

Koldner, J.L, Camp, P.J, Crismond, D., Fasses, J.G., Holbrook, J., Puntambekar, S., & Ryan, M. (2003). Problem-based learning meets case-based reasoning in the middle school science classroom. Putting learning by design into practice. *Journal of the Learning Sciences, 12*, 495-547. Retrieved from http://dx.doi.org/10.1207/S15327809JLS1204_2.

Lederman, N.G. (1992). Students and teachers' conceptions of the nature of science: A review of the research. *Journal of Research in Science Teaching, 29*(4), 331-359.

Lenze, I. & Dinham, S. (1994). Examining pedagogical content knowledge of college faculty new to teaching. Paper presented at the Annual Meeting of the American Educational Research Association. New Orleans, LA.

Mazur, E. (2009). Farewell, lecture. *Science, 323*, 50-51.

McKeachie, W.J., Pintrich, P.R., Lin, Y-G, Smith, D.A.F., & Sharma, R. (1990). *Teaching and Learning in the College Classroom. A Review of the Research Literature* (3rd ed.). Ann Arbor: University of Michigan Press.

McNally, J. (2006). Confidence and loose opportunism in the science classroom: Towards a pedagogy of investigative science for beginning teachers. *International Journal of Science Education, 28*(4), 423-438.

Metlife, Inc., (2013). *The Metlife survey of the American teacher: Challenges for School Leadership.* NY: New York.

Mislevy, R., & Duran, R. (2014). A sociocognitive perspective on assessing EL students in the age of Common Core and Next Generation Science Standards, *TESOL Quarterly, 48*(3), 560-585. DOI: 10.1002/tesq.177

Murphy, C., Neil, P., & Beggs, J. (2007). Primary science teacher confidence revisited. Ten year on. *Educational Research, 49*, 415-430.

National Academy of Sciences, National Academy of Engineering, and Institute of Medicine Committee on Science, Engineering, and Public Policy. (2007). Rising above the gathering storm: Energizing and employing America for a brighter economic future. The National Academies Press, Washington, D.C. Retrieved from http://www.nap.edu/catalog/11463.html (December 1, 2014).

National Research Council. (1996). National Science Education Standards. Washington D.C. National Academy Press.

National Research Council committee on a conceptual framework for new K-12 science education standards. (2012). A framework for K-12 science education: Practices, cross-cutting concepts and core ideas. The National Academies press, Washington, D.C. Retrieved from: http://www.nap.edu/openbook.php?recrd_id=13465 (November 17, 2014).

Nelson, C.E. (2008). Teaching evolution (and all of biology) more effectively: Strategies for engagement, critical reasoning, and confronting misconceptions. *Integrative and Comparative Biology, 48*, 213-225.

Next Generation Science Standards Lead States (NGSS Lead States). (2013). The Next Generation Science Standards. Achieve, Inc. on behalf of the twenty-six states and partners, Retrieved from http://www.nextgenscience.org/next-generation-science-standards (November 5, 2014).

Nicol, J., & Macfarlane-Dick, D. (2006). Formative assessment and self-regulated learning: A model and seven principles of good feedback practice. *Studies in Higher Education, 31*(2), 199-218.

Organization for Economic Cooperation and Development. (2009). Top of the class: High performers in science in PISA 2006. Retrieved from http://www.oecd.org/dataecd/44/7/42645389.pdf.

Rice, J. (2003). *Teacher quality: Understanding the effectiveness of teacher attributes.* Washington, DC: Economic Policy Institute.

Ripley, A. (2013). *The smartest kids in the world: And how they got that way.* New York, NY: Simon & Schuster.

Sahlbert, P. (2011). *Finnish Lessons: What can the world learn from educational change in Finland?* New York: Teachers College, Columbia University.

Sanders, W. (1998). Value-added assessment. *School Administrator, 55*(11), 24-27.

Sanders, W., & Rivers, J. (1996). *Cumulative and residual effects of teachers on future student academic achievement.* Knoxville: University of Tennessee Value-Added Research and Assessment Center.

Shallcross, T., Spink, E., Stephenson, P., & Warwick, P. (2002). How primary trainee teachers perceive the development of their own scientific knowledge: Links between confidence, content and competence? *International Journal of Science Education, 24*(12), 1293-1312.

Schoon, K., & Boone, W. (1998). Self-efficacy and alternative conceptions of science of pre-service elementary teachers. *Science Education, 82*(5), 553-568.

Schwartz, R., & Lederman, N. (2002). "It's the nature of the beast:" The influence of knowledge and intentions on learning and teaching nature of science. *Journal of Research in Science Teaching, 39*(3), 205-236.

Shulman, L. (1986). Those who understand: Knowledge growth in teaching. *Educational Researcher, 15*(2), 4-14.

Shulman, A.L. (1987). Knowledge and teaching: Foundations of the new reform. *Harvard Education Review, 57*(1), 1-22.

Supovitz, J.A., & Turner, H.M. (2000). The effects of professional development on science teaching practices and classroom culture. *Journal of Research in Science Teaching. 37*, 963-980.

Tassell, J., McDaniel, K., Johnson, H., Norman, T., Pankratz, R., & Tyler, R. (2012). Explore performance in mathematics and science: Why are middle school students unprepared for success in math and science? *International Journal of Innovation in Science and Mathematics Education, 20*(1), 1-23.

Tucker, M.S. (2011). Researching other countries' education systems. In M. S. Tucker (Ed.), *Surpassing Shanghai: An agenda for American education built on the world's leading systems* (pp. 1-18). Cambridge, MA: Harvard Education Press.

Young, B.J., & Kellog, T. (1993). Science attitudes and preparation of preservice elementary teachers. *Science Education, 77*(3), 279-291.

Wagner, T. (2008). *The global achievement gap.* New York, NY: Basic Books.

Chapter 6

It's Going to Get Messy: A Step by side-stepping process to align course Student Learning Outcomes, instructional strategies, and assessment practices with common standards

Ginni Fair

Messiness. If you stopped by my campus office, you might not think that a wee bit of messiness would bother me...that is, if you could see me past the clutter. If you stopped by my house, you would be convinced that I was entirely comfortable in an environment of disarray. With four young children, two crazy pups, and two full-time employed parents living there, every room has a pile of laundry (dirty or clean? Who knows?), a cache of toys (kids' or dogs'? Who can tell?), and, of course, a stack of books (his or hers? Definitely hers!). If I were to be honest, though, the messiness *does* bother me. I *prefer* to have things put away neatly. I would love to have *Southern Living* drop by for a visit in a photo-ready, always tidy living room. Such an environment, though, does not exist. At least not for me. BUT...and hear me out here... sometimes my messy is constructive, like when I have to take all my books out of my bookcase to better organize them. Or when I have to separate dirty clothes into piles in order to find the one dance outfit that I have to wash before my daughter can go to practice. Or even when I pull out documents to review so that I can choose the "just right" article for one of my classes.

You see, messiness can be productive. It may be uncomfortable, and it may be worrisome, but navigating through the messy to get to clarity is well worth the effort. It is through this perspective that I want to introduce you to the journey that we took at Eastern Kentucky University (EKU) to align General Education and Teacher Education Preparation courses to the Common Core. Although we will provide exact (sometimes messy!) instructions for the steps that we used in our journey, feel free to use and adapt them as a catalyst for addressing the unique alignment needs of your institution.

Before we go too deeply into the alignment process itself, it is prudent to briefly review the effectiveness and impact of that process at EKU. We considered both the product (i.e., aligned syllabi for targeted courses) and the process (i.e., using PLCs as the vehicle for change) as we designed and evaluated this initiative. The process was evaluated by an independent consultant, who ran on an online survey of faculty participants. The goal was to determine the extent, if any, to which the PLC process impacted faculty *knowledge* of related legislation, teacher preparation, teaching practices, and instructional design and faculty *perceptions* regarding the alignment process and the PLC model. Of 64 PLC participants, 37 (58%) responded, revealing the positive outcomes – a valuing of the hybrid PLC model, a greater understanding of teacher preparation, a greater knowledge of Common Core standards, a greater understanding of assessment and how to impact student learning, a commitment to implementing changes to their newly aligned courses, a recognition that the alignment process had a positive impact on them as educators, and a valuing of the inter- and intra-disciplinary collaboration – as well as some areas of weakness – some content areas (namely the sciences) felt the alignment process was tedious and somewhat unrelated to their content areas; and other responders indicated a need to disseminate and extend the work to additional faculty, namely adjuncts who would be teaching the newly aligned courses (Sweet, Blythe, Combs, Fair, & Hearn, 2012).

Faculty comments, both anecdotal and within the survey, also led us to the following conclusions:
- The PLCs were vital to the process: They allowed time for faculty members to collaborate, and faculty members were more likely to implement the updates when they were directly involved in the process. The embedded PLC model -

where different layers of PLCs worked both separately and collaboratively (see Chapter 3 for more discussion on this model)- promoted fidelity to the product and process and supported facilitators.
- Alignment is complex and heavily dependent on input from the experts who design and teach the affected courses. Because of this, targeted professional development is key.... And because of this, some resistance remains among faculty.
- The deeper layers of alignment, which will be addressed later in this chapter and which comprise the "messy" part of the process, needed clarity and ultimately impacted the faculty members' connections across outcomes, assessment, and instruction.
- Momentum, though difficult to maintain without active PLCs, is important for continued professional development, for new or adjunct faculty, and as new standards are released.

Getting Started

Before gathering the larger group of participants together for the first time, the Executive PLC met with and trained the Super PLC facilitators on the following issues: Senate Bill 1 (which was the legislation in Kentucky that mandated university alignment with Common Core), PLCs and how they would be utilized, and EKU's approach and goals for meeting the mandates of Senate Bill 1. While the Executive PLC group had chosen the facilitators for each of the content areas – English, Social Science, Natural Science, Teacher Education, and Math – we also asked the facilitators to help identify up to 12 people in their respective content areas who were involved in general education and teacher preparation courses. Ultimately, this discussion and resulting recruitment led to the identification of over 80 potential participants for the PLCs; 67 participants stayed the course.

The Executive PLC continued to meet regularly, sometimes 1-2 times monthly, and sometimes more; the Super met monthly as well. After a few months and several meetings, the Executive and Super PLCs were ready to host the first session for the initiative. This "Kick-Off" session was held as an all-day professional development experience prior to the start of the spring 2011 academic semester.

During this professional development, participants were:
a) updated on the retention and graduation rates of EKU's student population as a way to establish relevance of alignment to rigorous standards,
b) trained on Senate Bill 1 mandates,
c) trained on the content and structure of the Common Core standards (adopted in Kentucky as the Kentucky Core Academic Standards),
d) trained on the PLC model that would be utilized, and
c) asked to define their role and purpose as content PLCs, having recognized the mandates, the content of the standards, and their disciplinary goals.

While ultimately all PLC groups would align course syllabi, we wanted the PLC groups to initially explore their own goals related to their purpose.

It is important to note here that NO instruction on alignment took place at this juncture. Professional Learning Communities were expected, at this point, to begin the crucial task of collaborating and goal setting. Teams were asked to consider how PLCs in general defined their focus, purpose, training, use of scholarship, meeting schedules, and products and then to decide how their PLC specifically would fulfill those guidelines for their individual PLCs. While teams were asked to meet at least once a month, no further expectations were set for how often and when the PLCs would function. We did, however, ask that PLCs keep minutes according to a very general template, which had them record their focus for the meeting, the issue/problem/question discussed, the resources they utilized for their discussion or activities, the ideas/suggestions/recommendations that were generated, and the next steps/goal setting for subsequent meetings (see Appendix A for an example of English PLC minutes). Five months of embedded PLC meetings then followed.

> We believe that this time for PLCs to explore and wander a bit was entirely necessary and very productive. This time allowed the groups to begin functioning cohesively before a required product was thrust upon them.

At the continuing Super PLC meetings, various concerns and ideas were expressed, and it was clear that all PLCs were taking interesting and varied directions. One group was struggling to find its role in the process, another group was already thinking about assessment and outcomes, and still another group sought out data to determine the success of students within their individual programs. We believe that this time for PLCs to explore and wander a bit was entirely necessary and very productive. This time allowed the groups to begin functioning cohesively before a required product was thrust upon them. In addition, because we continued the Super PLC meetings during this time, inter- and intra-disciplinary conversations continued and new ideas from one group sparked interesting questions for others.

At the second whole group assembly, held in May of that same academic year, new goals for the PLCs were set and new information shared. We began the day by hosting breakout sessions on topics that had come up in our Super PLC meetings. Each PLC was asked to send representative group members to each session so that a debriefing time within each PLC could follow. Topics for these mini sessions included assessment for learning, best practices in pedagogy, content literacy standards, and professional learning communities at work. The rest of the day was dedicated to curriculum alignment.

What does the Literature Say about Alignment?

The alignment process itself will be *presented* linearly, but I must include a cautionary note: Do not expect to implement it in a true linear fashion; instead, expect to move back and forth between the steps as necessary to clarify nuances in the student learning outcomes and their course-specific impact on assessment and instruction. Before we get into the process itself, let's first take a look at what academicians have noted about curriculum and its relationship with alignment.

Ralph Tyler (1949) was one of the first to bring course objectives to the foreground in curriculum design. Though some researchers note flaws in Tyler's "Rationale," as it has come to be called (Kliebard, 1977; Laanemets & Kalamees-Ruubel, 2013), evidence of his approach is apparent in many classrooms today, and the most recent edition of his seminal text was published as recently as 2013. Four central questions, according to Tyler, are critical in determining a course's curriculum:

a) What educational purposes should the school seek to attain?
b) What educational experiences can be provided that are likely to attain these purposes?
c) How can these educational experiences be effectively organized?
d) How can we determine whether these purposes are being attained?

In other words, a four step process is necessary; an educator must state the objectives, choose "educational experiences," structure those experiences appropriately, and assess the objectives. When those objectives are stated in terms of what students should be able to do at the end of the course, student learning can be more efficient, and planning and delivery of the course aligns to student learning outcomes (Blumberg, 2009). In fact, Blumberg argues, "Consistency and alignment of the course objectives, content delivery and learning activities, and the assessment methods help students understand why they are taking this course and help them see how this course relates to other courses and to the overall program goals (Biggs, 1999)" (p. 96).

Tyler (1949) went on to explore potential sources for course objectives, including studies of learners, studies of contemporary life, and suggestions from subject-matter specialists. In short, Tyler recognized the influence of student, societal, and content-specific needs in the development of course objectives. According to Kliebard (1977), "The notion of needs as a basis for curriculum development was not a new one when Tyler used it in 1950. It had been a stable element in the curriculum literature for about three decades," (p. 59). At EKU specifically, when we reviewed the university's data about student retention and remediation and coupled that with the description of the Common Core standards' development, this

> ...Alignment requires that the teaching and learning experiences match the goals of the set outcomes/objectives.

issue of "needs" was one that we wanted to highlight. Our students' needs - described in detail for our participants through a "Know Your Audience" document (Sweet & Blythe, 2012) - combined with our students' societal expectations (the inclusion of Common Core standards at state colleges and universities was mandated by Senate Bill 1 in Kentucky) would influence the way in which our participants augmented or altered their disciplinary and course specific student learning outcomes (SLOs). Our journey, therefore, began in sync with Tyler's Rationale.

Then, of course, alignment requires that the teaching and learning experiences match the goals of the set outcomes/objectives. This, Kliebard (1977) argues, is a slippery slope:

> The problem is how can learning experiences be *selected* by a teacher or a curriculum maker when they are defined as the *interaction* between a student and his environment. By definition, then, the learning experience is in some part a function of the perceptions, interests, and previous experience of the student. At least this part of the learning experience is not within the power of the teacher to select. (p. 61)

Though Kliebard makes a valid point, educators can still support alignment with a careful choosing of teaching experiences (i.e., those activities the teacher chooses to do and use) and learning experiences (i.e., those activities the learners must complete and use). The instructor can still manipulate the learning environment in such a way as to stimulate the kind of learning that the outcome dictates. At EKU, we continued to remind our participants that choosing the best instructional activity and/or strategy heavily depended on the depth of knowledge required by the language of the student learning outcome. More on the specifics of that process later, though you may have already noted that we supplemented our large group professional development days with sessions related to instructional techniques. It was, in fact, an area where participants noted a need for their own classrooms, especially in regard to teaching content literacy skills. They realized that *assigning* activities for their students was quite different than *teaching* them... and this epiphany was one that validated the process: the relevance of alignment between the student outcomes, which were expected, and the instructional support, which was needed/provided, was secured.

Ultimately, according to the Tyler Rationale (Tyler, 1949; Kliebard, 1977; Laanemets & Kalamees-Ruubel, 2013), the process of alignment comes full circle when the student outcomes (objectives), teaching and learning experiences, and *assessment* practices completely align. If the evaluation(s) do not correctly align to the intended learning – or, for that matter, to the instructional experiences – then misalignment occurs and a great disservice is done to the students (Biggs, 1999). With our EKU cadre, we hosted our final whole group (and half day) professional development about assessment, both formative and summative.

Anderson (2002) explains that content validity (i.e., "to what extent does the test measure the important curricular objectives?" [p. 255]), content coverage (i.e., as determined by the relationship between instructional activities and materials and the assessments), and the opportunity to learn (by asking if the assessment tasks reflect the teaching that has occurred) are the observable measures that instructors can use to determine their course alignment. These three components, in fact, are the bond that cements the three elements of curricular alignment in place: he suggests that, like three sides to a triangle,

> ...curriculum alignment requires a strong link between objectives and assessments, between objectives and instructional activities and materials, *and* between assessments and instructional activities and materials. In other words, content validity, content coverage, and opportunity to learn are all included within the more general concept of 'curriculum alignment.' (p. 257)

Larkin and Richardson (2013) concur with this conclusion, going on to explain the exact process:

> Once intended learning outcomes have been defined, the next step as described by Biggs and Tang (2007) is to map the teaching activities and methods to the intended learning outcomes and ensure that what is being taught is directly linked to what students are expected to learn. Finally, authentic assessment tasks are developed that are aligned with both the teaching activities and the learning outcomes. (p. 199)

Within this process is where we deviated a bit. *Classroom Assessment for Student Learning: Doing it Right – Using it Well* (Stiggins, Arter, & Chappuis, 2007) was a seminal text that was used in Kentucky for the training of P-12 teachers for two primary purposes: helping teachers build capacity in deconstruction (i.e., the process of identifying the learning targets that were embedded in standards) and in promoting balanced assessment practices. Because of our group's work with this text, we rearranged the order and added a few important elements for our alignment. A review/revision of student learning outcomes, along with an understanding of deconstruction practices, came first. (I will explain each of these elements in more detail in the "Operationalizing the Curriculum Alignment" section within this chapter.) Then, instead of focusing on the instructional materials and activities next, we focused on the role and practices of assessment. We intentionally placed the assessment piece *before* the instructional activities because of our work with Kentucky's P-12 teachers. This was the process that they were expected to use, and quite frankly, it made more sense to us.

First, as Chappuis & Chappuis (2007/2008) indicate, part of students' knowing where they are "going" is to share with them the specific learning targets (from the broader standards or outcomes) *and* the criteria for success in demonstrating mastery of those learning targets. In other words, while students do not necessarily need to see a summative exam, they (and you, as the educator!) need to know what qualities are related to mastery: What rubric, what skills, what competencies will they be expected to demonstrate? If the assessment has not yet been determined at the early stages of the process, then it's much harder – if not impossible - for the teaching and learning activities to move students through the "Where am I going?" "Where am I now?" and "How can I close the gap?" stages that Chappuis & Chappuis espouse. Again, Kliebard (1977) is concerned that tying the objectives with evaluation outcomes is a "simplistic notion," as "it ignores what may be the more significant latent outcomes in favor of the manifest and anticipated ones, and it minimizes the vital relationship between ends and means" (p. 65). We humbly disagree. In a time where accountability and "evidence" of student success is paramount, measurable outcomes tied to assessment are critical. And, in fact, Wang, Su, Cheung, Wong, and Kwong (2013) found that constructively aligned courses encouraged students to engage in deep learning approaches and discouraged "surface learning."

Our alignment process, though, was different because of a critical factor: We were asking faculty to supplement their existing course student learning outcomes with relevant Common Core standards and then think about how they would assess that. This was difficult for faculty, since they weren't simply evaluating their existing course for alignment: They were evaluating if and how it would be aligned along with those Common Core standards, once they were embedded. Important to note, however, is that we, as organizers, did not mandate in any way which of the standards should be included in the courses – only that faculty evaluate their courses to see which ones were already embedded or that could be naturally embedded. Some found that they *taught* certain literacy skills, for example, but didn't assess them; still more realized that they *assessed* literacy skills but had never taught or clarified their expectations for them. Furthermore, additional misalignment woes were revealed. Blumberg (2009) cautions,

> If courses are misaligned, it is probably because instructors are using differing cognitive process levels in their objectives, teaching and learning activities, and assessment exercises. Often the objective requires a higher level of cognitive processing than do the teaching and learning activities and the assessment exercises. For example, instructors have misaligned courses when there are lofty goals stated for a course; but the assessment exercises only require recall of information. (p. 96)

Misalignment and non-alignment issues arose as faculty really began to study their course designs.

If those challenges weren't enough to make this process tedious, albeit revealing, for faculty, Fahey (2012) articulates a few more, especially in regard to change at the higher education level. She notes that one challenge is the difficulty for faculty of putting curricular intentions into practice. This was one concern that was somewhat validated in our survey. While most faculty participants who responded to the survey indicated that they would implement curricular changes because of the process, a few noted that they had completed the product (i.e., the revised syllabus) and were satisfied with that. This disappointing conclusion for a few participants revealed that they hadn't quite experienced the transformation that was intended. Tapa (as quoted by Laanemets & Kalamees-Ruubel, 2013) articulates it powerfully: "The curriculum cannot be regarded as a dead and summative body of all the materials, experiences and activities contained in the educational process. It is a living whole, comprised of experience actually going on in school. As such it is what it becomes in practice," (p.5).

Fahey (2012) actually recommends that curricular change should be accompanied by evaluation at higher levels: "When the teacher undertakes the curriculum evaluation as part of an internal professional mandate (an empowerment evaluation), the activity becomes part of her professional development as a researcher (McKernan, 2007)" (p. 707). This was not applicable to our alignment initiative, though ideally, it is something for other organizations to consider as they develop their own expectations for alignment. Fahey notes a second challenge as well – that of an institution's capacity and support for change. In our specific experience, and because compliance with state legislation was at stake, we had the support of our university's administration. In addition, our university prides itself on attention to teaching, and this particular initiative was strongly linked to student success through faculty development.

Defining Knowledge – That which is Embedded in Student Learning Outcomes

Having clearly established a rationale for the curriculum alignment process, it is necessary to explore the resources that impacted our view of student learning outcomes, the language used to classify them, and the layers of proficiency that are embedded within them. First of all, instead of using the term "objectives" on course syllabi, we at EKU use the phrase "Student Learning Outcomes" (SLOs). The previous discussion on objectives, however, is clearly relatable and was relevant to building a case for curricular alignment. Biggs (1999), Fink (2003), and Krathwohl (2002) all define knowledge in different (though related) ways, and all use their definitions of knowledge – or learning – to defend their processes for curricular alignment. Biggs, for example, determined that six types of objectives were suitable for college level courses:

1) **basic facts and terminology** – which require students to engage in recall and/or recognition;
2) **topic knowledge** – which requires students to comprehend topics and to recognize some relationships between topics;
3) **discipline knowledge** – which requires students to understand a unit "as a whole;"
4) **functioning knowledge** – which requires students to "put to work" **their** understanding;
5) **laboratory skills** – which require "procedural knowledge;" and
6) **monitoring and evaluation skills** – which impact students' "metacognitive knowledge" and "self-directed learning" (p. 30).

Fink (2003) also uses taxonomy to help faculty better understand and align objectives. His, however, include dimensions outside of content-specific knowledge:

1) **foundational knowledge** includes content, ideas, and course-specific information;
2) **application** includes the *thinking* that is required of students, including critical, creative, and practical thinking;
3) **integration** requires that different ideas across disciplines be connected;
4) **human dimension** includes those elements that help students learn more about themselves and others;
5) **caring** is the component that highlights students' abilities to develop new interests and values related to course content; and
6) **learning how to learn** promotes self-directed learning.

Add to these influential works the conclusions of Krathwohl (2002) in his overview of his and Anderson's work when they revised Bloom's Taxonomy. He and Anderson took Bloom's work and noted something interesting:

> Objectives that describe intended learning outcomes as the result of instruction are usually framed in terms of (a) some subject matter content and (b) a description of what is to be done with or

to that content. Thus, statements of objectives typically consist of a noun or noun phrase – the subject matter content – and a verb or verb phrase – the cognitive process(es)." (p. 213)

In order to give attention to both parts of the objective, then, Krathwohl and Anderson revised the taxonomy to account for both the noun part – to be described as the "Knowledge Dimension"- and the verb part – the "Cognitive Process Dimension." The Cognitive Process Dimension was altered to reflect the verb, or action, that was taking place. So, for example, "Knowledge," from the original taxonomy, became "Remember," in the revised one. Clarification of this level was supplied with additional descriptors: "Remember" included *recognizing* and *recalling*. "Comprehension" became "Understand," with the qualifiers of *interpreting, exemplifying, classifying, summarizing, inferring, comparing,* and *explaining* as the actions that demonstrate how to "understand." "Application" became "Apply," and no descriptors were included. "Analysis" became "Analyze" (which includes *differentiating, organizing,* and *attributing*). And a more substantive change in the revised taxonomy affects the last two levels: in Bloom's original taxonomy, "Synthesize" and "Evaluate" were the last two – and highest – levels. In the revised form, "Evaluate" (including *checking* and *critiquing*) and "Create" (including *generating, planning,* and *producing*) reflect the highest two levels.

Krathwohl's (2002) breakdown of the Knowledge Dimension is just as compelling:

1) The **Factual Knowledge** level includes *knowledge of terminology* and *specific details and elements.*
2) The **Conceptual Knowledge** level relies on interrelationships among course elements: *knowledge of classifications and categories; principles and generalizations;* and *theories, models, and structures.*
3) The **Procedural Knowledge** level implies that students must know to how do something and how to engage in disciplinary inquiry: *knowledge of subject-specific skills and algorithms, of subject-specific techniques and methods,* and *of criteria for determining when to use appropriate procedures.*
4) Finally, the **Metacognitive Knowledge** level requires that students be aware of themselves as learners: *strategic knowledge, knowledge about cognitive tasks, including*

appropriate contextual and conditional knowledge, and *self-knowledge* (p. 214).

Krathwohl (2002) explains that educators can analyze their objectives by charting them (see Figure 6.1) in order to classify their objectives. So, for example, if I were to chart two objectives from a "Teaching Grammar" course that were stated as follows - 1) Identify errors in use of grammar and mechanics, and 2) Describe English vernacular speakers and English Language Learners (ELLs) - then I may fill in the chart as indicated (see Figure 6.1).

This kind of analysis can reveal to educators several things. Outcomes can be charted to determine if higher level thinking is required of the course; the charting process can be a stepping stone in helping to later determine if instructional activities and assessments maintain the same level of rigor; and it can help educators recognize outcomes that have become almost meaningless, due to their too-vague or too-broad noun phrases or non-existent/non-measurable verb usage.

These three examinations of objectives-content helped us isolate the kind of knowledge that we wanted our participants to highlight and recognize in their own alignment work. All three researchers identify basic, foundational, and factual knowledge as relevant to course content. We did, too, so in our alignment, we wanted our faculty to identify – in regard to the Common Core standards – what their students needed to **KNOW**[1]. In other words, what facts, definitions, and concepts were important for students to recognize and explain in regard to the standards? Secondly, these three academicians recognized the importance of how students use what they know. In our alignment, then, we wanted faculty to consider how they asked students to **APPLY** the standards in their specific course. We further encouraged participants to think about whether they prompted students to apply certain literacy standards or whether they expected students to have developed enough automaticity with the standards to apply them without direct instruction telling them to do so. Furthermore, the three explored the role of metacognition in students' learning and course objectives. We, therefore, asked faculty to think about whether they required students to **MONITOR** their use of the standards, assessing their own success and evaluating what tools/resources would help them

Figure 6.1. Classification of Objectives with Krathwohl's (2002) model.

Cognitive Processes → / Knowledge Dimension ↓	Remember	Understand	Apply	Analyze	Evaluate	Create
Factual						
Conceptual		2) *Describe English vernacular speakers and English Language Learners (ELLs)*. Describe is used as a way of explaining, which is an *understand* verb. English vernacular speakers and ELLs represent categories of students that are part of the course content, thus *conceptual* knowledge.				
Procedural					1) *Identify errors in use of grammar and mechanics*. Though *identify* appears to be a lower level (Remember) verb, it is used in this case to locate errors, i.e., to *evaluate*. The appropriate use of grammar and mechanics is *procedural* knowledge.	
Metacognitive						

Figure 6.1. Krathwohl's (2002) model shows how two objectives that, in Bloom's original Taxonomy, appear to be at the "Remembering" Level, would be categorized at higher levels; 1) *Identify errors in use of grammar and mechanics*, would be at the "Evaluating" Level, and 2) *Describe English vernacular speakers and English Language Learners (ELLs)*, would be at the "Understanding" Level.

be more successful with the standards' implementation. Finally, because of the specific nature and expectations of the Common Core standards, some courses' objectives would include an expectation for students (as pre-service teachers) to **TEACH** the standards. This dimension would be relevant only to the teacher preparation courses that were being aligned, not to the general education courses. Overall, then, this KAM-T model (Know, Apply, Monitor, Teach) directs the deeper alignment of the applicable standards.

When faculty began this process of charting the standards, they needed lots of support from us as organizers. It was also this part of the process where we lost some of the enthusiasm from our Natural Sciences group. In hindsight, I think it would have been quite helpful to have shared elements of Biggs' (1999), Fink's (2003), and Krathwohl's (2002) work to help them understand the rationale and the thinking behind our specific classification system. While some of the teacher preparation faculty had engaged in alignment work many times, due to the nature of accreditation and the changing landscape of P-12 education, and were therefore more comfortable with terms like "metacognition" and "taxonomy," some of our colleagues were less so. Perhaps this transition could have been softened for some faculty with an intentional building of background knowledge. As co-coordinators of this project, Dorie Combs and I led this particular step in the alignment process, and as teacher educators ourselves, we underestimated the support that our participants might need in this step of the alignment. Because of the confusion that resulted in some groups, we had to back up and re-teach the categories. (Again, the exact steps and resources that we suggest will be addressed within the subsequent section of this chapter.)

Ultimately, the course alignment would be complete: Participants would evaluate, adjust, and explore their SLOs, embedding relevant Common Core standards; they would evaluate and adjust their assessments to determine if the levels of rigor in the SLOs matched the expectations and criteria established for student evaluation; and they would evaluate, adjust, and add to

> *The purpose of the process is not about filling in the provided chart: it is about the thinking and analysis that is required, which is what the chart facilitates.*

their repertoire of instructional activities to bridge the gap. So how, exactly, can *you* get there?

Operationalizing the Curriculum Alignment
Student Learning Outcomes

The first step is to analyze the course's Student Learning Outcomes (SLOs). Fallahi (2011) reminds of the necessity in shifting away from viewing a course's goals in terms of overall content to the skills and competencies that are to be retained after the course is complete. This establishment of course competencies is communicated to the students through the course's learning outcomes. The SLOs for each course are naturally different, but because you are aligning to the Common Core standards, then a pairing of the course standards with the Common Core is a necessary first step. Use the tool in Appendix B to facilitate this process. The purpose of the process is not about filling in the provided chart: it is about the thinking and analysis that is required, which is what the chart facilitates. Putting it in a form where faculty can, step by step, review their SLOs alongside the Common Core standards simply helps them take the journey with a map in hand. All applicable courses at EKU reviewed the Reading/Writing standards; others also reviewed the Speaking/Listening and Language standards. The math and natural science groups also reviewed the Math standards and Mathematical Practices.

The first step was to read through the standards and decide if, in fact, this standard was applicable to the course. If so, then the focus narrowed only to those standards. Then, faculty need to determine if the standard is *assessed* in the course. Assessment of the standard rarely is seen in paper-and-pencil testing situations (at least for the Reading/Writing and Speaking/Listening standards). Most often, faculty realized that they directly – or even tangentially – assessed some of these standards in students' responses to reading, in class discussions, in essay papers, in student projects, etc. You want faculty to think about *how* they assess these standards more deeply in later stages; at this point, though, they at least need to converse about it. If they are not assessing the standard, then it should not be linked to their SLO.

Once the standard has been identified in both areas (i.e., that it is applicable and assessed), then the faculty members are ready to link it directly to a course's SLO. If the course SLOs are numbered, then the faculty member can easily drop that number into the chart. Again, the point is not the filling out of the chart; it's the process of determining where the Common Core standard directly links to the SLO. Some standards may link to more than one SLO, just as some standards may not be applicable at all in some courses. As faculty complete this process, they will often find that their SLOs need to be revised or that they need to add a completely new SLO or two. That is the next step. Throughout this analysis, it is helpful for groups of faculty who teach the course in question to discuss this process. Such discussion reveals some inconsistencies in the ways that instructors envision the SLOs, the Common Core standards, and the relationships therein. These revelations are quite important to the alignment process, as they reveal both minor and major adjustments that may need to be made to the SLOs specifically or to the assessments, which will be analyzed later. When all of these questions and possible inconsistencies have been hashed out, the faculty member is ready to go to the syllabus itself and indicate how the Common Core aligns. In one of our courses at EKU, a "Foundations of Reading" course, one SLO looks like this: *4. Describe the five key components of reading instruction (phonics, phonemic awareness, vocabulary, comprehension, and fluency) and evaluate the instructional efficacy of strategies for each. (CCR.R.1, CCCR.R.2, CCR.R.3, CCR.R.7, CCR.R.8).* Notice the parenthetical notation that indicates that these five reading standards are taught AND assessed as students in the course demonstrate mastery of this SLO.

Expect this first phase to take some time in each PLC. PLC facilitators need training and practice in this phase before they take the process back to their PLC groups. That way, the PLCs have an "expert" among them when they seek clarification. Once this piece of the process is complete, some faculty might believe that the aligned SLOs are the finished product and that the course is fully aligned. We recommend, however, that you keep moving forward. Remember, true course alignment is in the matching of SLOs to assessment and instruction. And to carefully match the SLO to assessment and instruction, the SLO (with aligned Common Core) needs to be carefully explored for its layers of expected proficiency. This is where the muddy but extremely important taxonomical analysis comes in to play.

Linking Student Learning Outcomes to Assessment

Use the chart in Appendix C to help you navigate the next phase. Figure 6.2 is an excerpt from that chart. The first step is to transfer your student learning outcomes into the document. In this way, you isolate and carefully analyze each one. As you look at your first SLO, noting the CCR standard that is embedded, take the time to verbalize and record the connection that you made. See Figure 6.2 as an example. In the italicized statement, I have indicated the exact reason for my decision to include the reading standards 4 and 10 with this SLO. This step accomplishes a few things: First of all, it helps me determine later on exactly how I intend to assess it; and secondly, it communicates to everyone who teaches the course what the expectation is for embedding the content of the standards. Otherwise, the CCR references simply become numbers on the document. Until faculty think deeply about how they intend to assess the standards as part of the learning outcomes, the alignment is incomplete; assessment and instruction are less intentional and, therefore, less effective.

Step Two is to think about the formative assessment that helps you and your students know if they are mastering that outcome. Formative assessments don't take specific forms; rather, the intent behind the assessment determines if it is formative. If, for example, I take a class poll (electronically or with hand signals) about the content that I'm teaching and use that to influence my instruction, then that poll is a formative exercise. I haven't collected papers to grade and score, but I still am able to determine my students' learning needs and to adjust my instruction. In some cases, I could use class discussions, quizzes, written responses, clicker systems/ questions, labs, etc. as tools to formatively assess my students on their learning. The inclusion of formative assessment is vital, both for the instructor, who can determine what learning is occurring, and for the students, who become aware of the expectations for mastery of the learning outcome that is targeted. You may find, as you complete this step, that some professional development (e.g., journal readings, PLC discussions, seminars, etc.) related to formative and summative assessment would be useful to you and your faculty workgroups. Obviously, formative assessment will look different in a freshman level history class with 150 students than it would in a senior level core class with 25. In both scenarios, formative assessment is critical, but it must be practical and useful, as well. In the case presented in Figure 6.2, the example course is a methods course with approximately 20 students; students regularly complete reading response/reflections on the readings that they complete. In this scenario, students complete some reading and discussion on this very topic, so formatively, I can determine their developing mastery of this outcome through their related reading response.

Figure 6.2. Example of Alignment Process for Assessment.

Student Learning Outcome	Assessment: Formative	Assessment: Summative	KAM-T	Follow Up Notes
1 Define and analyze different theories of learning, relating each to the development of adolescent readers and writers. (CCR.R.4, CCR.R.10 – *these CC standards mean that students will use technical language and concepts in their analysis and that they will choose age-appropriate texts and resources for adolescents to use, based on those theories of learning.*)	Reading Response	Unit Plan Reflection	R4: A, M R10: M	Review rubrics for language related to **vocabulary** (CCR4) and **textual resources** (CCR10) for adolescents. Create a question in the Unit Plan reflection based on this SLO.

Figure 6.2. This Example of the Alignment Process for Assessment depicts the Student Learning Outcome (SLO), Formative and Summative Assessments of that SLO, the level of learning expected (KAM-T) and the faculty's follow-up notes.

The next column in the chart indicates that the SLO must be aligned to a summative assessment. A summative assessment, unlike the formative assessment, is not used to determine instructional and learning "next steps." Its function is to ultimately determine what level of mastery the students demonstrate. Final exams, projects, performances, etc., usually fall into this category. While instructors should still give feedback to students on these final assessments, they do not provide follow up instruction related to students' learning needs. At the higher education level, this is often because the course is ending or because the class is moving on to another module or different content. In the example in Figure 6.2, the students in this course develop an instructional unit and must reflect on the choices that they made, related to the learning needs of adolescents. That reflection should demonstrate their mastery of this SLO.

Every SLO should be both formatively and summatively assessed. Again, conversations among faculty who teach the courses being aligned will help those faculty members sort out practical methods in which to do this. Faculty need to carefully consider whether the assessment they link to the SLO actually requires students to demonstrate mastery of the SLO as it is written. For example, if the intent of the SLO is for students to use reasoning and/or application, but the assessment does not require that level of thinking, then the assessment is not neatly aligned with the SLO. Without aligned assessment, the teacher and students cannot determine the success of the learning. Without determining the success of the learners, the instructor cannot determine the appropriateness of instruction. And without appropriateness of instruction, there cannot be mastery of the SLOs. Are you seeing the cycle at work here? The circumspect consideration of each SLO and its alignment to the assessment in the course will reveal many things to the faculty who participate. This is an example of how course evaluation is actually professional development for faculty, a difference, as Kubitskey and Fishman (2006) explain, in "knowing that" and "knowing how." The powerful conversations that arise impact the course design and the teaching/learning that will take place.

> *Without aligned assessment, the teacher and students cannot determine the success of the learning. Without determining the success of the learners, the instructor cannot determine the appropriateness of instruction. And without appropriateness of instruction, there cannot be mastery of the SLOs.*

The next step is a tricky one. At this juncture, faculty will need to spend some time thinking about the KAM-T model that was described earlier. In relation to the Common Core standards (note the language in the SLO column of Figure 6.2), what connection is made and how do faculty expect students to demonstrate that standard within the SLO? That connection will help them decide if the intent is for students to demonstrate **KNOWLEDGE** of the standard (i.e., do they need to identify important words, concepts, or language within the standard and demonstrate an ability to define or describe the content of the standard itself?); if they need to demonstrate **APPLICATION** of the standard (i.e., will they be using the skill within the standard as they complete the course assessment related to that SLO?); if they need to demonstrate MONITORING/**METACOGNITION** related to the standard (i.e., do they need to demonstrate an awareness of how the standard impacts their teaching and learning?); or do they need to **TEACH** the standard (i.e., does the related SLO indicate that they will need to demonstrate a readiness to teach this standard to P-12 students?). The purpose of this step is to really help faculty navigate the ways that they are embedding the CC standards. Using a taxonomy such as this one assists faculty in making the related assessments meaningful for students. If, for example, the instructor intends for students in an early general education English course to respond to text by tracing a central idea and its development throughout a text (CCR.2), but does not establish whether students have KNOWLEDGE about this concept (i.e., of analyzing central ideas and their development), then certainly students are ill-equipped to APPLY that concept. What faculty may realize is that they are expecting students to demonstrate proficiency in ways for which they are not prepared.

At this point in the conversation, faculty usually respond with the following: "Isn't this what these students are supposed to be learning in high school?" To which I counter: "And how many of your students, then, are able to demonstrate this skill consistently and proficiently?" Whether it is the P-12 system's "job" is really moot: If the students in our courses are not prepared for the kind of thinking and responding that we espouse, then we as faculty need to do our part in helping them get there. Furthermore, in defense of those high school teacher scapegoats, as the texts and resources that we in higher education utilize, the skills noted in the Common

Core standards get more and more difficult to utilize. The rigor of the standards (and the literacy standards in particular) increases as text levels and complexity increases. Thus, the textual resources that are used in higher education *should be* more complex than those students experienced in high school; they need scaffolded instruction at that higher level to utilize those skills in disciplinary-specific and more rigorous levels. A student may, for example, be fully able to trace thematic development in Shirley Jackson's "The Lottery" in high school but may need assistance in tracing such development in Franz Kafka's "The Metamorphosis." Before students are able to apply the skill of tracing thematic development, they may need some knowledge about what it means to do so with complex texts.

These are the kinds of discussions that faculty must have in relation to their SLOs. This also helps faculty understand that their responsibility is not only to deepen students' content knowledge but also to strengthen their skills for learning and utilizing that content knowledge. This may be a paradigm shift for some faculty, so don't rush this process. Faculty need to muddle, to debate, to seek precision, to challenge. Out of this ambiguous process comes clarity and purpose. Oftentimes, discussions related to this part will cross courses, too. So, faculty may indicate that in HIS 101, students will be provided with explicit instruction related to a few of the standards, and in HIS 102, there will be less explicit instruction and more application. There are no right answers or perfect conclusions to be drawn. For that very reason, the process itself is equally challenging and enlightening for faculty.

An important note should be made here, too, about how very different this process is in relation to the math standards. While the Mathematical Practices are process-dependent and may prompt the kinds of discussions among faculty that the literacy standards promote, the mathematical standards themselves are more content based. The domains within the math standards indicate that students must know and apply specific concepts as opposed to broad processes and proficiencies. This will result in different kinds of discussions among the math faculty; that, too, is to be expected and encouraged.

As faculty navigate this KAM-T process, they should record on their chart the level of proficiency – with the Common Core standard – that they expect students to demonstrate. The chart itself is the tool for their journey, but it is also something that a facilitator can copy and review. Are there standards that are notably missing? Are there standards that never are taught at the knowledge level but that are expected to be applied throughout the discipline? Are students ever expected to think metacognitively about the standards' impact on them as learners? These are bigger questions that a facilitator can generate for disciplinary whole group discussions.

Finally, faculty can reflect on what follow-up work they need to do with their assessments to ensure that fidelity to the standards and the learning outcomes is intact. For example, in the course indicated in Figure 6.2, I had to ensure that my rubric/guidelines for the reading response formative assessment clearly indicated that students needed to incorporate the discipline-specific vocabulary and concepts that are required by CCR.4. Otherwise, neither the students nor I as the instructor focus on that as an important component for that assessment. Similarly, while the students were already completing a unit plan reflection, I wasn't sure that I asked them to directly reflect on the theories of learning that impacted their resource choices for their adolescent scenario. I needed to double-check to ensure that I had clearly articulated that expectation for that final product. By completing these follow up activities, I ensured that my assessment communicated the importance of the SLO (with the embedded standards) to my students. In addition, I ensured that my assessment of students' learning would directly relate to the SLO that was deemed so important. This entire process is quite an undertaking, and courses may be changed: SLOs may need to be added; SLOs may need to be altered; SLOs may need to be reduced. The important conclusion is for the course to be manageable but focused; to be rigorous but structured; to be systematically evaluated and carefully aligned.

> *The important conclusion is for the course to be manageable but focused; to be rigorous but structured; to be systematically evaluated and carefully aligned.*

Again, the PLC facilitator should work on this process with a course he/she has taught or is teaching. Having the experience of working through the process will better enable him/her to foresee problems and questions that may arise. This stage of the alignment process takes time; don't expect one PLC session to suffice for this work. It will be important, however, to take some time to train faculty (as needed) on assessment and the KAM-T model, to allow for the work group(s) to discuss their course(s), and to debrief.

Linking Student Learning Outcomes and Assessment to Instruction

The final step is to link instruction to the assessment. Scholars agree that an aligned course yields positive student learning results (Anderson, 2002; Blumberg, 1999; Biggs, 2009; Larkin & Richardson, 2013; Wang, Su, Cheung, Wong, & Kwong, 2013). Wang et al. (2013) concluded that their research

> provided evidence that a more constructively aligned teaching and learning environment would lead students to adjust their learning approaches in a way that a more deep situational learning approach and a less surface situational learning approach would be employed in their study, despite their pre-existing individual differences in the preferred learning approaches. (p. 487)

Unlike the previous parts of this alignment process, however, it is not essential for faculty members who teach common courses to identify or use identical instructional techniques for their shared courses. The intent of this exercise is not to design a "canned" course; allowances for faculty members' own styles and preferences are ideal. Because of this, the guidelines in Appendix D may or may not be stringently applied in your PLCs. While the breakdown of the SLOs with the Common Core standards is helpful to many in determining appropriate learning activities, the use of this document is simply one of many options. While scholars have yet to promote a system for aligning to Common Core (until now, of course!), much has been written about course alignment in regard to general assessment and instructional choices. I offer my process as one within the larger group of models that are available.

That being said, should you choose to continue with my mapping process, here are the guidelines for the work:
- Isolate each SLO in order to thoroughly explore each one. Go ahead and again record the assessments that will be utilized; as you think about instruction, you should always keep that assessment in mind. Then begin to break down that SLO. Using the provided columns (see example in Figure

6.3), identify the key verbs and the content specific topics that make up the SLO. Be sure to embed the language of the CCSS that impacts both the assessment and instruction.
- Next, begin thinking about the instructional steps/activities that will guide the students in mastering the SLO. The instructional activity needs to relate directly to the verb and content. The instructional activity should match the level of verb. You may note, too, the level of expectation for the Common Core standards. In the example provided, you will note the references to those KAM-T labels.
- Don't forget to also attend to the difference in teaching activities and learning activities. This process builds on the constructivist nature of learning: If the instructor does all of the thinking and explaining, for example, then the students have little opportunity to practice the skill at the level where they may be assessed. For instance, if students are expected to analyze, then lecture as the only instructional activity is insufficient, as it does not give *students* an opportunity to analyze. (See Figure 6.3.)

Perhaps, too, an SLO might indicate that students will defend a position related to the content. The instructor may even use an instructional assessment (such as a written essay) that forces students to defend a position. The alignment seems solid so far.... If, however, the instructor assigns provocative texts and then uses class discussion to review the themes within those texts, the students may still be ill-equipped to thoroughly defend a position. That instructor needs to consider the instructional support that he/she can provide in teaching students *how* to defend a position (e.g., looking at the example texts not simply for the argument within, but helping students recognize how the author is making an argument; setting up conferences with students to chat about the argument they will be making; organizing a trip to the writing center to make the students aware of outside supports, etc.)

This instructional exploration may be a bit intimidating to faculty, especially if they have had little experience or exposure to different instructional approaches. That is why faculty should be patient with the process, why they should widen their professional development priorities, and why they should continue working

Figure 6.3. Completing the SLO, Assessment, and Instructional Cycle

Student Learning Outcome	Assessments: (F) Formative and (S) Summative	Key Verbs (embedded with language of standards)	+ Content Specific Topics	= Appropriate Instructional Activities
Define and ***analyze*** different theories of learning, relating each to the development of adolescent readers and writers. (CCR.R.4, CCR.R.10 – these CC standards mean that students will use technical language and concepts in their analysis and that they will choose age-appropriate texts and resources for adolescents to use, based on those theories of learning.)	Reading Response (F) Unit Plan Reflection (S)	***Define*** *(using technical language and concepts)* ***Analyze*** *(using technical language and concepts)* ***Relate*** *(choose age-appropriate texts and resources)*	Theories of Learning Development of adolescent readers and writers	1. Concept attainment exercise (for definition) 2. Mini-lecture with webbing exercise that analyzes elements of the theories and how they link to adolescent development (emphasize *Application of the CCR*) 3. Class exercise using materials and resources for adolescents, evaluating their appropriateness based upon theories of learning (emphasize *Metacognition* with CCR)

Figure 6.3. Completing the SLO, Assessment, and Instructional Cycle shows how the Student Learning Outcome is clearly aligned with the assessments, course specific content, and appropriate instructional activities.

with colleagues to extend their instructional strategy toolboxes. Be creative in how you expose faculty within your workgroups to new ideas. Is there a teaching center on your campus that can provide some support? Are there colleagues who have ideas to share? Could PLC groups each research and present instructional ideas in a campus-wide mini conference? A variety of resources are available online, at national teaching and learning conferences for higher education, and through appropriate professional texts.

From start to finish, the alignment process, which begins with an introduction to the Common Core standards themselves, all the way to the instructional decision-making that aligns with the SLOs and assessment, takes time – several semesters, in fact. It takes hard work. It takes commitment. The tools provided for you here are the result of one university's journey through that process. Our journey enabled us to refine the process and to clarify the purpose. This text is just a tool: use it, adapt it, make it work for the journey that your faculty need to take.

The Work That Remains

Individual course alignment may only be the initial phase toward program alignment within your university. The tools and process shared here have focused on course alignment rather than programmatic alignment. Although a few references were made to program alignment (e.g., in reviewing various documents to look for overlap and/or gaps), this text does not really guide that process. It may be a valuable task to consider, however, especially as accreditation and legislative bodies begin to look carefully at teacher preparation programs for evidence of alignment and demonstrations of pre-service candidates' exposure to the Common Core.

In addition, the recommendations in this text rely heavily on the input of faculty. Rather than being a top-down, forced process, the alignment has ownership from the faculty. Depending upon the situation in which you are using this text, faculty may be "forced" to go through the process, but they certainly own the work. Their insights, their expertise, and their instructional input are not simply valued: they are essential. Maintaining that respect for faculty presence as the courses are updated, implemented, and revised is necessary, too...both for fidelity to the alignment and for faculty development (Fahey, 2012). In addition, faculty interests and questions should drive related professional development opportunities. At EKU specifically, faculty have explored professional development texts and resources related to grading practices, rubric development, textbook choices, and mini conferences for adjuncts, to name a few.

Ultimately, and to validate the impact of the curriculum alignment on student learning, faculty should think about how they can determine impact on student learning. What scholarship opportunities for faculty exist in their course re-alignment, in their journey, and in the implementation of the "new" course?

As you and your faculty PLCs navigate the activities shared here in regard to alignment with Common Core, to assessment, and to instruction, I conclude with a reminder from Fahey (2012) about the influence of faculty in this process:

> A curriculum should be considered as content, form, and design that can be assessed by the teacher in a professional role as a practitioner and researcher. The curriculum should be changed, revised, and modified (following McKernan 2007: 56, Stenhouse 1981: 109) as internal and external-to-the-university demands dictate such, as changing needs of society or students. (p. 708)

Certainly the influence of the Common Core standards falls under the category of "external" demands.

You have the tools and the rationale for beginning your curriculum alignment. Are you ready to get started? More importantly, are you prepared to get a little messy?

References

Anderson, L.W. (2002). Curricular alignment: A re-examination. *Theory into Practice, 41*(4), 255-260. Retrieved from http://www.unco.edu/cetl/sir/stating_outcome/documents/Krathwohl.pdf

Biggs, J. (1999). Teaching for quality learning at university (pp. 165-203). Buckingham, UK: SRHE and Open University Press. Retrieved from http://www.ntu.edu.vn/Portals/96/Tu%20lieu%20tham%20khao/Phuong%20phap%20giang%20day/teaching%20for%20quality%20learning-j.biggs.pdf

Blumberg, P. (2009). Maximizing learning through course alignment and experience with different types of knowledge. *Innovation in Higher Education, 34*: 93-103. doi 10.1007/s10755-009-9095-2

Chappuis, S., & Chappuis, J. (2007/2008). The best value in formative assessment. *Educational Leadership, 65*(4), 14-19. Retrieved from http://www.ascd.

org/publications/educational-leadership/dec07/vol65/num04/The-Best-Value-in-Formative-Assessment.aspx

Fahey, S.J. (2012). Curriculum change and climate change: Inside outside pressures in higher education. *Journal of Curriculum Studies, 44*(5), 703-722.

Fallahi, C. (2011). Using Fink's taxonomy in course design. *Observer, 24*(7).

Fink, L. D. (2003). *Creating significant learning experiences: An integrated approach to designing college courses.* San Francisco, CA: Jossey-Bass.

Kliebard, H.M. (1977). The Tyler rationale. In A.A. Bellack & H.M. Kliebard, (Eds.) *Curriculum and Evaluation: Readings in Educational Research* (pp. 56-67). Berkeley, CA: McCutchan Publishing Corporation.

Krathwohl, D.R. (2002). Revising Bloom's taxonomy. *Theory into Practice, 41*(4), 212-218. Retrieved from http://www.unco.edu/cetl/sir/stating_outcome/documents/Krathwohl.pdf

Kubitskey, B., & Fishman, B. (2006, April). *Professional development design for systemic curriculum change.* Paper presented at the Annual Meeting of the American Educational Research Association, San Francisco, CA.

Laanemets, U. & Kalamees-Ruubel, K. (2013). The Taba-Tyler rationales. *Journal of the American Association for the Advancement of Curriculum Studies.* Retrieved from http://www.uwstout.edu/soe/jaaacs/upload/2013-05-1-Urve.pdf

Larkin, H., & Richardson, B. (2013). Creating high challenge/high support academic environments through constructive alignment: student outcomes. *Teaching in Higher Education, 18*(2), 192-204. http://dx.doi.org/10.1080/13562517.2012.696541

Stiggins, R.J., Arter, J.A., & Chappuis, J. (2007). *Classroom assessment for student learning: Doing it right – using it well.* Upper Saddle River, NJ: Prentice Hall.

Sweet, C. & Blythe, H. (2012). *Know your audience.* Retrieved from http://tlc.eku.edu/sites/tlc.eku.edu/files/TLCAppenB.pdf

Sweet, C., Blythe, H., Combs, D., Fair, G., and Hearn, J. (2012). A reflection on CARTE as Eastern Kentucky University's response to Senate Bill 1. *Kentucky Journal of Excellence in College Teaching and Learning,* 20-26. Retrieved from http://kjectl.eku.edu/sites/kjectl.eku.edu/files/files/Journal%2012/SweetEtAl2012.pdf

Tyler, R.W. (1949). *Basic principles of curriculum and instruction.* Chicago, IL: University of Chicago Press.

Wang, X., Su, Y., Cheung, S., Wong, E., & Kwong, T. (2013). An exploration of Biggs' constructive alignment in course design and its impact on students' learning approaches. *Assessment & Evaluation in Higher Education, 38*(4), 477-491. http://dx.doi.org/10.1080/02602938.2012.658018

Endnotes

[1]In our original documents and process, we classified this breakdown as FIP-M (Factual, Interpretive, Procedural, and Metacognitive). Over time and based upon some confusion that arose

among participants, we tidied up the description and descriptors for this analysis. Factual became Know; Interpretive and Procedural, whose nuances were difficult for participants to navigate, became Apply; Metacognitive remained; and we added Teach to remind some course instructors that their students needed to know how to *teach* those standards as well. Initially, the courses that included the "teach" component completed other charts. This new KAM-T model is cleaner and clearer.

Appendix A

Notes from PLC Meeting---Eastern Initiative

Department of English and Theatre
April 6, 2011

Present: T-------, K-------, L-------, C---------, K--------, G--------, S--------

Ideas/suggestions/recommendations and next steps

The group discussed the article by Gerald Graff, "Why Assessment," and agreed with the premise that overcoming teacher and curricular isolation is valuable, as is discussion of what we teach, how we teach and why we teach what we do.

Discussion about assessment included the following points:
- the difficulties of assessing learning outcomes in literary studies and the humanities
- assessment allows teachers to critically reflect on what and how they teach but faculty members have limited time to reflect and make changes in teaching.
- assessment should determine the syllabus, the focus for understanding what works and implementing curricular and pedagogical changes.
- need to incorporate latest brain research in our pedagogy.
- used to have more opportunity for critical reflection with our colleagues: we don't have forums anymore. CIVIC was working for a while---there was more cohesion
- it would be nice to have smaller groups meet---American Lit group; comp group---share ideas about teaching. This group is a good start.

The Writing project should be involved in reflecting and re-thinking ENG 101 and 102. Some mentioned not even knowing what the gen ed assessments are for ENG 101 and 102: some have never seen the results of those assessments.

G--------- discussed his review of the Common Core standards, what steps he takes to get to outcomes. Looking at the standards helps him see holes in his approach: he is doing #7 well but says #8 is harder to do.

S---------- said that in her Adolescent Lit class she sees students having the most difficulty with citing strong textual evidence---in finding explicit evidence as well as inferential evidence. She focuses on helping students see authors as purposeful and asks them to reflect on how authors create text---analysis of rhetorical strategies.

Next Steps: S--------- suggested that it would valuable to the PLC to see the developmental process across the standards, from middle school through high school, then to extrapolate where we take it from there. L--------- asked if she and G------- would share that at the next meeting. She also asked if K----------- and R---------- would share their experiences deconstructing standards with area secondary education teachers at the next meeting.

K------ noted that the dept is hiring two new rhetoric/comp people and that this a good time to re-think the comp program. He suggested that we ask related faculty to join us in talking about ideas for changing these courses. The Writing Project wants to be involved in that as well. We could invite M-------- to a PLC meeting in the early fall term.

Resources/research: L--------- will work on collecting some data about
- grade distributions in our classes (developmental plus ENG 101, 102, 210, 301, 302,)
- pass rates in our classes
- retention rates in our classes
- retention rates for developmental students into mainstream classes
- graduation rates of our majors (especially in the teacher ed option)
- Praxis scores and pass rates

Issue/Problem/Question Discussed:
In the last general education reform, assessment did not serve the English department well. We've gone from 40 people teaching 200 level courses to 10-12 people teaching 200 level courses.

In the past, ENG faculty were more interested in teaching freshman composition. The culture has changed. This is partly because our department has been decimated: lost 10-12 tenure-track lines past few years. Hired many more adjuncts. 98% of EKU ENG 101 and 102 is taught by adjuncts---this is a national trend –a system that is "cost effective" but may be negatively impacting student learning and retention. Some said that it is a crisis.

L-------- expressed concern that ENR 112 will be cut from general education curriculum, especially since ENG 101 does not always help students who need explicit instruction in critical reading skills. Although that is an objective of ENG 101, many instructors probably do not teach "reading." It was noted that adjuncts have a difficult time especially making the reading/writing connection in ENG 101. Sometimes writing assignments are not related to the reading and some instructors say that they don't know what to do with the readings in *World of Ideas*.

Also discussed ENG 102, that it is a difficult course to teach and not very interesting to teach. Dull for students; problem of the artificiality of research course. Many adjuncts just teach MLA style in a rote manner. MLA citation should not be the focus of the course but of just one or two lessons. Maybe it should be literature-based? More of a seminar course like the honors course 105. Especially since fewer students take ENG 211, 212 or 210 now. Discussed another college's freshman seminar model. 101 should be taught as critical thinking and expression course. 102 should be taught as an argument course.

P---------- suggested (via email to L---------) that we team teach ENG 095, 101 and 301 and students exchange papers with one another on a common reading (such as Letter from Birmingham Jail or the Declaration of Independence).

How can we make 101 and 102 more rigorous and interesting experiences for students? Would that impact retention? One person commented that students are not getting prepared in 101 for 102. Students don't think they need 102 after 101, yet students in Shakespeare course are at a complete loss to write a research paper.

Discussed the need to include adjuncts in any re-thinking of 101 and 102—their input would be valuable.

Adjuncts need professional development to better help students with reading and writing. Adjuncts are asking for PD (for example, through the FAIR organization). They only get 6 hours in the summer: 3 hours is all business and 3 in instruction. A week would be very valuable. Maybe the SB 1 CPE grant has money for professional development for 101 and 102 instructors? L----- will find out.

There are 65 adjunct instructors teaching freshman comp. 40 would possibly come to summer PD: would pay them $400 per week and would have to pay the faculty who develop and facilitate the PD.

Next Meeting: Wed April 27, 2:30.

Appendix B

Analyzing the Student Learning Outcomes: Where does the Common Core fit?

STEP ONE: Put a checkmark in the indicated column if this standard is applicable to your course.

STEP TWO: Put a checkmark in the next column if this standard is assessed in some way in your course.

STEP THREE: Put the course's exact SLO number (i.e., 1, 2, 3, etc.) in the next column **IF** it is applicable **AND** assessed in your course.

STEP FOUR: Put a checkmark in the last column if you need to revise, reword, or add a new student learning out come to your syllabus. Make those adjustments to your SLOs as needed

STEP FIVE: Go to your syllabus and indicate how you've aligned to the Common Core. See below for an example from a Foundations of Reading Course:

4. Describe the five key components of reading instruction (phonics, phonemic awareness, vocabulary, comprehension, and fluency) and evaluate the instructional efficacy of strategies for each. (CCR.R.1, CCCR.R.2, CCR. R.3, CCR.R.7, CCR.R.8)

College and Career Readiness Anchor Standards for Reading

Key Ideas and Details		Applies	Assessed	Matching SLO	Revision needed
CCR.R.1	Read closely to determine what the text says explicitly and to make logical inferences from it; cite specific textual evidence when writing or speaking to support conclusions drawn from the text.				
CCR.R.2	Determine central ideas or themes of a text and analyze their development; summarize the key supporting details and ideas.				

CCR.R.3	Analyze how and why individuals, events, and ideas develop and interact over the course of a text.					
Craft and Structure						
CCR.R.4	Interpret words and phrases as they are used in a text, including determining technical, connotative, and figurative meanings, and analyze how specific word choices shape meaning or tone.					
CCR.R.5	Analyze the structure of texts, including how specific sentences, paragraphs, and larger portions of the text (e.g., a section, chapter, scene, or stanza) relate to each other and the whole.					
CCR.R.6	Assess how point of view or purpose shapes the content and style of a text.					
Integration of Knowledge and Ideas						
CCR.R.7	Integrate and evaluate content presented in diverse media and formats, including visually and quantitatively, as well as in words.					
CCR.R.8	Delineate and evaluate the argument and specific claims in a text, including the validity of the reasoning as well as the relevance and sufficiency of the evidence.					

		Applies	Assessed	Matching SLO	Revision Needed
CCR.R.9	Analyze how two or more texts address similar themes or topics in order to build knowledge or to compare the approaches the authors take.				
Range of Reading and Level of Text Complexity					
CCR.R.10	Read and comprehend complex literary and informational texts independently and proficiently.				

College and Career Readiness Anchor Standards for Writing

Text Types and Purposes		Applies	Assessed	Matching SLO	Revision Needed
CCR.W.1	Write arguments to support claims in an analysis of substantive topics or texts, using valid reasoning and relevant and sufficient evidence.				
CCR.W.2	Write informative/explanatory texts to examine and convey complex ideas and information clearly and accurately through the effective selection, organization, and analysis of content.				
CCR.W.3	Write narratives to develop real or imagined experiences or events using effective technique, well-chosen details, and well-structured even sequences.				
Production and Distribution of Writing					
CCR.W.4	Produce clear and coherent writing in which the development, organization, and style are appropriate to task, purpose, and audience.				

CCR.W.5	Develop and strengthen writing as needed by planning, revising, editing, rewriting, or trying a new approach.				
CCR.W.6	Use technology, including the internet, to produce and publish writing and to interact and collaborate with others.				
Research to Build and Present Knowledge					
CCR.W.7	Conduct short as well as more sustained research projects based on focused questions, demonstrating understanding of the subject under investigation.				
CCR.W.8	Gather relevant information from multiple print and digital sources, assess the credibility and accuracy of each source, and integrate the information while avoiding plagiarism.				
CCR.W.9	Draw evidence from literary or informational texts to support analysis, reflection, and research.				

Appendix C

Matching the SLOs to Course Assessments: Think Taxonomy!

STEP ONE: Copy your course's Student Learning Outcomes into the chart below (the first row is an example for you). As you review your first SLO, note the CCR standard(s) that is embedded. After discussing with your colleagues the intent of the standard as it relates to this specific SLO, record the connection that you have made. See the example in the first row and note the italicized addition as the discussion of how these particular standards relate. *(Please note: not all of your SLOs may include CC standards. Include those SLOs in the chart anyway, though you will not need to complete the latter part of this first step. Steps two, three, and five will still be applicable to your course alignment.)*

STEP TWO: Indicate, for each SLO, how you assess student learning formatively. In other words, what assessment in class helps you adjust your instruction according to what students are learning or not learning? (These may take the form of class discussions, written responses, hand signals, "clicker" questions, online polls, etc. The important factor is not the *form* it takes, but rather the purpose of the assessment.)

STEP THREE: Indicate, for each SLO, how you assess student learning summatively. How do you – and the students – ultimately know whether they have learned the content? These assessments may take the form of course exams, written essays, performance assessments, etc. Again, the form of the assessment is not as important as its purpose. If the intent of this assessment is an ultimate determination of student learning – and not a guide for future instruction for this group of students – then the assessment is summative in nature.

STEP FOUR: Use the KAM-T column to designate whether the Common Core skill will be assessed (and therefore taught) at the Knowledge level, the Application level, or the Metacognitive level. Perhaps, too, if this is a Teacher Education course, the students in the class will be expected to demonstrate a readiness to Teach this standard to P-12 students.

STEP FIVE: Review the actual assessments (where applicable) to determine if any tweaking is necessary. Do your assessments themselves reflect the learning that is required by the SLO? Do rubrics, instructions, or procedures need to be altered? Make a note in the last column as a reminder about the follow up steps that are required.

SLO and Assessment Chart
Course:_____ Lead Instructor: _____

	Student Learning Outcome	Assessment: Formative	Assessment: Summative	KAM-T	Follow Up Notes
1	Define and analyze different theories of learning, relating each to the development of adolescent readers and writers. (CCR.R.4, CCR.R.10 – *these CC standards mean that students will use technical language and concepts in their analysis and that they will choose age-appropriate texts and resources for adolescents to use, based on those theories of learning.*)	Reading Response	Unit Plan Reflection	R4: A, M R10: M	Review rubrics for language related to **vocabulary** (CCR4) and **textual resources** (CCR10) for adolescents. Create a question in the Unit Plan reflection based on this SLO.

Appendix D

Choosing the Best Instructional Techniques

STEP ONE: If your PLC is choosing to use this particular process for aligning your instruction, copy your course's SLOs and assessments into the chart.

STEP TWO: Dissect your SLO further: identify the key verbs and the content in the separately labeled columns. Make a note about where the Common Core standards (where applicable) fit into the learning.

STEP THREE: Consider the instructional steps/activities that will assist in helping students master the SLO. The instructional activity needs to relate directly to the verb and content. The instructional activity should match the level of verb. For example, if students are expected to analyze, then lecture as the only instructional activity is insufficient, as it does not give students an opportunity to analyze. Consider, too, the level of expectation for the Common Core standards. In the example provided, you will note the references to those KAM-T labels.

STEP FOUR: Use your PLC group to determine what areas related to instruction are weaknesses or areas that require further study. What resources could be useful to your group as you look to deepen or strengthen your instructional repertoire? Please note, too, that your instructional choices do not have to match among every instructor teaching the course. Allow for individual styles and preferences while still matching the instructional activities to the level of mastery required by the SLO.

Instructional Design: Completing the Cycle
Course: _____   Lead Instructor: _____

	Student Learning Outcome	Assessments: (F) and (S) Formative	Key Verbs (embedded with language of standards)	+ Content Specific Topics	= Appropriate Instructional Activities
1	Define and analyze different theories of learning, relating each to the development of adolescent readers and writers. (CCR.R.4, CCR.R.10 – these CC standards mean that students will use technical language and concepts in their analysis and that they will choose age-appropriate texts and resources for adolescents to use, based on those theories of learning.)	Reading Response (F) Unit Plan Reflection (S)	**Define** (using technical language and concepts) **Analyze** (using technical language and concepts) **Relate** (choose age-appropriate texts and resources)	Theories of Learning Development of adolescent readers and writers	1. Concept attainment exercise (for definition) 2. Mini-lecture with webbing exercise that analyzes elements of the theories and how they link to adolescent development (emphasize *Application* of the CCR) 3. Class exercise using materials and resources for adolescents, evaluating their appropriateness based upon theories of learning (emphasize *Metacognition* with CCR)

Chapter 7

So That's the Problem: Why Literacy Standards Matter in General Education

Gill Hunter

In 2009, Eastern Kentucky University responded to Kentucky's Senate Bill 1 by aligning curriculum for courses in the College of Education and select courses in the College of Arts and Sciences with Kentucky's K-12 Core Academic Standards, the State's adopted version of the Common Core State Standards. Instructors of courses with high concentrations of pre-service teachers worked in departments to connect established student learning outcomes to English Language Arts Anchor Standards. We kept inventing problems, since we imagined clear distinctions between what happens on a college campus and what happens in K-12 schools. However, the exercise required us to think critically about classes' outcomes and envision overlap with the Standards. By overtly depicting these connections on syllabi, instructors could show education majors where their academic training connects to their teaching careers. At the same time, instructors could see the skills the next generation of college students would bring to campus. All we'd have to do, then, is build from there.

So we altered syllabi to tack a cryptic series of standards-speak letters (W, RL, RI, SL, L) – which refers to the Anchor Standards' strands/domains, like writing, reading literature, reading informational, speaking/listening, and language - and numbers (1-10) to the list of student learning outcomes prominently displayed on the front page of every syllabus. Magically, our classes were aligned to the Standards. However, other than those cosmetic adjustments to the syllabus, nothing had to change. Adding a layer to outcomes didn't necessarily mean classes were altered. It certainly didn't mean students would have to pay more attention to the Standards; it didn't even mean instruction would have to change in any way. It could, because instructors had the same opportunity as with any revision to the outcomes of a course. But it raises the same question that has always existed in relation to established, publicized, mandated, even assessed student learning outcomes: What difference do (can) they make to the instruction in the classroom?

In order to explore that potential for difference, this chapter begins with the assumption that standards, or "student learning outcomes," matter. That exploration will demonstrate why standards matter and how they make a difference to student learning and instructional design. The same logic can be narrowed to consider why literacy standards specifically matter and, then, why literacy standards matter in general education courses, students' first exposure to college. General education is the bridge between the college-readiness of high school and the career-readiness of upper-level courses in students' majors. Finally, all of this matters because close examination of the Core Standards provides the rationale for not only including connections to the standards on the syllabus but using them to rethink and intentionally design courses throughout a college's general education program. It's not just that standards matter, or that literacy standards do, because they're easily dismissed after a syllabus' first page; but instructors have the opportunity to make these standards – the college-readiness standards K-12 districts throughout Kentucky and across much of the nation have adopted, and so the kind and level of thinking students will be doing as they begin college – matter.

We can make courses matter more than ever before as we seamlessly transition students from their formative K-12 years to their broad-based general education programs to the career-readiness courses of their majors...

Simply declaring standards' importance, however, gets us no farther than dumping that list of outcomes on the syllabus. We can deliberately build from them, by planning for the logical ways in which these standards should be incorporated into college classes, and by considering how to teach students who have learned through the standards and, for education majors, will teach to the standards. We can make courses matter more than ever before as we seamlessly transition students from their formative K-12 years to their broad-based general education programs to the career-readiness courses of their majors, spiraling through knowledge and building skills they need for success in college and in their lives beyond.

Standards Matter

College has mattered since the late 11th century, when teaching began at Oxford University (Oxford) or, in America, since the mid-17th century, when Harvard College (Harvard) opened. And despite the advent of online learning, dual enrollment programs, study abroad, and internships, the college classroom and a lot of instructional practice looks a lot like it did in 1636 or even 1096. The research behind some Common Core decisions is questionable (Whitney & Shannon, 2014). But study of the Standards' K-12 progression shows that careful attention has been paid to the sequential building and necessary spiraling of skills, and the vertical alignment of essential knowledge. In response, K-12 teachers are changing the way they teach. The Standards point toward college, and college faculty members have to be ready to teach from the Standards' endpoint. Our firm reliance on tradition must be reconsidered.

The Standards point toward college, and college faculty members have to be ready to teach from the Standards' endpoint. Our firm reliance on tradition must be reconsidered.

Most of us must resist the inclination to teach the way we were taught. We know too much about how learning happens to rely on the teacher-centered lecture model that defined the college classroom experience of so many faculty members. A problem is that we're disinclined to do so, because college worked for us: we were engaged in our disciplines and liked the atmosphere. These students, benefitting from ever-earlier pushes to consider college and careers, aren't arriving on campus to learn how to be professors. A functional pedagogical change must follow. Freshman composition courses, sophomore communications courses, general education anthropology and literature and history and sociology and political science and humanities and psychology courses aren't preparation for careers in those fields so much as an education in ways of thinking, or habits of mind. The Standards introduce those mental processes that each general education discipline builds on and deepens. The instructional practice that honors this process must be flexible, dynamic, and current. Ideally, students will come to college ready to learn within the disciplines, but their expectations for how learning happens, and what instruction looks like, have changed.

The good news is that college faculty members have the opportunity to respond. The first step is to recognize the potential of course standards – student learning outcomes – to shape instructional practices. In fact, such standards are the first step, our starting point in designing a course: "In the best designs form follows function. In other words, all the methods and materials we use are shaped by a clear conception of the vision of desired results. That means that we must be able to state with clarity what the student should understand and be able to do" (Wiggins & McTighe, 2005, p. 14). So we start with the standard. We design a course backwards by asking what students need to know and be able to do and then committing to that knowledge set instead of assuming that those skills displayed on the syllabus' front page will probably be picked up along the way. Then we test it. So many instructors willfully oppose "teaching to the test" but by doing so miss opportunities to test what they teach. The test, then, becomes not only an assessment of student achievement, but also a way for an instructor to measure instructional effectiveness. I still hear colleagues complaining that a "whole class" failed a test. Each time I wonder whether form follows function in their classroom, whether they're testing what they taught, and what they're going to do with the knowledge that a "whole class" hasn't succeeded. If instructors are committed to their outcomes – if they've established outcomes that are truly necessary for success in the course and have designed instruction around them – then they feel compelled to remediate. But the traditional college syllabus and class schedule probably allow little

> So many instructors willfully oppose "teaching to the test" but by doing so miss opportunities to test what they teach.

space for re-teaching. The result? That "whole class" misses out, and the instructor marches on.

The antidote to missing out and marching on rests with the learning we want students to accomplish in our classes. Starting, and ending, with the standard puts students "at the centre of the learning experience by using learning outcomes to focus attention more directly on the activities and the achievements of students, rather than simply on the teaching of the curriculum content" (Brooks, Dobbins, Scott, Rawlinson, & Norman, 2014, p. 722). So standards decenter both the instructor and the textbook as they encourage revision of curriculum. Students learn when actively engaged; clear learning outcomes that students can understand, can engage with, and will build on keeps them invested in a class from its first moments to its last. Wiggins and McTighe (2014) recognize that this is a new way of thinking, pushing instructors "away from starting with such questions as 'What book will we read?' or 'What activities will we do?' or 'What will we discuss?' to 'What should they walk out the door able to understand, regardless of what activities or texts we use?' and 'What is evidence of such ability?' and, therefore, 'What texts, activities, and methods will best enable such a result?'" (p. 17).

> *Students learn when actively engaged; clear learning outcomes students can understand, can engage with, and will build on keeps them invested in a class from its first moments to its last.*

Haven't you planned courses by deciding what books you want to teach, or maybe by choosing a particular catchy theme, or finding a dazzling anchor text that sets up the activities you want students to try? It's the way we were taught, and it worked for us. We made connections with work we did and between disparate parts of the semester because we were eager to absorb new information and our minds more or less automatically engaged in a dialectic process to make sense of it. When prioritizing standards, key, controllable elements of those approaches remain. A well-chosen collection of texts comes together to accomplish the class' goals; a provocative theme runs through a semester's weeks as students build knowledge; a class begins with an unforgettable touchstone reading that students return to and work from. Heeding standards does not dismiss any of those course structures. Instead, paying attention to learning outcomes first gives purpose to other decisions. A text is an approach, a medium through which to address a standard, and a clear standard shows students the connections an instructor wants for them, the learning that is essential for success in the course. Students glean from a learning outcome an objective, a goal, a reason for reading, writing, and thinking. In fact, Brooks (2014) shows that students are inclined to "use the outcomes to structure their study and note-taking... as a kind of syllabus of their course" (p. 727). Students do this already. They see those outcomes plastered on the front page of the syllabus and expect to see them again. Why not intentionally give them a reason for paying attention to them, returning to them, and remembering them?

Literacy Standards Matter

If instructors agree that standards matter, and prepare to shape instructional practice around student learning outcomes, then the question emerges: Exactly what kind of outcomes should we be focusing on? Nothing says an instructor starts from scratch. In fact, the material that defines an expertise is the right medium with which to work. For most disciplines, that means the reading, writing, and thinking instructors want students to do is the work through which clear standards will be taught and assessed. Ultimately, we are all doing the same thing: teaching students to think and, once they can do that, to think critically. This means that literacy, then, is the essential objective. We want students to be literate generally, because "literacy – defined simply as the basic activities of decoding print – has been related to heightened moral and intellectual categories" (Kalman, 2008, p. 525). We also expect students to gain more specific forms of literacy as they learn within disciplines, in order to benefit from the nuances of multiple perspectives and the critical work of making meaning in a variety of contexts.

It's probably not news to instructors that "particular literacy practices are unique to each discipline" (Manderino & Wickens, 2014, p. 29). But students don't come to us thinking that way; they don't know that thinking shifts to suit the discipline, and they don't know how to shift their thinking to meet the texts they read and are expected to write. The fact is, though, that "literacy skills/strategies and disciplinary content are inextricably intertwined and

... without literate practices, the social and cognitive practices that make the disciplines and their advancement possible cannot be engaged" (Fang & Coatoam, 2013, p. 628). So how do we scaffold the knowledge mastered by those within a discipline so that students can begin to gain familiarity with it? We begin by reflecting this goal in our outcomes. Then we teach to the first steps of it, the foundational qualities, then assess student progress and teach the next steps – and reteach the first ones when necessary. In other words, we design our course so that students grow ever-more comfortable with the language and ways of thinking of our discipline. We use reading as mentor texts, so that students are not just learning content but also seeing models of how writers and practitioners think and communicate in the field. We use writing assignments as opportunities to first make sense of the reading students do without the pressure of trying to immediately do the same sort of writing themselves. Students "need practice thinking, and thereby talking, like a scientist, historian, or literary critic. It is through academic talk that students can reason their way through increasingly complex and abstract ideas" (Manderino & Wickens, 2014, p. 35). Students come to class to make sense of the material they've read, to engage in developmental conversations where they hear how others, including experts and novices, make meaning, and test out ideas formatively to get feedback on them before committing more formally to the discourse of the discipline.

College cannot represent a step backward through courses that rely on textbooks to build content knowledge. Literacy is not a canned and pre-packaged skill. Students need strategies and skills for dealing with the complexities of real materials.

Embedded within students' discipline-specific talk is the cross-curricular meaning-making central to the college experience. For students, the Common Core State Standards scaffold the most important thinking college classes require. College-readiness means schools include "a discipline-based model of literacy instruction, [that] while not necessarily ensuring that all high school graduates become junior scientists, historians, or mathematicians, is needed to prepare critical thinkers who are capable of comprehending and critiquing the materials they read" (Fang & Coatoam, 2013, p.

628). Will the next generation of college students arrive on campus better prepared to handle the reading and writing expectations of their courses? They will have a better idea of what to expect. They will have experience with complex texts written for authentic audiences and purposes. Instructors, in turn, can have a better idea of the thinking on which their classes need to build. College cannot represent a step backward through courses that rely on textbooks to build content knowledge. Literacy is not a canned and pre-packaged skill. Students need strategies and skills for dealing with the complexities of real materials. This is cause for celebration: An aptitude for working with such materials and an enjoyment in doing so is why we entered our profession in the first place. Translating our strategies for interpreting and, eventually, creating, such texts – without leaning on, hiding behind, or passing through a textbook to do so – becomes a primary instructional goal.

How do we translate what we know into terms with which students can work? Manderino and Wickens (2014) summarize the task clearly: "The role of the teacher is to provide the appropriate scaffolds in order to move students toward disciplinary knowledge construction" (p. 37). Student learning outcomes can reflect those scaffolds. Our course design consists of the careful placement and deliberate removal of those scaffolds. Instructional strategies – including course materials, activities, and assessments – build on what students know when they enter the course and make plain what students will be able to do by the end. Students will not achieve proficiency in a discipline through a single course, but a deliberate plan centered on knowledge students need to build and the materials and methods through which they'll build it helps them grow familiar with the habits of mind of those within the field. And as a single course's depth combines with a multitude of classes to create breadth, students develop career-readiness ways of thinking no matter what they do after college.

Literacy Standards Matter in General Education

The fulcrum on which the Common Core State Standards' two primary tenets – college-readiness and career-readiness – rest is a college's general education program. If the college-readiness goal has been met, then students begin their freshman year prepared for the academic rigors that await them. The problem is that many of them will not be adequately prepared. Enter a more responsive instructional design to bridge the gap. Another problem is that all of us – K-12 teachers and college instructors alike – know the career-readiness goal won't be reached. For most college-bound students, it can't possibly be. When students enter college without a declared major there is no possibility of being prepared for a specific career. Even those students who arrive on campus knowing how they'll spend their lives after college quickly realize how much they have to learn. The solution, then, is to create in students a desire for continual learning and an ability to incorporate new information. The cornerstones of this career-readiness foundation are the literacy skills of interpreting disciplinary texts and clearly communicating for a variety of audiences. K-12 education, therefore, builds toward a college's general education program like never before because general education programs expose students to diverse ways of thinking and promote breadth. Therefore, general education courses have the opportunity to build upon the skills students will bring with them in unprecedented ways.

> *K-12 education, therefore, builds toward a college's general education program like never before because general education programs expose students to diverse ways of thinking and promote breadth.*

Reasons for emphasizing literacy for new college students are central to the overlap of general education missions and the broadest definitions of career-readiness: "Some have considered reading and writing key for achieving democracy, economic growth and stability, social harmony and, most recently, competitiveness in world markets" (Kalman, 2008, p. 524). Colleges respond to the need to produce contributing members of a range of societies by prioritizing students' well-rounded education before, or alongside, the ever-deepening immersion into the coursework of their major. The endpoint looks like this:

> *This work is not only an academic expectation reflected in a student learning outcome; it's a pedagogy, an instructional practice.*

...stronger exposure to liberal types of education resulted in such positive outcomes as greater reading comprehension, critical thinking, science reasoning, writing skills, openness to diversity/challenge, learning for self-understanding, sense of responsibility for one's own academic success, preference for deep and difficult intellectual work, and positive attitude toward literacy. (Laird, Niskode-Dossett, & Kuh, 2009, p. 66)

The instruction that leads to such results is less isolated than that which consists only of unique courses in individual disciplines. It makes use of teaching that is aware of the cumulative effect of having students learn by grappling with real problems, engaging with real texts, and thinking deeply and repeatedly about real issues in order to write in real ways for real purposes. This work is not only an academic expectation reflected in a student learning outcome; it's a pedagogy, an instructional practice. Because we know that "these skills and competencies are critical for success in advanced course work in the major as well as in students' lives after college," instruction must prioritize literacy skills and assess those competencies (Laird et al., 2009, p. 80). Students cannot successfully move into the work of their majors without personal literacy strategies, and are ill-equipped for life after college without being competent as readers, writers, and thinkers. We teach such skills because we value the mission of the university and privilege the life of the mind. We structure our courses from these skills-as-outcomes because we understand that too many students initially resist the introspection and struggle that brings competency, much less mastery. We show the flexibility to reteach material and re-envision courses because we know that this learning happens developmentally and incrementally, and specific course goals are holistic program goals. All of that is important so that students can enter the careers they envision for themselves and so that we might someday have the world we think is possible.

The Common Core English Language Arts Standards Matter in General Education

Whether those student learning outcomes have been prominent in course design or not, standards will soon matter to college instructors more than at any time before. Along with details of colleges' strategic plans, and established departmental objectives (those, too, might need revisiting), standards matter because these standards – the Common Core State Standards – matter. The Standards define the education students now receive, and so will define the skills students possess as they begin college. The Standards carry their own language; K-12 teachers speak it and students are becoming versed in it. Therefore, as students' literacy skills develop, so too does their awareness of their learning and their ability to talk about it. The progress of mindful college-readiness cannot be halted when students actually arrive on campus.

Students will spend years preparing for the kind of intellectual work on which college relies. Shifted K-12 literacy practices result from Reading Standards that "suggest that the most important type of writing students must do – perhaps the only type they must do – is straightforward, analytic writing about their reading" (Jolliffe, 2013, p. 141). While some, including Jolliffe, bemoan the reduced emphasis on narrative, it's clear that the Standards exist to prepare students for the work they'll do in their postsecondary years. General education classes expect students to read complex texts and demonstrate straightforward, analytic thinking. K-12 teachers are therefore laying a foundation of increasingly complex texts to read and writing and thinking assignments that require students to demonstrate mastery of concepts and styles within those texts. General education classes need students to be critical readers (Jolliffe, 2013), so the Standards lead students to research to support ideas and to argue, and to gain multiple perspectives by reading informational texts in conjunction with each other and paired, too, with literary fiction. And general education classes want students to be close readers, focusing on details, remembering them and finding ways to combine them with information from other sources. So K-12 teachers emphasize close reading like never before. Student writers comfortably talk to each other about details – finding ways to develop ideas – at every step of the writing process.

> ...general education classes want students to be close readers, focusing on details, remembering them and finding ways to combine them with information from other sources. So K-12 teachers emphasize close reading like never before.

Responsively, colleges' general education courses must be prepared to build upon the analytic thinking, the critical reading, and the close reading students are being taught to do. In other words, college instructors will teach students what to do with that analytic thinking, and how to access the next level(s) of such thought. They'll work with students to discover new reasons for reading critically and help students find the skills to think through increasingly complex problems. And these instructors will challenge students with more difficult texts in a variety of disciplines and, at each step, give them strategies for making sense of new material and increasingly challenging real work to do with it as they gain proficiency. How exactly to do that is the same question K-12 teachers asked when first presented with the Common Core State Standards. Those teachers' first, tentative answers, informed by experimentation and near-constant collaboration, are now the opportunity and responsibility of college instructors. We have to work together, to try new things, to seek new ways of reaching new learners.

Calkins, Ehrenworth, and Lehman recognized teachers' questions and wrote *Pathways to the Common Core* (2012) as a guide for K-12 teachers in understanding and implementing the Standards in their classrooms and schools. The writers take pains to remain balanced and neutral, exploring all sides of the contentious process of debating and adopting the standards and then systematically unpacking the English Language Arts Standards for teachers. Calkins carries great credibility with elementary school teachers, adding this book to a career's worth of theory and resources for teaching literacy. Her agenda with *Pathways to the Common Core* is noble. It also casts a glaring light on the college instructor, who needs a pathway *from* the Common Core. The problem is that there's not just one path, no easy answers. But there are answers; there is a process to finding them, and it starts with the standards.

Pathways from the Common Core

Lindsey Tepe, of the New America Education Policy Program, voices the need for colleges to respond to the Standards: "the Common Core standards appear at the moment to end at the college gate, representing the completion of an indistinct goal – 'college readiness' – rather than as another deliberate step on a student's journey toward a college degree" (Education, 2014). To solve the problem Tepe identifies, it is necessary to extrapolate from the established Standards. To end this chapter I want to start the process of envisioning literacy possibilities for general education courses that meaningfully grow out of the Standards. I'm no Lucy Calkins, so this effort is far more speculative than authoritative, but I start the same place Calkins does, with the relevant Standards themselves.

Reading Standard 1

The first reading standard focuses on citing textual evidence to support analysis. The analysis the standard prioritizes involves text-based interpretation ("explicit") and inferences. The leap that high school students make from grades 9-10 to grades 11-12 is in their ability to identify places where writers demonstrate the complexity of the topics with which they work. "Determining where the text leaves matters uncertain" proves a college-readiness skill because it primes students to ask questions of texts. General education courses, then, spiral through this type of learning, asking students to engage with ideas and ask questions of increasingly complex texts, and to identify research questions within reading they do. Of course, while asking questions alone is a valuable critical reading strategy, the practice also leads to the pursuit-of-answers-process identified in the second reading standard.

Reading Standard 2

High school students learn to synthesize as they matriculate, moving from close reading of a single idea within a single text to working with multiple ideas within a single text by the time they graduate. This lays a foundation on which college classes build when they require students to synthesize, gathering multiple ideas from a variety of sources and organizing their own thoughts around those ideas. College students are expected to write from ideas, organizing essays around one or more writers' thoughts, building arguments from their own thinking. College courses will expect students to summarize increasingly complex texts, but summaries are a means to closer reading and more purposeful use of texts' ideas. Students will build on established skills to draw upon ideas from a range of sources within a single assignment.

Reading Standard 3

The third reading standard requires students to read like a writer, a valuable skill across all disciplines. In demonstrating achievement of the third reading standard, high school students will not read for content only. Instead, in grades 9 and 10 students will explore characterization in literature and similarly independent portions of text in nonfiction works, isolating single features of text to consider writers' decisions. By grades 11 and 12 students will consider all choices writers make, reading texts on multiple levels in order to create similar texts in college classes.

> They will "read" so they can write. They will analyze and interpret so they can create.

This close relationship between reading and writing foregrounds students' active reading approach. College students will read to acquire additional content knowledge and will begin to understand how texts are put together as they examine and rehearse the skills of practitioners in the discipline. As instructors focus on content and the process underlying the creation of texts students will encounter in college classes and a range of professional fields, students will gain a broader, more sophisticated definition of text, one that joins the traditional written word to ideas, experiences, and anything else able to be studied and interpreted. They will "read" so they can write. They will analyze and interpret so they can create.

Reading Standard 4

While the fourth standard seems straightforward, it remains relevant at all levels of education, because the texts with which students engage become increasingly complex. Strategies for reading actively, for making meaning of new vocabulary, and for unpacking sentences written for a range of audiences are not quick-hit solutions to reading problems. Instead, every time college students read, they should learn more about how to read difficult text; by reading like a writer, every complex text becomes a primer for how to read complex

> *If every college instructor shared with students how he or she reads the material students read, then students would leave each semester with a wealth of strategies with which they could experiment.*

texts. If every college instructor shared with students how he or she reads the material students read, then students would leave each semester with a wealth of strategies with which they could experiment. Some would stick, and students would be ever-better prepared to encounter, work with, and use unfamiliar text in the future.

Reading Standard 5

As with the third reading standard, the fifth focuses on text structures, or how texts are put together. This is not a skill students master in high school and bring with them to college ready to apply to any new text. Because college-level texts are often so much more complex than those with which students most often work in high school, foundational thinking about structure must be ever-developed. Students in high school are being prepared to not only analyze and interpret texts and ideas but also evaluate them, and this, the upper end of Bloom's taxonomy, requires the spiraling that brings students back to the skill of evaluation each time they encounter a new text, a new argument, or a new idea. This is the critical thinking objective general education programs throughout the country share. We want our students to be independent thinkers, to critically explore possibilities and make informed, well-reasoned choices; they have to continually learn to do so as problems they face become harder and the ways in which those problems are discussed become more complex.

Reading Standard 6

The Common Core Standards treat "point of view" in an interesting way. Rather, they treat it in multiple ways. K-12 teachers do their best to make sure students can accurately identify both a writer's point of view and her or his perspective, or worldview. College instructors, while usually not too concerned with students identifying whether a work of fiction is written in first-person or third-person, limited or omniscient, can build on the worldview awareness students are primed to consider. The liberal aesthetic of a general education program requires students to consider perspectives other than their own. This is the hallmark of the well-roundedness of the general education certified student. Both point of view and perspective signal writers' purposes, and students do well to include among the questions they ask of a text, "what is this author's purpose in writing?" Seeking answers to purpose shows students the reasons a writer writes, the choices she or he makes, and the rhetorical and aesthetic impact of the published text. In turn, college students learn ways to structure their own writing, finding solutions to issues of idea development and counterarguments, even finding chances to consider the contentious issue of whether or not to use the first-person I in academic writing. Students need to know they have choices, and they need to see the possibilities before them. By reading for writers' choices they inform themselves about their own.

Reading Standard 7

As with the sixth, the seventh reading standard captures the essence of a broad-based general education program. It encourages variety, multiple perspectives, and diverse methods of receiving and presenting information. It pushes students to think broadly and deeply and does not limit students to traditional methods of acquiring information. What does this mean for the college instructor? Organizing a course around a textbook will no longer carry the same relevance for students. Assigning the same papers students have written for years carries new risk. Students will arrive on campus ready to read broadly, and ready to create texts using multiple media for real audiences beyond the classroom. Though some of their questions are the same ones students have been asking for a generation, some will be new; and they'll all have new ways of finding answers and be ready to experiment with new ways of making those answers known.

> *Students will arrive on campus ready to read broadly, and ready to create texts using multiple media for real audiences beyond the classroom.*

Reading Standard 8

While as an English teacher I am frustrated that the framers of the Common Core declare that the eighth standard does not apply to literature, the logical progression of the standard in working with nonfiction texts leads directly to the sort of work that happens in college courses. Where students in grades 9 and 10 explore the arguments of any single texts, students in grades 11 and 12 explore the arguments in specific texts (specifically American historical texts or foundational scientific texts). The skill students develop is to unpack an argument, first in a highly controlled situation, then – because this is how scaffolding works – in a less controlled situation, with more and more complex texts available. In college, then, students should be able to analyze arguments, moving between relatively narrow, single focuses of individual classes and the breadth of perspectives in general education programs and, ultimately, the career-directed sequence of courses in a major. Broad application of the skills of analysis is precisely what college expects. We want students to know how to make sense of the ideas in the texts they read. We want them to be able to contribute to the conversations they hear in those texts. Reading Standard 8 suggests that students will be better equipped than ever to understand and participate in those conversations.

Reading Standard 9

The same understanding of ongoing conversations lies at the center of the ninth reading standard. Focused on source material, students in grades 9 and 10 are encouraged to explore intertextuality, considering ways in which one text, or one author, influences or is influenced by another. Students in grades 11 and 12 are expected to extend this same thinking to include ideas, "themes and topics," as they relate to one another over time and across contexts. The implication for college success, and the opportunity for practical extension into college courses, is notable, because the skill that helps students succeed more than any other is the ability to transfer knowledge from one context to another. This sort of retention has been explained away by the summer slide/brain drain, or by the highly-specific content focus of individual academic disciplines. But we want students to make connections. We want them to remember what they read and what they learn in class. To do so they have to learn deeply and have to have occasion for applying knowledge they add. The ninth reading standard foregrounds just this kind of thinking by showing how writers do this over time and across disciplines, and by suggesting how students can join the discussions others have initiated and picked up on before them.

Reading Standard 10

The tenth reading standard is certainly the most straightforward, or the least surprising, of any of the standards. But instructors will do well to consider the language of the standard carefully as we think about applications to the college classroom. In short, the standard makes clear that students should achieve a certain level of proficiency – being able to comprehend appropriately complex texts – by the end of grades 10 and 12. To continue that trend, colleges' general education programs should be considered holistically – what do we want students to know and be able to do by the end of their sophomore year? It is not logical to expect students to demonstrate mastery of 10th grade material during the first days of 9th grade, but this is what we do with college freshmen who are given the option of taking a wide range of "introductory" courses.

Only by teaching students how to read the material in our classes and how to think and write like professionals in the field will we overcome the problem of students who can't do the work we value. We have to reconsider the work we want students to do, maybe even what academic work means and what it looks like. We can only do that by first reconsidering the work we're willing to do and what our work in the classroom and in designing a course needs to be.

References

Brooks, S., Dobbins, K., Scott, J.J.A., Rawlinson, M., & Norman, R.I. (2014). Learning about learning outcomes: The student perspective. *Teaching in Higher Education*, 19(6), 721-33.

Education Advisory Board. (2014). Higher ed must embrace Common Core, says policy expert. Retrieved from http://www.eab.com/daily-briefing/2014/12/19/higher-ed-must-embrace-common-core-says-policy-expert?elq_cid=1385946

Fang, Z. & Coatoam, S. (2013). Disciplinary literacy: What you want to know about it. *Journal of Adolescent and Adult Literacy*, 56(8), 627-32.

Harvard College. (2014). Historical facts. Retrieved from http://www.harvard.edu/historical-facts

Jolliffe, D. (2013). The Common Core Standards and preparation for reading and writing in college. In A.S. Horning & E.W. Kraemer (Eds.), *Reconnecting Reading and Writing*. (134-53). Anderson, SC: Parlor Press.

Kalman, J. (2008). Beyond definition: Central concepts for understanding literacy. *International Review of Education*, 54, 523-538.

Laird, T.F.N., Niskode-Dossett, A.S., & Kuh, G.D. (2009). What general education courses contribute to essential learning outcomes. *JGE: The Journal of General Education*, 58(2), 65-84.

Manderino, M. & Wickens, C. (2014). Addressing disciplinary literacy in the Common Core State Standards. *Illinois Reading Council Journal*, 42(2), 28-39.

National Governors Association Center for Best Practices & Council of Chief State School Officers. (2010). *Common Core State Standards for English language arts and literacy in history/social studies, science, and technical subjects.* Washington, DC: Authors. http://www.corestandards.org/ELA-Literacy/

Smarter Balanced Assessment Consortium. Retrieved from http://www.smarterbalanced.org/k-12-education/common-core-state-standards-tools-resources/

University of Oxford. Introduction and history. Retrieved from http://www.ox.ac.uk/about/organisation/history

Whitney, A. & Shannon P. (2014). Metaphors, frames, and fact (checks) about the Common Core. *English Journal*, 104(2), 61-71.

Wiggins, G. & McTighe J. (2005). *Understanding by design.* 2nd edition. Upper Saddle River, NJ: Merrill/Prentice Hall (ASCD).

Chapter 8
Teacher Education – Standards at a whole new level

Karen Kidwell and Saundra Hamon

Not since the Kentucky Education Reform Act (1990) has there been more intensive effort to improve outcomes for students and educators in the Commonwealth than in the last five years. Kentucky legislators passed Senate Bill 1 (2009), laying the foundation for Unbridled Learning, the name given to the new era of public education in the Commonwealth of Kentucky. In this new era, every system's input, process, output, and outcome have been examined with a laser-like focus; and efforts were aligned to ensure every school/district is led by effective leaders, every class is taught by an effective teacher, and every student, then, graduates ready for college, career, and civic life.

The design for Unbridled Learning is the *guarantee that every student graduates from high school ready for college, career, and civic engagement and success.* To achieve that guarantee, it is essential to identify the components necessary by deconstructing the language of that statement:

1. *Kids graduate*—all of them—which means they need to be engaged, experience success, and sense that learning matters to keep them in school.
2. They are *ready for success (college, career, civic engagement)*—which means they have access to learning the essentials for those next steps. For example, they need their learning experiences to prepare them to do complex, authentic, inquiry-based learning that requires creativity, critical thinking and problem-solving, not just work for school. Having clearly defined, aligned, and important/

rigorous standards that have been vetted through each/all of those lenses is critical to setting the bar or expectations.
3. They have to *persist in learning until they meet the benchmarks for success*—which means not only that they have the opportunity to learn the essentials, but they have learning opportunities that guarantee and provide defensible evidence of their learning successes and challenges, getting feedback along the way so that they see their targets clearly and feel confident they can reach them. This means more than evidence generated from standardized tests. Defensible evidence must be gathered from observing important and relevant skills and competencies in action.
4. Engineering those kinds of learning (and assessment) experiences will require *highly effective teachers and leaders*—people who are committed to students first, but are also skilled instructional designers. These instructional and assessment experiences must not only require students to demonstrate their knowledge and skills, but also keep them engaged in "winning streaks" that promote persistence.
5. Rigorous expectations for teachers/leaders will demand *opportunities for all educators to learn* a variety of skills and competencies and have *access to rich resources* (for their own learning *and* their students') so that they can customize learning for each and every student in the interest of success—success that matters for post-secondary pursuits such as college, a career, civic participation.

This is why Kentucky is working on things like implementing college/career-ready standards pre-K thru high school; defining characteristics of highly effective educators; identifying and sharing resources, tools, and strategies that support rigorous and engaging classroom practices; defining Career Pathways; implementing aligned assessments; and creating networks of educators that focus on learning and solving challenging problems together. Each of these is not an initiative or component on its own, the education panacea du jour. Each contributes to the support of that systemic goal of *all students graduating college, career, and civic life ready.*

Ensuring, then, that all pre-service students have the opportunity to gain the knowledge and practice the skills that will enable them to enter into a school setting and be able to engage and contribute to student growth from the very beginning must be a priority for schools of education. Research by Carrie R. Leana (2011) suggests, "In trying to improve American public schools, educators, policymakers, and philanthropists are overselling the role of the highly skilled individual teacher and undervaluing the benefits that come from teacher collaborations that strengthen skills, competence, and a school's overall social capital" (p. 30). If the expectation, then, is that new teachers will work together in learning teams to ensure that students have the competencies necessary for success, they need the opportunity to engage in those very kinds of situations prior to their hiring in a school. These learning teams, sometimes referred to as professional learning communities (PLCs), must be more than a study group or work group in a class. They should center on the authentic tasks that educators are faced with daily in their efforts to plan and implement standards-based learning experiences, such as co-constructing learning experiences that are explicitly designed to get at the intent of key learning standards, analyzing student work in order to uncover patterns in thinking and working that may be unproductive to learning, designing tasks and questions that provide diagnostic information for next steps in teaching and learning, and reflecting on particular instructional practices for the sake of growing as practitioners.

Effective implementation of standards in classrooms is not nearly as simple or straightforward as it may appear. The work conducted by the Kentucky Department of Education's Leadership Networks in Kentucky over the past five years in supporting the implementation of new standards has revealed a number of findings:

1. Most educators have had little to no experience in analyzing or deconstructing standards in order to understand the true intent of them and in order to identify the key knowledge, reasoning, and skills that must be intentionally addressed if students are to be able to attain them.
2. Most educators have had little to no opportunity to develop necessary assessment literacy, particularly in understanding how to design effective tasks, questions, and items that provide students the opportunity to demonstrate attainment of particular standards/targets or to be able

to discern the appropriate and inappropriate uses of information/resulting inferences from both standardized and non-standardized assessments.
3. Many educators have not participated in true learning teams that focus on the two items above. Rather, they have typically been assigned to a team, which may be called a PLC but doesn't focus deeply on colleagues learning together to develop the competencies above, but which functions more as a work team to complete assignments handed down to them by administrators that may or may not actually enhance their work with students.

Focusing intentionally in pre-service education on those three specific tasks of analyzing standards, becoming assessment literate, and engaging in true professional learning will do much to support the critical work needed and required in all schools.

Analyzing Standards

The notion of analyzing and then deconstructing (also sometimes called unpacking) standards has been, unfortunately, reduced to a rote activity in some cases. Teachers have been told to just pick out key verbs and concepts/vocabulary and that is sufficient. However, in reality, that is far from sufficient. Even prior to Kentucky's adoption of new standards, analysis of student work, interviews with teachers, and reviews of classroom assignments and assessments revealed that teachers often have vastly different interpretations of the intent of standards. This difference in interpretation leads to a great disparity in opportunity to learn among students, not to mention expectations for demonstrating attainment through assessment. This is not done with any ill intent on the part of teachers, however. When there is not a formalized process or expectation that teachers collaborate to analyze each standard carefully to clarify the intent, then that deep analysis often

Standards will change over time, but learning how to study standards and determine intent along with required student competencies (including enabling knowledge and skills) is an essential skill for all teachers to develop and hone over time.

doesn't occur. Consider the example presented in Figure 8.1.

Figure 8.1 Example of a Deconstructed Standard

Students will:
Distinguish between elements and compounds and classify them according to their properties.
Classify substances according to their chemical/reactive properties.
Infer real life applications for substances based on chemical/reactive properties.

In chemical reactions, the total mass is conserved. Substances are often classified into groups if they react in similar ways. The patterns which allow classification can be used to infer or understand real life applications for those substances.

*(note: this is a sample from work done with Kentucky's 2006-2013 standards)

	Weak Analysis/ Unpacking	Strong Analysis/Deconstruction
Knowledge	Element Compound Periodic Table Physical property Chemical property	Observe, describe and identify properties of elements Observe, describe and identify properties of compounds Use properties to identify elements and compounds Identify the Periodic Table as a resource containing information about certain properties of all known elements Recognize that a substance is a compound if it's not an element. Recognize that groups of elements have similar properties, including highly reactive metals, less-reactive metals, highly reactive non-metals, and some completely non-reactive gases.
Reasoning	**classify** substances **infer** real life applications	**distinguish** between elements and compounds distinguish physical properties from chemical properties **classify** elements, compounds and substances according to their chemical/reactive properties **Classify/sort** materials as elements or compounds; metals or nonmetals using properties (boiling point, melting point, density, solubility, ductility, malleability, conductivity) **propose** real life applications for substances based on chemical/reactive properties **Support/evaluate** applications using evidence/ information about the properties of substances **Infer** why particular elements or compounds were selected for use in real life applications

Skills	make observations sort substances based on physical and chemical properties draw conclusions	**observe** substances for distinguishing properties **Develop operational definitions** of physical properties and of chemical properties **Identify** relevant information **from narratives/charts/graphs** that focus on uses and properties of elements/compounds/substances **Investigate** some common substances in order to identify and describe the relationship of their properties with their common or typical uses **organize data** to support **conclusions about the characteristics and uses of substances** **draw conclusions** about a substance based on data
Products	*No products explicitly called for in the standard*	*No products explicitly called for in the standard*

Figure 8.1 The example of a deconstructed (unpacked) standard shows how one standard should be analyzed for intent and deconstructed into requisite learning targets or objectives necessary for attainment of the standard, with examples of weak and strong analysis

In the process of analysis for intent and deconstruction of standards, educators are asked to consider what students will need to know and be able to do in order to demonstrate attainment of the standard as intended. To determine the intent of a standard, teams of teachers must be prepared to think about where the standard occurs in the overall progression of learning. By considering what comes before and what follows the particular standard(s) in question, the team ensures that students' learning experiences build upon each other and deepen over time around key conceptual ideas. In short, it keeps every grade that has the content of "chemical property" from teaching the exact same ideas or targets or staying at the same level of depth or complexity.

Teachers have varying degrees of knowledge and understanding about particular concepts and skills. A key task, then, is to engage in a study of the topic or concept among the team, including researching common misconceptions and identifying essential underpinning or foundational knowledge and skills upon which to build, as well as how the concept or topic is connected to past, present or future learning. The key idea is not to omit or minimalize the need or time for learning among the teachers themselves. Otherwise, what is actually translated into practice will likely vary greatly from the intent of the standard and necessarily create inequity among students in terms of opportunity to learn.

An important distinction to make is that standards define the *what* for learning and doing, but not the *how*, which is the art of effective curriculum design and instructional planning. Teams often want to jump directly into activity planning instead of spending enough time on clarifying the specific targets for learning. In working with educators in Kentucky, the process of standards deconstruction found in the book *Classroom Assessment for Student Learning: Doing it Right, Using it Well* by Chappuis, Stiggins, Chappuis, and Arter (2012) has ben used. The deconstruction process involves uncovering the intent of a standard and then being able to translate it into a set of key learning targets. Teams should consider what the overall standard is requiring for competency, as well as what knowledge, reasoning, skills or products are the essential building blocks to achieving the overall standard. The process aims at maintaining the integrity of the entire standard instead of segmenting or reducing every standard down to just a series of discreet 'knows' and *does* without ever connecting the pieces back together.

One component of the standard in the example above states "classify substances according to their chemical/reactive properties." That is very explicit. If teachers stopped at the verb-subject level which some consider unpacking, they may have students spending a great deal of time "classifying substances" in any number of ways that may not focus on their chemical properties. However, when taking the time to think deeply, educators must consider the progression of learning related to chemical properties, and then consider the knowledge, reasoning and skills that the entire standard calls for; as a result, some very specific and congruent targets begin to emerge. The deconstruction process guides more effective teaching and learning experiences in a classroom because it forces the production of clear targets which are essential for designing congruent assessments and learning experiences. After all, it is hard to hit a target that has not been set or shown. However, the transformational result is not just compiling a set of targets from the standard, but understanding and actually engaging in the process that led to that product. Simply sharing a list of key learning targets that someone else derived from the standards is of limited value. There is no substitute for the conversations and thinking that occur among a group of teachers whose job it is to actually implement those standards and assure that students have attained them. Standards will change over time, but learning how to study standards and determine intent along with required student competencies (including enabling knowledge and skills) is an essential skill for all teachers to develop and hone over time.

Assessment Literacy

Because it is the process of digging deeply into standards that builds the entire foundation for clarifying what it is that students really must know and be able to do, educators must be knowledgeable about selecting, designing and using assessments and learning tasks that allow students to demonstrate their attainment of those standards. James Popham, in a Harvard Education Group Publishing blog, says "Assessment literacy is present when a person possesses the assessment-related knowledge and skills needed for the competent performance of that person's responsibilities" (2009, para. 4). This means that teachers must know how to effectively gather defensible evidence of student attainment of the standards they are expected to teach. It means they must have such a grasp of what the standards intend as well as the myriad ways that evidence can be obtained and how that evidence can enable inferences about student learning, as well as how it cannot or should not be used. It means teachers must think about what information students need to improve their learning; what parents need to support their children; and what the school and district leaders, and even the state or federal government, need to know about their students' capabilities. After all, it is the job of all teachers to ensure that student learning is producing evidence that can be used to support inferences about their successes and challenges.

> *There just is no substitute for the conversations and thinking that occur among a group of teachers whose job it is to actually implement those standards and assure that students have attained them.*

Assessment can be used to certify or evaluate learning, as in summative assessments, also considered assessment *of* learning. It can also be used regularly to promote learning, as in assessment *for* learning. Much emphasis has been placed on assessment *for* learning or formative assessment; however there are disparities that exist among educators at every level around that phrase. Kentucky has adopted the definition created by the Council of Chief State School Officer's Formative Assessment for Students and Teachers collaborative: "Formative assessment is a ***process*** used by teachers and students during instruction to adjust ongoing teaching and learning to improve students' achievement of intended instructional outcomes" (Council of Chief State School Officers, 2012, p.4). Placing an emphasis on the process during pre-service experiences can equip new teachers to think systemically about how they engineer their interactions with students around the content. Research is clear that those teachers who understand the process of formative assessment and use it consistently enable students to achieve at higher levels. In the seminal article by Paul Black and Dylan Wiliam (1998), "Inside the black box: Raising standards through classroom assessment," the authors cite key issues or barriers to student learning, particularly as we expect more of students via higher standards:

- The tests used by teachers encouraged rote and superficial learning even when teachers said they wanted to develop understanding; many teachers seemed unaware of the inconsistency.
- The questions and other methods teachers used were not shared with other teachers in the same school, and they were not critically reviewed in relation to what they actually assessed.
- For primary teachers particularly, there was a tendency to emphasize quantity and presentation of work and to neglect its quality in relation to learning (p. 4).

Fortunately, key actions or skills that can remedy these problems have been suggested (Thompson & Wiliam, 2007, p. 7). These include the following:

- clarifying, understanding, and sharing learning intentions;
- engineering effective classroom discussions, tasks and activities that elicit evidence of learning;
- providing feedback that moves learners forward;
- activating students as learning resources for one another; and

- activating students as owners of their own learning.

Again, these only produce strong results when done within the context of deep understanding of the standards for particular classes or courses. In other words, focusing on these skills or practices apart from the content standards/resulting learning targets teachers will be expected to teach will not yield expected high results. Effective pre-service programs must model these practices, not just talk about or cover them as topics in education courses. It is widely recognized that when challenges occur in classrooms, teachers revert to the way they were taught. There is the opportunity to change this—and that opportunity must be taken in their pre-service courses if it is to really take hold in practice.

Professional Learning

In the Leana (2011) study, an incredible finding was revealed: Most striking, students showed higher gains in math achievement when their teachers reported frequent conversations with their peers that centered on math, and when there was a feeling of trust or closeness among teachers.

The power of teachers learning together cannot be discounted. However, merely putting some people on a team does not ensure that they actually function as a true or effective learning team. Kentucky recently adopted new Standards for Professional Learning (Kentucky Department of Education, 2014).

> *Expectations should exist for teacher candidates to identify and solve authentic problems of practice (especially regarding teaching and learning of standards) as a member of a learning team.*

There are seven intrinsically linked standards, one of which is learning communities. These standards cannot be isolated if they are to be fully achieved. So, while some may consider learning communities one standard that *may* be addressed, the intent of the new professional learning standards is to consider learning communities as one standard that *must be addressed in conjunction with the other six*—all the time. The other six are leadership, resources, data, learning designs, implementation, and outcomes. Taken together, they create a formula for orchestrating opportunities for teacher learning that is manifested in student success. While there are times that teachers will need to engage in independent learning, that should be a by-product of teacher reflection on their own teaching and learning or from information uncovered when the learning team comes together to address problems of practice impacting teaching and learning.

Pre-service educators have a responsibility to assist their students in understanding the professional learning standards just as they should the academic standards. Professors should help aspiring teachers learn how to use protocols and norms to facilitate productivity and focus within learning teams. Expectations should exist for teacher candidates to identify and solve authentic problems of practice (especially regarding teaching and learning of standards) as a member of a learning team. Experiences should involve pre-selected teams as well as self-selected teams. Adequate time and attention should be paid to analyzing the outcomes of those learning teams, as well as analyzing processes that enabled or impeded success.

The desire to be a teacher—*THAT* teacher—who forges great connections with other educators and students in pursuit of meaningful learning and whose students attain success is ubiquitous. Too often, though, new teachers become disillusioned because their reality quickly overwhelms them. Though they desire to implement standards through effective teaching and learning practices, they end up resorting to practices that are most familiar –how they themselves experienced school. It is imperative to design teacher education programs that model the very practices that can enable a teacher to navigate the challenges in the profession in the interest of seeing students succeed.

References

Council of Chief State School Officers. (2012). Distinguishing formative assessment form other educational Assessment labels. Retrieved from http://www.ccsso.org/Documents/FASTLabels.pdf

Leana, C. (2011). The missing link in school reform. Retrieved from http://www2.ed.gov/programs/slcp/2011progdirmtg/mislinkinrfm.pdf

Black, P. & Wiliam, D. (1998). Inside the black box: Raising standards through classroom assessment. *Phi Delta Kappan 80*(2), 139-148. Retrieved from http://www.dpi.state.nc.us/docs/accountability/educators/insidetheblackbox1998.pdf

Chappuis, J., Stiggins, R., Chappuis, S., & Arter, J. (2012). *Classroom assessment for Student Learning: Doing it Right-Using It Well* (2nd ed.). Upper Saddle River, New Jersey: Pearson.

Kentucky Department of Education. (2014). Guidance for professional learning. Retrieved from http://education.ky.gov/teachers/PD/Documents/KY%20Professional%20Learning%20Guidance.pdf

Popham, J. (June 4, 2009). Is assessment literacy the "magic bullet?" Harvard Education Publishing Group Voices in Education Blog. Retrieved from http://hepg.org/blog/is-assessment-literacy-the-magic-bullet

Thompson, M., & Wiliam, D. (2007, April) Tight but loose: A conceptual framework for scaling up school reforms. Paper presented at the annual meeting of the American Educational Research Association, Chicago, IL.

Chapter 9
The Landscape of K-16 Assessment

Shannon Gilkey and Cody Davidson

It's hard to imagine a conversation about K-12 education in the United States without the terms "standards" or "assessments." Standardized testing and assessment systems, while commonplace in the education dialogue today, were not always ubiquitous with elementary and secondary education. Assessments which measure students transitioning into higher education have historically been used for admission and placement. While all colleges and universities may rely on different systems of assessment to ensure students meet their specific admission requirements, postsecondary institutions also wish to pinpoint varying degrees of academic preparation in order to ensure each student is successful in his/her pursuit of a degree.

Beginning in 2009, states adopted K-12 academic standards which focus on expectations students must meet as they enter colleges and universities. The Common Core State Standards (CCSS) were purposely designed to increase the level of students' preparation as they enter college-level, credit bearing coursework. The CCSS also provided an opportunity for assessment system alignment as K-12 and higher education sectors considered their respective systems of assessment in light of new cohorts of students who were required to meet aligned academic expectations.

The purpose of this chapter is to provide context for both the K-12 and higher education assessment systems leading up to the adoption of the Common Core State Standards. While educators from both systems respectfully consider the implications, this chapter will suggest areas of further consideration in hopes of providing fruitful discussion as implementation of both the standards and their aligned assessments continue.

Background of K-12 Assessments

Although this chapter is not intended to provide a thorough history of the national education reform movement and the interplay between federal, state, and local policy, all levels of government legislative initiatives play crucial roles when shifting American education onto a standards-based platform (Ravitch, 1995). Today's K-12 assessment system, originated in revisions to Title 1 section of the Improving America's Schools Act of 1994 (IASA) (Debray, 2006). Title 1 spending has historically provided the largest portion of federal spending for schools across the country. Revisions made in the mid-nineties to Title 1 required states, within five years, to develop learning standards and aligned assessments that measure student progress (No Child Left Behind Act, 2002). This change in Title 1 spending dramatically shifted the focus from educational inputs to educational outputs (Debray, 2006). Specifically, legislation within Title 1 required assessment of students in grades third-fifth, sixth-eighth, and tenth-twelfth.

In January of 2001, President George W. Bush sent his No Child Left Behind (NCLB) proposal to Capitol Hill, which began a legislative process that would become the largest expansion of the federal role in education since 1965 (Debray, 2006). While many states had already implemented assessment systems as part of the IASA Act, the NCLB Act required all states to have such systems and required math and reading tests in grades 3-8 and once during high school (No Child Left Behind Act, 2002). According to data collected by the Pew Center, before NCLB, no more than thirteen states passed this new requirement (Pellegrino, 1999).

Beginning in 2002, states began aligning assessment systems with new requirements passed in the No Child Left Behind Act. A decade later, state assessment systems were present in all fifty states. This resulted from a shift in education policy, brokered through bi-partisan legislation, beginning with financial incentives through Title 1 funding reform to mandates enforced by No Child Left Behind. By 2012, forty-five states contributed to assessment systems that totaled more than 650 million dollars, ranging from $7 to $127 in per pupil spending (Chingos, 2012). The assessment marketplace consisted of six primary vendors (Pearson, McGraw-Hill Education CTB, and the Educational Testing Service, for example) controlling more than 90% of the assessment system market (Cavanaugh, 2014;

Chingos, 2012). In state contexts, assessment vendors worked with state-developed learning outcomes to customize an assessment system to measure academic progress for school grades 3-8, then once in Grade 11. States, school districts, and individual schools are then held accountable for progress made year to year, through provisions passed in the 2002 No Child Left Behind Act.

CCSS Aligned Assessments: Two Consortia, Similar Objectives, Different Approaches

From 2000-2013, states continued to execute state-based assessment systems; however, in 2009 the National Governors Association and the Council of Chief State School Officers sponsored an initiative to develop a set K-12 standards, also known as Common Core State Standards (CCSS) as outlined in Chapter Two of this book. After forty-five states agreed to adopt these new K-12 standards that same year, state assessment systems, as mandated in NCLB, required renewed alignment. The US Department of Education, supported implementation of revised K-12 standards by offering grant funds (U.S. Department of Education, 2009). These grants, derived from the 2009 American Recovery and Reinvestment Act, became a competitive grant program called Race to the Top Program (RTT).

Intended to instill comprehensive reform in four key areas, a small portion of RTT funds were used to launch a competitive grant pro- gram in April of 2010. Awarded funds supported one or more consortia of states that agreed to develop and implement assessments aligned to newly adopted K-12 standards. Since the CCSS are internationally benchmarked and build toward "college and career readiness," students graduating from high school may have a greater opportunity to enter postsecondary education: with the necessary academic preparation to succeed or to pursue a chosen career (US Department of Education, 2009).

Later the same year, the Partnership for Assessment of Readiness for College and Careers (PARCC) and the Smarter Balanced Assessments (Smarter Balanced) were awarded $15.9 million each to develop assessment systems that are valid, support and inform instruction, provide accurate information about what students know and can do, and measure student achievement against standards designed to ensure that all students gain the knowledge and skills needed to succeed in college and the workplace (US Department of Education, 2009). Both PARCC and Smarter Balanced designed a multi-state, computer- based, assessment system to measure student progress aligned with the Common Core State Standards in grades 3-8 and 11. Both assessment consortia, state-led through state memberships, are made up of a collection of different states across the U.S. As of fall 2014, the PARCC consortia membership includes thirteen governing state members and one participating state. PARCC identifies a "governing state" as a consortia member who "makes the strongest commitment to PARCC and therefore has the most decision-making authority" (Partnership for Assessment of Readiness for College and Careers, 2012). Governing states' chief school officers serve on the consortia's governing board, which approves "assessment system design, make[s] decisions on major expenditures, common achievement levels for assessments, modification to PARCC's governance structure and provide[s] direction to the fiscal agent and to the project management partner." Participating states agree to participate in the design of PARCC's assessment system by piloting and field- testing the PARCC assessment system components in 2012–13 and 2013–14, but have the option to participate in more than one assessment consortium during that same period (State Roles in the Partnership for Assessment of Readiness for College and Careers, 2012, p.2).

Similarly to PARCC, Smarter Balanced was developed and organized as a result of states' wishing to consolidate efforts to assess students. As of fall 2014, Smarter Balanced maintained a membership of 19 governing states, two advisory states, and one affiliate member. Within the Smarter Balanced governance structure, a governing state is committed to implementing the Smarter Balanced assessments and has authority to vote on policy decisions adopted by the consortium. Advisory states participate in the development of the assessment systems; however, they relinquish the right to vote on the direction of the consortium. Affiliates are territories or U.S. Department of Defense Education Activity (DoDEa) and/or the United States. Each participating state selects representatives from K-12 and higher education to direct the consortium's leadership and work-group committees (Smarter Balanced Assessment Consortium, 2013).

PARCC and Smarter Balanced Assessment Design

The PARCC assessment is a four-component system for evaluation of student progress towards achievement as determined by the CCSS within the subject areas of English and language arts (ELA) and mathematics, administered in grades three-eight and the "full range of CCSS standards" for high school (Partnership for Assessment of Readiness for College and Careers, 2012).

The assessment's four components consist of a (1) diagnostic, (2) mid-year, 3) performance, and (4) end-of-year exams. Each assessment component is delivered by non-adaptive, computer-based exams.

According to the consortia, the Performance-Based Assessment will focus on CCSS's "hard-to-measure" standards and is intended to be used in conjunction with the end-of-the-year exam to assist with determining a summative score. These assessments, for English and language arts, will contain two types of tasks, one focused on stimulation of a student's research skillset based on informational texts while the other tasks focuses on literary text. In addition, these tasks focus on analyzing texts then challenging the student to compose a written response using text-supportive evidence in their responses.

The Smarter Balanced Assessment is a three-component system aligned to the Common Core State Standards, which currently examines English and language arts/literacy (ELA/literacy) and mathematics for grades three through eight and grade eleven. The three components include a summative assessment administered during the last twelve weeks of the school year, optional interim assessments administered throughout the year, and a digital library for professional development, and instructional materials on the formative assessment process.

The summative assessment, which will be used to measure a student's progress toward meeting the CCSS, is two-part. One part utilizes computer adaptive testing, unlike the PARCC system, and the second part, which consists of performance tasks, is taken on a computer, but is not adaptive.

> **Performance tasks** challenge students to apply their knowledge and skills to respond to complex real-world problems. They can best be described as collections of questions and activities that

are coherently connected to a single theme or scenario. These activities are meant to measure capacities such as depth of understanding, writing and research skills, and complex analysis, which cannot be adequately assessed with traditional assessment questions (PARCC, 2014, p.5).

Uses of PARCC and Smarter Balanced: K-12 and Higher Education

The PARCC and Smarter Balanced assessment systems are aimed at measuring student achievement growth. For PARCC, a summative assessment score is composed of two summative/accountability components – performance-based assessments (PBAs) and end-of-year (EOY) assessments – given as close to the end of the school year as possible. PARCC developed the Model Content Frameworks, which include descriptions of the major content and skills to be emphasized in each grade/course. A draft assessment blueprint aligned to the Model Content Frameworks outlines a preliminary set of claims to be made about student knowledge, skills and abilities, sample forms of evidence accepted, and examples of the types of tasks to be utilized.

In 2014, the Smarter Balanced Assessment Consortium convened panels of teachers, higher education faculty, business and community leaders, and parents to provide input for the design of the "achievement levels." After these panels concluded, a subset of representatives from the panels reviewed each achievement level to ensure that alignment from grade to grade is achieved. In their final stages, the member states of Smarter Balanced will meet to review and endorse the achievement levels (Smarter Balanced Consortium, 2014). For grade eleven, higher education representatives will participate to ensure the achievement levels in the eleventh grade represent the expectations of postsecondary education.

Both PARCC and Smarter Balanced proclaim their tests are not designed to use as admission exams for higher education. The exams are aligned to the CCSS, which have been developed for the purpose of meeting expectations of colleges and universities. In sum, the eleventh grade assessment is a reflection of the student's readiness for entry-level, credit-bearing postsecondary coursework in English and Mathematics (PARCC, 2014). As both consortia aim at these exams providing an evaluation of this sort, this begs the question: What is the current landscape of higher education assessments for students leaving K-12 education and entering our colleges and universities?

Background of Higher Ed Assessments: Admissions and Placement

Understanding the landscape for which college admission and placement exams are built is important for positioning the Common Core aligned assessments or standards aimed at producing students ready to enter and successfully complete postsecondary coursework. For decades, colleges and universities utilized assessment practices for both admissions and course placement in an attempt to understand the level of pre-college preparation students have acquired and also the likelihood they may be 'successful'.

In 1900, the College Entrance Exam Board, formed by 12 college presidents, administered admission tests in an attempt "to standardize the admissions process administratively and to force New England boarding schools to adopt a uniform curriculum" (Chandler, 1999, para 1). Based on this development and execution of the intelligence quotient (IQ) test in 1905, Alfred Brigham was placed in charge of a committee to develop a follow-up exam, which would later be called the Scholastic Aptitude Test (SAT), and which was first administered to high school students in 1926. In 1934, Harvard began using the SAT to select students for an institutional scholar- ship program aimed at assisting "intellectually promising" students from poor and modest backgrounds to have the same opportunities at Harvard as students from elite backgrounds. One year later, all Harvard students were required to take the SAT. Eleven years later, in 1959, the American College Testing (ACT) was introduced by University of Iowa education professor E.F. Lindquist (ACT, n.d.; Chandler, 1999).

Since their creation, the SAT and ACT have become the dominant admissions tests for college entrance. In 2012, 1,664,479 students took the SAT and 1,666,017 students took the ACT, which was the first year more students took the ACT compared to the SAT. Also, in 2013, 13 states required students to take the ACT and three states required students to take the SAT (Lewin, 2013). Growth of assessments used by colleges and universities to select students for admission into higher education has not successfully prescribed how students arrive, prepared or underprepared, in specific subject areas, based on specific institutions' expectations.

In 1986 Abraham noted, "there is very little consensus on what college-level work is" (p. 2). To complicate matters, he went on to note, "In discussions of entry-level standards for college, it is often confusing whether placement standards or admission standards are being addressed" (p. 2). Based on surveys administered to 186 four-year (88% response rate) and 303 two-year (79% response rate) public colleges, Abraham reported "almost 100 combinations of about 70 different tests...are used to place students" (p. 3). The most frequently used subject area specific placement tests used were: Nelson-Danny (reading), English portion of the American College Test (ACT) (writing) and an in-house/institution- ally development test (math). Overall, ACT, SAT, Math Assessment Preparation for Students (MAPS), Assessment for Skills for Successful Entry and Transfer (ASSET) and in-house/institutionally and state/system developed tests were the most popular. Abraham noted some institutions were using more than one test. After assessing cut scores for various tests, Abraham stated, "the notion of 'college-ready' obviously varies greatly among public two-year and four-year institutions in the SREB region. In fact, depending on the test selected, these data indicate that entry-level placement is based on scores that vary from as low as the 1st percentile to as high as the 94th percentile" (p. 4).

In the twenty years following Abraham's survey, the growth of exams used by institutions to place students rapidly grew. Lewis and Farris (1996), using the fall 1995 cohort, reported 58%-63% of all institutions practiced giving all entering students a placement test in each subject area (e.g., reading, writing, math). Students who did not have or had scores below a certain level on the ACT or the SAT or had a low high school grade point average (GPA) were often selected for placement testing in 22%-25% of institutions and were "required or encouraged" to enroll in 8%-10% of institutions (p. 21). Any student who was deemed not college ready was not allowed to enroll in a particular course and, subsequently, placed into remedial education. Five years after Lewis and Farris (1996), Parsad and Lewis (2003) collected similar data and reported 57%-61% (58%-63% in 1995) of all institutions practiced giving all entering students a placement test in each subject area (e.g., reading, writing, math); this was the most common means of determining the need for a remedial course. Students who did not have test scores or had scores below a certain level on the ACT or SAT or had a low high school GPA were often selected for placement testing in 25%-29% (22%-25% in 1995) of the institutions and were "required or encouraged" to enroll in remedial education 10%-12% (8%-10% in 1995) of institutions (p. 21).

Higher Education State Policy Catching Up with Established Institutional Practice

By the end of the twentieth century, placement exams extended into state higher education policy, becoming an issue of statewide policies in the community college sector. In 2002, Jenkins and Boswell reported on state placement policies based on a national survey of community colleges. At that time, 20 states had a state level policy (by statute, board or combination of both), seven states had state mandated college placement exams, and other states allowed the institutions to make this decision. Only Maryland had a common placement exam and cut score. Also, 21 states required remedial education based on college-level performance criteria, while three states advised, but do not require, remediation, and some states did not require remediation if the student enrolled less than full-time.

In 2007, based on a study of 29 two-year community and/or technical schools, Gerlaugh, Thompson, Boylan and Davis, reported 92.4% of institutions had mandatory assessment. They also found 69% of institutions used more than one assessment instrument. The majority (97%) of these institutions used ACT, Computerized Adaptive Placement Assessment and Support Systems (COMPASS) or Educational Testing Service's ACCUPLACER with COMPASS being the most popular. Also, the ASSET (paper-and-pencil) was used by 41.4% of the institutions, 21% of the institutions developed their own assessment instruments, and 7% used non-cognitive (e.g., time management, motivation, personality, etc.) assessments.

Lastly, Fulton (2012) reported state policies on common assessment, cut score, assessment/cut score reviews, multiple measures and intake process advising/review. He found 13 states (Arkansas, Colorado, Florida, Kentucky, Louisiana, Massachusetts, Mississippi, Nevada, North Dakota, Oklahoma, South Dakota, Texas and West

Virginia) and 17 (typically community colleges) systems (Alabama, California, Connecticut, Delaware, District of Columbia, Georgia, Hawaii, Indiana, Maryland, Minnesota, Montana, New Jersey, New York, North Carolina, South Carolina, Tennessee, Virginia) had policies for placement assessment and cut scores. Typically, states that had common assessments also had common cut scores, the exceptions being California and South Carolina. California allowed campuses to select cut scores. Georgia, Kentucky, Mississippi, Montana, New York, Oklahoma, and South Carolina have similar arrangements in which there is some variation of the state or system selecting the test and/or cut scores, then allowing institutions to set their own cut scores and/or secondary test and cut scores. Minnesota, Oklahoma, and Tennessee had policies related to the evaluation of assessment and/or cut scores. California, Minnesota, Mississippi, and Oklahoma had policies related to multiple measures, and only California had a policy related to the intake process for students for assessment and placement.

K-12 and Higher Ed Assessment Alignment: An Opportunity for Consideration

An aligned system of assessments used by both K-12 and higher education may offer reduction of assessments given to students, and potentially a reduction in public resources spent on multiple exams. Colleges and universities receiving cohorts of students that have met college readiness standards as set forth by CCSS with assessment data providing an account of the level of academic preparation is a promising notion for higher education institutions to ensure more students reach graduation. As educators ponder aligning the Common Core State Standards and their assessments for P-20 education, considerations should be highlighted in hopes of increasing impact on student achievement.

Multiple Measures

Recently, Scott-Clayton (2012) reported on four cohorts of first-time degree-seeking students who took the COMPASS placement test at an anonymous large urban community college system (LUCCS) between the fall 2004 and fall 2007 (N = 68,220). Using

analysis of variance correlation coefficients, Scott-Clayton determined:
1. Placement tests are more predictive in math than English courses;
2. Placement tests are better at predicting who will do well compared to who will fail in a college level, credit-bearing course;
3. Placement test scores are poorer predictors of student success compared to high school academic achievement (e.g., grade point average);
4. Using placement test scores with high school achievement could lower rates or remediation without compromising student success; and,
5. Even though multiple measures (e.g., placement test score, high school academic background, student motivation) would lower severe placement errors (by 15%), these factors would not eliminate all errors.

Alongside Clayton-Scott's findings, Belfield and Crosta (2012) examined placement test scores and high school data to predict course grades and college performance (e.g., grade point average) from students who entered an anonymous statewide community college system (SWCCS) between fall 2008 and summer 2010. SWCCS used over 40 placement tests, but this analysis only considered ACCUPLACER and COMPASS. They found placement tests "do not have much explanatory power" in college grade point averages, credit accumulation and success in math and English gatekeeper courses (Belfield & Crosta, 2012, p. 39). Nonetheless, high school grade point average is an "extremely good and consistent predictor of college performance" (Belfield & Crosta, 2012, p. 39). Similar to Scott-Clayton (2012), Belfield and Crosta (2012) found placement tests have larger severe error rates; however, high school grade point average has error rates half as large. Lastly, they found a strong relationship between high school and college grade point averages, to the extent that this sole measure could accurately be used for placement purposes.

Even though studies exploring multiple measures have increased, the implementation of policy and practice is not wide spread. Fulton (2012) reported only four states (e.g., California,

Minnesota, Mississippi and Oklahoma) used multiple measures and Colorado is expected to do so. Even though four states have multiple measure language in policy, only California's policy "requires" they be used. California's Seymour-Campbell Matriculation Act (1986) requires California Community Colleges to use multiple measures to determine course placement for students (Lagunoff, Michaels, Morris, & Yeagley, 2012). California Community Colleges were given the freedom to select which placement tests to use, placement tests and how to determine placement based on the selected multiple measures. Nog, Kwon, Melguizo, Prather, and Bos (2013) examined multiple measures in seven of the nine colleges in the Los Angeles Community College District (LACCD). Using ordinary least squares and controlling for age, race, sex and other data elements, and based on students enrolled in developmental math between 2005 and 2008, they found students placed into higher math classes based on prior math background and high school grade point aver- age had similar course passing rates and credit completion as their peers. Recently, North Carolina State Board of Community Colleges approved a multiple measures approach to student placement (Morrissey, 2013). First, if a student has a recent high school grade point average of 2.6 or higher, the student is placed into "gateway" math and English classes. Second, if the student does not meet the grade point average, then ACT or SAT subject area test scores are used to determine placement. Third, if the student does not meet the high school grade point average or the minimum ACT or SAT subject score, then the college will administer a diagnostic placement test. Lastly, if a student does not have a recent high school transcript or ACT/SAT scores, then the college will administer a diagnostic test (Morrissey, 2013).

Third-Party Assessment Validation

Scott-Clayton said, "While there is a long history of empiri- cal research into the predictive validity of college entrance exams, only a handful of studies have examined these high-stakes college placement exams. Most of these studies have been conducted by the test makers themselves" (2012, p. 2). As Scott-Clayton noted, there has been limited research related to a number of considerations related to placement testing: (a) guidance on how to set cut cores (Morgan, 2010; Morgan & Michaelides, 2005); (b) specific cut scores for commercial tests (e.g., WritePlacer) (Morgan & Hardin, 2009); and, (c) the validity of popular (e.g., ACCUPLACER) (James, 2006; Mattern & Packman, 2009) and institutionally developed (Parker, 2005) placement tests. There has been considerably more academic research related to placement test scores. Researchers have measured the association of the placement test scores while considering other factors (e.g., high school grade point average, gender, race, socio-economic status, etc.) as it relates to student success using methodological techniques such as logistic regression (Armstrong, 2000; Horn, McCoy, Campbell, & Brock, 2009; Hoyt & Sorensen, 2001; Schumacher & Smith, 2008; Secolsky, Krishnan, & Judd, 2013). Recently, there have been a growing number of studies that have addressed the implications of course placement policies using more sophisticated quasi-experimental research designs, which allow the researcher to make causal inferences related to placement and student success (Bettinger & Long, 2005, 2009; Calcagno & Long, 2008; Martorell & McFarlin, 2011; Moss & Yeaton, 2006; Moss, Yeaton & Lloyd, 2014).

Summary

The landscape of assessments used by both K-12 and higher education has entered an exciting moment for increased collaboration. After a history of separate assessment enterprises, with intentions to ensure American citizens are provided a "quality" public education, K-12 and higher education have a unique op- portunity to further ensure that the expectations of students entering higher education institutions are not only clearly articulated to K-12 educators, but that they are also measured. "Aligned" assessments to the Common Core States Standards offer an entry-point to this shared space in education and provide a renewed foundation for shared ownership of student achievement.

References

Abraham, A. (1986). College-level study: What is it? Variations in college placement tests and standards in the SREB state. *Issues in Higher Education, 22*.

Armstrong, W. B. (2000). The association among student success in courses, placement test scores, student background data, and instructor grading policies. *Community College Journal of Research & Practice, 24*(8), 681-695.

ACT. (n.d.). ACT history. Retrieved from http://www.act.org/aboutact/history.html

Belfield, C. R., & Crosta, P. M. (2012, February). Predicting success in college: The importance of placement tests in high school transcripts. (CCRC Working Paper No. 42). Retrieved from Community College Research Center website: http://ccrc.tc.columbia.edu/media/k2/attachments/predicting-success-placement-tests-transcripts.pdf

Bettinger, E. P., & Long, B. T. (2005). Remediation at the community college: Student participation and outcomes. In C. A. Kozeracki (Ed.), Responding to the challenges of developmental education (New Directions for Community Colleges, 129, 33-41). San Francisco, CA: Jossey-Bass. doi: 10.1002/cc.182

Bettinger, E. P., & Long, B. T. (2009). Addressing the needs of underprepared students in higher education: Does college remediation work? *Journal of Human Resources, 44*(3), 736-771.

Center for K-12 Assessment and Performance Management. (2012). Coming together to raise achievement: New assessments for the Common Core State Standards. K12 Center at ETS. Retrieved from http://www.k12center.org/rsc/pdf/Assessments_for_the_Common_Core_Standards.pdf

Calcagno, J. C., & Long, B. T. (2008). The impact of postsecondary remediation using a regression discontinuity approach: Addressing endogenous sorting and noncompliance. (NBER Working Paper 14194). Cambridge, MA: National Bureau of Economic Research.

Cavanaugh, S. (2014, September 30). Common-Core testing contracts favor big vendors. Education Week. Retrieved from http://www.edweek.org/ew/articles/2014/10/01/06contract.h34.html

Chandler, M. (1999). History of the SAT: A timeline. In M. Chandler (Producer), Frontline. Boston, MA: WBGH Cam Bay Productions. Retrieved from http://www.pbs.org/wgbh/pages/frontline/shows/sats/where/timeline.html

Chingos, M. M. (2012). Strength in numbers: State spending on K-12 assessment systems. Washington D.C.: Brookings Institute Brown Center on Education Policy.

Debray, E. H. (2006). Politics, ideology, & education: federal policy during the Clinton and Bush administrations. New York NY: Teachers College, Columbia University.

Fulton, M. (2012, May). Using state policies to ensure effective assessment and placement in remedial education. Retrieved from http://www.ecs.org/clearinghouse/01/02/28/10228.pdf

Fulton, M., Gianneschi, M., Blanco, C., & DeMaria, P. (2014, April). Developmental strategies for college readiness and success. Denver, CO: Education Commission of the States.

Gerlaugh, K., Thompson, L., Boylan H., & Davis H. (2007). National study of developmental education II: Baseline data for community colleges. *Research in Developmental Education, 20*(4), 1-4.

Horn, C., McCoy, Z., Campbell, L., & Brock, C. (2009). Remedial testing and placement in community colleges. *Community College Journal of Research and Practice, 33*(6), 510-526. doi: 10.1080/10668920802662412

Hoyt, J. E., & Sorensen, C. T. (2001). High school preparation, placement testing, and college remediation. *Journal of Developmental Education, 25*(2), 26-28, 30, 32-34.

James, C. (2006). ACCUPLACER Online: accurate placement tool for developmental programs? *Journal of Developmental Education, 30*(2), 2-4, 6-8.

Jenkins, D., & Boswell, K. (2002, September). State polices on community college remedial education: Findings from a national survey. Retrieved from http://www.ecs.org/html/Document.asp?chouseid=4081

Lagunoff, R., Michaels, H., Morris, P., & Yeagley, P. (2012). A framework for evaluating the technical quality of multiple measures used in California community college placement. Sacramento, CA: WestEd.

Lewin, T. (2013, August 2). Testing, testing: More students are taking both the ACT and SAT. New York Times, Retrieved from http://www.nytimes.com/2013/08/04/education/edlife/more-students-are-taking-both-the-act-and-sat.html?pagewanted=all&_r=0

Lewis, L., & Farris, E. (1996, October). Remedial education at higher education institutions in fall 1995. U. S. Department of Education, National Center for Education Statistics. Retrieved from http://nces.ed.gov/pubs/97584.pdf

Martorell, P., & McFarlin, I. J. (2011). Help or hindrance? The effects of college remediation on academic and labor market outcomes. *Review of Economics and Statistics, 93*, 436-454. doi: 10.1162/REST_a_00098

Mattern, K. D., & Packman, S. (2009). Predictive validity of ACCUPLACER scores for course placement: A meta-analysis. (2009-2). Retrieved from https://research.collegeboard.org/sites/default/files/publications/2012/7/researchreport-2009-2-predictive-validity-accuplacer-scores-course-placement.pdf

Morgan, D. L. (2010, September). Best practices for setting placement cut scores in postsecondary education. Retrieved from http://www.postsecondaryresearch.org/conference/PDF/NCPR_Panel%202_MorganPaper.pdf

Morgan, D. L., & Hardin, E. (2009). Setting cut scores with WritePlacer. Retrieved from http://professionals.collegeboard.com/profdownload/writeplacer-setting-cut-scores.pdf

Morgan, D. L., & Michaelides, M. P. (2005). Setting cut scores for college placement. (2005-9). Retrieved from https://research.collegeboard.org/sites/default/files/publications/2012/7/researchreport-2005-9-setting-cut-scores-college-placement.pdf

Morrisseey, S. (2013, March 19). State Board of Community College placement policies. Retrieved from http://www.successnc.org/sites/default/files/inititiative-docs/SBCC%20Placement%20Policies.pdf

Moss, B. G., & Yeaton, W. H. (2006). Shaping policies related to developmental education: An evaluation using the regression-discontinuity design. *Educational Evaluation and Policy Analysis, 28*, 215-229. doi: 10.3102/01623737028003215

Moss, B. G., Yeaton, W. H., & Lloyd, J. E. (2014). Evaluating the effectiveness of developmental mathematics by embedding a randomized experiment within a regression discontinuity design. *Educational Evaluation and Policy Analysis, 36*, 170-229. doi:10.3102/0162373713504988

Ngo, F., Kwon, W., Melguizo, T., Prather, G., & Bos, J, M. (2013). Course placement in developmental math: Do multiple measures work? Retrieved from http://www.uscrossier.org/pullias/research/projects/sc-community-college

No Child Left Behind Act of 2001, P.L. 107-110, 20 U.S.C. § 6319 (2002).

Parker, M. (2005). Placement, retention, and success: A longitudinal study of mathematics and retention. *The Journal of General Education, 54*(1), 22-40. doi: 10.11353/jge.2005.0016

Parsad, B., & Lewis, L (2003, November). Remedial education at degree-granting postsecondary institutions in fall 2000. (NCES 2004-101). U. S. Department of Education, National Center for Education Statistics. Retrieved from http://nces.ed.gov/pubs2004/2004010.pdf

Partnership for Assessment of Readiness for College and Careers. (2012). State Roles in the Partnership for Assessment of Readiness for College and Careers. Washington D.C.: PARCC. Retrieved from http://parcconline.org/sites/parcc/files/PARCC_State_Roles_APRIL2013.pdf

Pellegrino, J. W. (1999). *The evolution of educational assessment: Considering the past and imagining the future.* Princeton, NJ.; Educational Testing Service Policy Evaluation and Research Center.

U. S. Department of Education. (2009). Race to the Top Fund executive summary: Notice of proposed priorities, requirements, definitions, and selection criteria. (2009) (pp. 1–8). Washington D.C. Retrieved from http://www2.ed.gov/programs/racetothetop/executive-summary.pdf

Ravitch, D. (1995). *National standards in American education: A citizen's guide.* Washington D.C.: Brookings Institution.

Schumacher, P. A., & Smith, R. M. (2008). A comparison of placement in first-year university mathematics courses using paper and online administration of a placement test. International *Electronic Journal of Mathematics Education, 3*(3), 193-202.

Scott-Clayton, J. (2012, February). Do high-stakes placement exams predict college success? (CCRC Working Paper No. 41). Retrieved from Community College Research Center website: http://ccrc.tc.columbia.edu/media/k2/attachments/high-stakes-predict-success.pdf

Secolsky, C., Krishnan, S., & Judd, T. (2013, April). Using logistic regression for validating or invalidating initial statewide cut-off scores on basic skills placement tests at the community college level. *Research in Higher Education Journal, 19*. 101-105.

Smarter Balanced Assessment Consortium. (2012). Governance Structure Document. Retrieved from http://www.moagainstcommoncore.com/Smarter-Balanced-Governance%20w-exit%20rules-1.pdf

Smarter Balanced Assessment Consortium. (2014). Frequently Asked Questions. Retrieved from http://www.smarterbalanced.org/resources-events/faqs/

Chapter 10

Creativity to the Core: Developing Creativity in a Standards-based Era

Dorie Combs

Clearly embedded in the Common Core State Standards (CCSS) is an expectation that students will be able to independently analyze complex text, generate solutions to difficult problems, and express ideas orally and in writing, creating new products. As the lead authors of the CCSS explain, "To help students meet the new standards, educators will need to pursue, with equal intensity, three aspects of rigor in the major work of each grade: conceptual understanding, procedural skill and fluency, and applications" (Coleman, Pimental, & Zimba, 2012, p. 12).

The CCSS promote a more rigorous curriculum and demand that teachers make significant changes in their own knowledge. While these standards do not specifically dictate *how to teach*, critical shifts in both the English language arts and math standards are resulting in change in some instructional practices. Even though the standards are more complex, the implementation of these standards at the local level seems to be having an unintended consequence. In the rush to implement and assess the CCSS, we have missed the caveat that these are the *minimum expectations,* not the whole of what *can* or *should* be taught. As the Common Core developers clearly state, "No set of grade-specific standards can fully reflect the great variety of abilities, needs, learning rates, and achievement levels of students in any given classroom" (NGA Center & CCSSO, 2015, para. 9). Some believe that a standards-based curriculum will eliminate the joy and art of teaching, while promoting boring, rote learning of low-level knowledge and skills. In a *USA Today* op-ed, former social studies teacher and member of "Save our Schools," David Greene states what seems to be a common belief about the Common Core Standards:

> To try to live up to the new demands and ensure better test scores, states, districts and schools have purchased resources, materials and scripted curricular modules solely developed for test success. Being lost is the practical wisdom and planned spontaneity necessary to work with 20 to 35 individuals in a classroom. Academic creativity has been drained from degraded and overworked experienced teachers. Uniformity has sucked the life out of teaching and learning. (2013, para. 14)

In an introduction to a special edition of the *Kentucky Journal on Excellence in College Teaching* focused on the standards, Sweet and Blythe go so far as to proclaim that "one could make a good argument that the imposition of the CCSS in a test-heavy environment will actually destroy the creative impulse" (2013, p. 18). In the 2014 Gallup Poll, 65% of those who oppose the Common Core Standards responded that the most important reason for their opinion was that the standards "will limit the flexibility that teachers have to teach what they think is best" (as cited by Rothman, 2014).

In 2013, *EdWeek* reported that 76% of the teacher respondents agreed that the Common Core Standards are helping them improve their instructional practice, even though only 44% agreed that their textbooks were aligned to the standards. Over 70% of these teachers also indicated that more planning time and access to better aligned instructional materials and assessments would help them be better prepared (Editorial Projects in Education, 2013).

A more recent survey by Scholastic, supported by the Bill and Melinda Gates Foundation, indicates that this is not the case. *The Primary Sources Survey Update: Teachers' Views on the Common Core Standards* (2014) reveals that most teachers have positive attitudes about the implementation of the Common Core Standards and the effects on their students' knowledge and skills. Key findings from this national survey of 20,000 P-12 public school teachers reveal:

- While the percentage of teachers overall who report that they are "enthusiastic" about the standards has slightly declined from 2013 - 2014 (68% in 2014 vs. 73% in 2013, 84% of teachers who have implemented the CCSS for more than a year report that they are "enthusiastic" about the implementation of the standards.
- Sixty-eight percent (68%) of teachers indicate that implementation of the new standards is "going well," an increase of 7% in a year;

- The majority of teachers report that they are seeing positive effects in their classrooms and are more likely to say so if they have been implementing the standards longer. Fifty-three percent (53%) report a positive impact on their students' ability to think critically and use reasoning skills, and 68% who report they are in schools where implementation was fully complete for at least a year report so.
- Seventy-nine percent (79%) of those surveyed believe teachers are better prepared to implement the standards, up from 71% in 2013.

At the heart and soul of the Common Core Standards is a belief that all children can learn at high levels – a belief that is also the core of American democratic principles. The standards were created to "spell out the academic knowledge and skills all students need at each grade level to be ready for college and careers" at the end of high school (Coleman et al., 2012, p. 9). In fact, these standards are supposed to raise the level of critical and creative thinking.

In her blog Creativiteach, author Alaine Starko (2014) points out three principles to keep in mind regarding creativity and the CCSS:
1. The standards should not represent the entire curriculum.
2. The standards do not dictate *how* teachers teach.
3. The standards do not say what students are allowed to *do* with the standards.

The narrowing of the curriculum is due not to the standards themselves, but to the use of high-stakes testing for accountability and the evaluation of schools and teachers. The tests are not necessarily the problem - it is *how* the results are used and the *amount of instructional time* delegated to testing. If districts, schools, and individual teachers are going to be scored and ranked based solely on traditional, short-answer tests, then we shouldn't be surprised that the instructional focus will be on what is tested. Sir Ken Robinson, renowned author and expert in the development of creativity and innovation, explains:

> The regime of standardized testing has led us all to believe that if you can't count it, it doesn't count. Actually, in every creative approach some of the things we're looking for are hard, if not impossible, to quantify. But that doesn't mean they don't matter. (Azzam, 2009, p. 26)

Creativity can be assessed but not on easily administered and scored tests (Azzam, 2009; Bellanca, Fogarty, & Pete, 2012; Drapeau, 2014). Teachers at all levels should employ a variety of assessment methods to ensure student mastery of all learning outcomes. The CCSS are not intended to kill creative teaching, and in fact, as we understand more about the creative thinking process, maybe the CCSS can actually promote creativity.

What is Creativity?

When defining creativity, we tend to think of individuals who are artists and make unusual, unique works and spend time in playful, random thought. There is considerable agreement among experts that creativity is "the ability to produce work that is both novel and appropriate (or useful)" (Sternberg & Lubart, 1999, p. 3) or "imaginative processes with outcomes that are original and of value" (Robinson, 2001, p. 118). Csikszentmihalyi (1996, 1999) points out that, while the mental activity required for creativity is a documented cognitive process, there is also a societal component to that process.

The creation of something that is both unique and useful requires a strong foundation of knowledge and skills. One must be able to analyze the current status of a problem and then generate possible solutions. This is impossible without having a deep understanding of the domain, its language, and methodologies. It is myth that geniuses are born with innate knowledge and skill. Creativity is a highly "disciplined process" (Azzam, 2009, p. 23) that requires daily commitment and technical, analytical thinking (Rutledge, 2008). One must clearly understand and be able to think critically in the particular field (Sternberg, 2006). The elegance of the creation often belies the time, effort and errors that preceded it. As Beghetto and Kaufman (2013) explain, "You have to learn to think inside the box before you can think outside of it" (p. 139).

Creativity requires both the divergent thinking necessary to generate ideas as well as the analytical skills to evaluate and make revisions. Current research in neuroscience is finding that creativity involves different brain processes that interact with each other. These include the spontaneous and emotional functions we commonly associate with creativity, as well as those that are deliberate and cognitive. While "emotions do not require specific knowledge, insights based on emotional processing are not domain specific ... (However), creative work based on these insights might require specific skills for appropriate expression," (Dietrich, 2004, p. 1020).

While there are certainly some "creatives" who have expertise in more than one domain (da Vinci, for example), most hold vast, deep knowledge and skill within only one field. They are artists, or musicians, or mathematicians, or astronomers, or writers who commit to a lifetime of study and practice (Csikszentmihalyi, 1996). Certainly they may find inspiration, respite, or metaphor in other domains, but they are rarely experts in that area.

It is estimated that true creatives spend 10 years or 10,000 hours learning and perfecting their skill before their first successful creation (Sternberg, Grigorenko, & Singer, 2004; Gladwell, 2008; Coyle, 2009). Those who have been successful in their fields as very young adults or teens either began their studies as young children (Bach and Mozart, for example) or worked intensively, learning and practicing their craft over a shorter time (such as Bill Gates and the Beatles). Whatever the start date, true creativity can only occur with a solid foundation of domain-specific knowledge and skills. Although the new standards can certainly provide that foundation, creative thinking and production require more than knowledge and skill.

Creative thinking can be described in two different levels, "Big-C" and "Little- c." The great creatives possess the "Big-C," while those who use creative thinking to solve routine tasks at home or work practice "Little-c." Beghetto and Kaufman (2013) propose a Four-C Model that provides a framework for integrating creativity in Birth – 12 learning environments:

- **Mini-c – Interpretive creativity** represents individual "aha's" or discoveries that are creative to the child, and may be valued by the child's social group and family, but do not necessarily have a value to the society at large. This would encompass children's artwork, structures built with blocks, stories and poems, and problem solving, to name a few. Within the child's world, the discoveries are unique and are valued by family, friends, teachers, and peers.
- **Little-c – Everyday creativity** describes the day-to-day problem solving and innovations that require some degree of domain-specific knowledge. Examples might be building

a unique garden, making up a new recipe or class project, or a teenager crafting a poem, artwork, or song. These innovations may solve problems, be individual artistic expressions, or result from a class assignment, but they are none-the-less unique and valued by the social group, though representative of relatively low levels of knowledge and skill.

- **Pro-C – Expert or Professional Creativity** designates professional innovations built from years of deliberate practice. These include research, books, works of art, music, and engineering innovations that may contribute to the field, but not necessarily have a long-term impact or result in a paradigm shift.
- **Big-C – Legendary Creativity** refers to those groundbreaking developments that are recognized over time to have long-term value and / or paradigm-shifting breakthroughs. While often acknowledged at the time of the creation (Polio vaccine, the light bulb, radio, etc.), these may not be valued initially or even during the creator's lifetime and might initially be categorized as Pro-C.

> *Communities, schools, colleges, and workplaces must provide the opportunities, experiences and environments children need in order to practice creativity. The Common Core Standards can be the vehicle to accomplish this goal.*

Using this model, the goal of public education should be to develop Mini- c and Little-c skills in our youth in order to prepare them to move into Pro-C (college and career), and just maybe, Big-C. Communities, schools, colleges, and workplaces must provide the opportunities, experiences, and environments children need in order to practice creativity. The Common Core Standards can be the vehicle to accomplish this goal.

Creative Habits of Mind

There are certain habits of mind that are the hallmark of successful creatives. First, creativity requires a strong work ethic – a willingness to focus on a task for hours, days, and even years. To be innovative, one must not only generate ideas but set goals and monitor progress toward these goals (Combs, Cennamo, & Newbill, 2009). We assume that Bach was born a great composer or that Monet invented Impressionism without any prior study.

Bach began his music studies at an early age because his father was a "piper" (one who builds and repairs organs), and many of his relatives were musicians. He was the first of his family to complete school (Latin School) at the age of 18 and took his first professional post with a church soon after, mostly doing menial, non-music related tasks. He began composing works in his mid-20s but wasn't immediately recognized as the genius we know today ("Johann Sebastian Bach," 2015).

Monet began studying art at the age of 11 and had several influential teachers and mentors before he began to find success as an artist. Impressionism was largely a collaborative creation involving experimentation and trial and error among a group of innovative artists. While he had some acclaim as early as 25, he was not initially accepted by the established art community, and the style that is now known as Impressionism was not recognized in a formal exhibit until 1874, when Monet was 34. His paintings did not begin to bring substantial income until he was middle-aged ("Claude Monet," 2015).

Michael Jordan, recognized as both a gifted and creative athlete, was cut from his high school basketball team his sophomore year of high school, later allowed back on the team after a growth spurt sent him to 6' 3". But his success is due less to his height and more to his commitment to practice (National Basketball Association, 2014).

In his book, *The Talent Code*, Dan Coyle (2009) stresses the role of focused, intensive practice in athletics and music. The success of the many young Chinese pianists is largely due to the fact that they begin lessons as children and practice 3 - 5 hours daily. Through her research, Carol Dweck has found that some individuals develop the belief that they can improve with practice, that failure is an opportunity to learn something new. She has termed this the "Growth Mindset" (Dweck, 2009). Individuals with a Growth Mindset are intellectual risk-takers who do not fear making a mistake and do not give up when their first attempt to solve a problem fails. These individuals believe that they can control their performance through trial and error and effort. Those with the opposite, "Fixed Mindset," are threatened by difficult situations, believing their own or others' success is due to "talent" or an inborn "gift." Dweck (2009) has found that students can be taught to have a Growth Mindset, and she has developed a series of training materials and web-based resources that parents and teachers can easily implement (Dweck, 2009). With the success of his book *The Talent Code*, Coyle (2009) has also developed an extensive website that primarily focuses on the role of "deep practice" on athletic performance. We can teach our students, at any age, to develop a Growth Mindset and learn to value practice, trial and error, and effort. To do this, we must help our children recognize what they know and what they need to know. We must give our students control of their learning.

The Math Common Core Standards include Math Practices that address some of these habits of mind. For example, CCSS MP.1 requires that students "Make sense of problems and persevere in solving them," and MP.6 asks that they "attend to precision" (NGA Center & CCSSO, 2010a).

To develop something unique or find a solution to a problem, one has to be open not only to new ideas, but to new combinations of ideas. Whether mixing oil paints, trying out new rhythms, or splicing genes, experimentation is necessary to the process. Of course, more often than not, these new combinations and trials will end in failure. The work ethic and commitment to the task is what leads them on. When one of Thomas Edison's colleagues expressed disappointment in the lack of progress on a project, he is quoted as responding, "I have gotten a lot of results! I know several thousand things that won't work" (O'Toole, 2015).

Creativity is not limited to what occurs "inside people's heads, but [lies] in the interaction between a person's thoughts and a sociocultural context. It is a systemic rather than an individual phenomenon" (Csikszentmihalyi, 2009, p. 313). There is no doubt that sometimes the utility or appreciation of an invention or work of art may at first elude understanding (Picasso, the Beatles, and Galileo, to name a few) but in time, these great works are recognized as groundbreaking and highly valued.

Trying new ideas, therefore, can take a certain amount of emotional courage or cognitive risk-taking. There are countless stories of great scientists and artists who were criticized or even punished by others in their field, the church, or even the government. Their single-minded focus on their own knowledge was more powerful than any public scorn.

The opportunity to learn an art or musical skill, at least at a rudimentary level, seems to be another factor that contributes to the development of creative thinking (Root-Bernstein & Root-Bernstein, 2013). While the great creatives are not necessarily accomplished artists or musicians, experience in the arts seems to provide the mental skills to think metaphorically, envision possibilities, and generate options. We have become a society in which only those with access to specialized training can truly develop their artistic skill through private lessons or out of school activities like camps and select schools. Schools must ensure that every child, regardless of income, has regular access to experience art, music, theater and dance. All students need to learn about art, to learn through the arts, and to do art.

> We have become a society in which only those with access to specialized training can truly develop their artistic skill through private lessons or out of school activities like camps and select schools.

Generating ideas takes time. It is a mental process that often takes place unconscientiously during "defocused attention" such as rest, play, or even sleep. "Associative combinational creativity during altered states such as dreaming or daydreaming can play a vital part in the creative process for the arts and the sciences" (Dietrich, 2004, p. 1018). Human beings need to have time to let our minds go and to simply let our thoughts wander. The best environment for this is nature. Research has demonstrated that simply being outside can improve cognitive functions (Jonides, 2010). Actual exercise is even better (Medina, 2008). Eliminating recess in an attempt to increase time on task in the classroom is pure folly. We cannot function without water, food, or sleep – and we cannot learn and think effectively without exercise and simply spending time outside.

> Eliminating recess in an attempt to increase time on task in the classroom is pure folly. We cannot function without water, food, or sleep – and we cannot learn and think effectively without exercise and simply spending time outside.

Can We Explicitly Teach Creative Thinking?

Could these new Core Standards actually encourage innovation? The Common Core Standards are not a checklist of facts and skills. These standards identify knowledge and skills that must be developed with increasing complexity as student progress from grade to grade. Embedded within the standards is the expectation that we will ask our students to think more deeply, to apply what they learn to real situations, and to create unique products and models.

Creativity *can* be explicitly taught, but this will require a fusion of knowledge, skills, and instructional methods. Our students must have opportunities to learn about creative individuals and how they work. But they must also have opportunities to identify and practice the thinking process that are associated with creativity. Most importantly, our students must be taught in an environment that supports and fosters creative thinking across the curriculum. Teachers should not only encourage experimentation and risk-taking but demonstrate these attitudes in their instruction.

Which standards explicitly require creative thinking skills? If creativity is a building, the standards are the foundation and framework. Just as a building has many systems (electrical, heating, plumbing, exterior, décor, for example), the curriculum is equally complex. The specific content represents the type of building; the grade level represents the complexity; the actual instruction and learning experiences represent the architectural design. The standards should be intertwined and integrated across and within content, spiraling up the grades, much like the electrical systems that connect all of our structures. Figure 10.1 describes a model for teaching creativity. Teachers can plan instruction to teach students knowledge and understanding *about creativity,* allow their students to demonstrate learning in creative ways, and provide opportunities to create new and effective products and processes.

Figure 10.1 The Creative Teaching Model

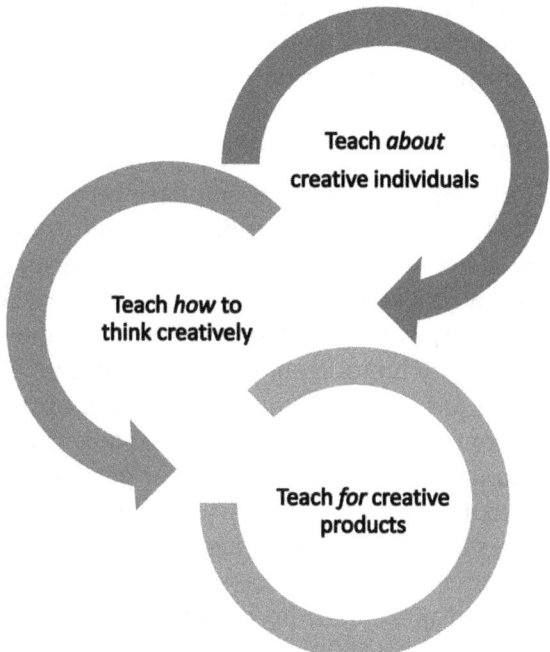

Figure 10.1 **The Creative Teaching Model suggests** that we should facilitate students' knowledge and understanding *about creativity,* allow students to *demonstrate creative thinking,* and provide opportunities for students to *create new and effective products and processes.*

Creative thinking is not the top of the thinking pyramid so much as it is part of the problem-solving process that leads to innovation and invention. Creative thinking skills "are the cornerstones of productive, generative thinking in the rich, rigorous, and relevant curriculum espoused in the CCSS" (Bellanca et al., 2012). In their book, *How to Teach Thinking Skills within the Common Core,* Bellanca, Fogarty and Pete (2012) analyzed the CCSS to identify the high-frequency words that describe the expected thinking skills. In this exhaustive list, "create" is found 11 times in the K-5 ELA and Math Standards and 30 times in the 6-12 standards. Related terms, such as

> *Teaching for mastery of the standards is not mutually exclusive of teaching for creativity. We can also use creative thinking skills, strategies and assessments as a means to teach any standard.*

"write," "develop," and "produce" also appear frequently. We can also use creative thinking skills, strategies and assessments as *a means to teach* any standard. Teaching for mastery of the standards is not mutually exclusive of teaching for creativity.

Teach about Creative People

With the CCSS English Language Arts emphasis on non-fiction, it is not difficult to incorporate biographical and informational text about creative individuals in any subject area at any level, P – college. These texts, available at any Lexile level, in picture books, short texts, or more complex biographies, can be used to meet any of the reading standards for literature or informational texts. Teachers of any subject can use this background knowledge to support instruction of their content; whether it is a picture book of an artist or musician prior to studying a particular style or period, or short biographies of key mathematicians, scientists or inventors, teachers will find resources online and in their school libraries. Teachers can embed the specific content within these texts (or other media). Examples of highly rated appropriate books are *Mathematicians are People, Too* (Reimer & Reimer, 1994), *Albert Einstein and Relativity for Kids: His Life and Ideas* (Pohlen, 2012), *Marvelous Mattie: How Margaret E. Knight Became an Inventor* (McCulley, 2006), *Lincoln: A Photobiography* (Freedman, 1989), and *Amazing American Inventors of the 20th Century* (Jeffrey, 2013). Instructors must take care to find accurate, reliable texts and ensure representation of women and minorities in both authors and subjects. What is important is that the teacher guide students to *analyze the text* and *identify* these individuals' *backgrounds and work habits.* Our young people need to recognize that creativity involves effort, time, and quite often, initial failure. We must teach them to accept these failures, learn from them, and try again. Our students need to believe in their own creative efficacy.

Practice Creative Thinking Strategies

Besides a strong knowledge and skill base, creativity requires individuals to fluently *employ* higher order thinking processes. Bellanca and his colleagues (2012) have identified three creative thinking skills that can be explicitly taught across content and throughout the grade levels: generating, associating, and hypothesizing. They propose a three-step instructional process for each thinking skill. First, the skills must be explicitly taught, the "talk-through" phase. This is a critical component, as the teacher provides the students with a clear explanation of the thinking skill through a concept development process. The teacher first defines and helps students recognize and practice the skill. Then the teacher helps the students assess their skill proficiency, reflecting metacognitively about their progress. The second phase is the "walk through" in which teachers guide students to practice the skill with the specific content. In the third phase, the teacher can use a "drive through" in which the students use the skill in a specific, standards-based assessment task. This three-phase, scaffolding approach is grounded in Vygotsky's theory and the gradual release of responsibility. "The teacher teaches the skill explicitly, demonstrating and vocalizing the learning; the teacher and student try it together, with the teacher monitoring and providing guidance and finally the student performs the skill on his or her own with confidence" (Bellanca et al., 2012, p. 5).

Common Core Standards that specifically require these include the following:

- CCRA R.4 **Interpret words and phrases** as they are used in a text, including determining technical, connotative, and figurative meanings, and analyze how specific word choices shape meaning or tone.
- CCRA R.5 **Analyze** how knowing the author's point of view helps the reader identify the true meaning of the text.
- CCRA.SL.2 **Integrate and evaluate information** presented in diverse media and formats, including visually, quantitatively, and orally.
- CCRA.SL.3 **Evaluate** a speaker's point of view, reasoning, and use of evidence and rhetoric.
- CCRA R.7 **Integrate and evaluate** content presented in diverse media and formats, including visually and quantitatively, as well as in words.
- CCRA R.9 **Analyze how two or more texts address similar themes or topics** in order to build knowledge or to compare the approaches the authors take.
- CCRA W.8 **Gather relevant information** from multiple print and digital sources, assess the credibility and accuracy of each source, and integrate the information while avoiding plagiarism.

- CCRA W.9 ***Draw evidence from literary or informational texts*** to support analysis, reflection, and research.
- CCSMP.1 ***Make sense of problems and persevere in solving them.***
- CCSS.Math.Practice.MP2 ***Reason abstractly*** and quantitatively.
- CCSS.Math.Practice.MP3 ***Construct viable arguments*** and critique the reasoning of others.
- CCSS.Math.Practice.MP8 Look for and express regularity in ***repeated reasoning***.[1] (NGA Center & CCSSO, 2010b)

The selection of skills to be taught and the timing of that instruction depends upon the grade and subject area. However, schools and professional learning communities should vertically and horizontally align their curriculum to ensure all skills are addressed across all subjects and grades.

Incorporate Student Developed Creative Products

Standards that promote creative achievements include the following:
- CCRA.W.2 ***Write informative/explanatory texts*** to examine and convey complex ideas and information clearly and accurately through the effective selection, organization, and analysis of content.
- CCRA.W.3 ***Write narratives to develop real or imagined experiences or events*** using effective technique, well-chosen details, and well-structured event sequences.
- CCRA.W.6 ***Use technology, including the Internet, to produce and publish*** writing and to interact and collaborate with others.
- CCRA.W.7 ***Conduct short as well as more sustained research projects*** based on focused questions, demonstrating understanding of the subject under investigation.
- CCRA.W.10 ***Write routinely*** over extended time frames (time for research, reflection, and revision) and shorter time frames (a single sitting or a day or two) for a range of tasks, purposes, and audiences.
- CCSS.Math.Practice.MP4 ***Model*** with mathematics. (NGA Center & CCSSO, 2010b)

If each of these standards can be addressed in developmentally appropriate ways throughout the grades, then creative endeavors can be integrated as well, initially as "Mini-c" tasks, then as "Little-c" products. Web resources such as the Partnership for 21st Century Schools (www.p21.org) and the Buck Institute's Project Based Learning methods (www.bie.org) provide the tools and guidance to facilitate this mode of instruction. Schools must redesign curriculum so that it integrates discipline-based content, infuses that instruction with the standards, and provides the environment and experiences to encourage creative achievements that apply those standards.

Anderson and Krathwohl's revision to Bloom's Taxonomy (Anderson, Krathwohl, Airasian, Cruikshank, Marer, Pintrich, & Wittrock, 2001) clearly depicts the relationships among the cognitive processes (remembering, understanding, applying, analyzing, evaluating, and creating) and knowledge dimensions (factual, conceptual, procedural, and metacognitive). As Fair explains (see Chapter Six), teachers can use the taxonomy to chart student learning outcomes across both dimensions. Figure 10.2 presents the Revised Taxonomy with additional indicators to show where creative thinking can be integrated within a standards-based curriculum. (See Figure 10.2.)

Develop and Maintain a Creativity-Safe School and Classroom

In order to ensure that we teach our students to think creatively, we have to provide classrooms that encourage, support and value creativity. Teachers have to be willing to model and even articulate their own creativity, whether that be through their classroom décor, crafts and hobbies, or, more importantly, their instructional methods. They should be willing to point out to students when they are trying something new, and acknowledge when the trial was ineffective. When appropriate, they may share their professional accomplishments, such as presentations, writings, or projects. But teachers should not feel like they have to be artists or musicians. In order to develop creativity promoting atmospheres, schools and classrooms must provide:
- specific instruction for the development of broad general foundational knowledge and skills;

Figure 10.2. Classification of Objectives with Krathwohl's (2002) model.

Cognitive Processes → Knowledge Dimension ↓	Remember define, describe, identify, label, match, name	Understand comprehend, distinguish, extend, interpret	Apply change, compute, construct, discover, modify	Analyze analyze, break down, separate, compare, deconstruct	Evaluate appraise, conclude, evaluate, interpret, justify	Create compose, create, devise, generate, reconstruct, write
Factual Basic elements students must know to be acquainted with a discipline or solve problems, including *creative individuals*.	List	Paraphrase	Classify	Outline	Rank	Categorize
Conceptual Concrete or abstract class of items, words, or ideas known by a common name, including creative concepts.	Recall	Explain	Demonstrate	Contrast	Criticize	Modify
Procedural How to do something, methods of inquiry, and criteria for using skills, algorithms, techniques, and methods *to create*.	Outline	Estimate	Produce	Diagram	Defend	Design
Metacognitive Knowledge of cognition, as well as awareness and knowledge of one's own cognition & *creativity*.	Reproduce	Give An Example	Relate	Identify	Critique	Plan

Figure 10.2. Krathwohl's (2002) model can be used to plot student learning outcomes to cognitive processes and knowledge domains and identify potential connections to creative thinking.

- access to develop deep knowledge and skill in at least one domain;
- opportunities for sustained and coached practice in one or more specialty areas;
- the development of, and appreciation for, hard work and persistence by promoting a Growth Mindset and valuing experimentation and inquiry;
- opportunity for all children and youth to experience, develop skills in and practice the arts;
- regular play, collaboration, and brainstorming within a community of learners;
- an environment that supports intellectual risk-taking and the safety to learn from failure;
- opportunities to apply knowledge and skills and to create unique models, writings, and products; and,
- regular periods of exercise, recess, and time in nature.

The Common Core Standards do not prevent or discourage the teaching of creativity. The assumptions made by school leadership, teachers, and the general public are what impose constraints on the curriculum. The Common Core State Standards provide the bricks and mortar to reinvent schooling. But just as innovations in electricity and plumping have changed the way we build our homes, these standards demand change in our schools. We cannot continue to teach as we did even ten years ago. If we are to guide the next generation to be innovative, we must be innovative in our approach to instruction. Our school organization, schedules, and even their physical structures will have to adapt. Teachers will have to work hard and have the intellectual courage to apply their own Pro-C creativity, and instructional leaders will have to support and value their efforts.

References

Anderson, L., Krathwohl, D., Airasian, P., Cruikshank, K., Marer, R., Pintrich, J., & Wittrock, M. (2001). *A taxonomy for learning, teaching, and assessing: A revision of Bloom's taxonomy of educational objectives.* Boston: Pearson Education Group.

Azzam, A. (2009). Why creativity now? A conversation with Sir Ken Robinson. *Educational Leadership*, 67(1), 22 - 26.

Beghetto, R. & Kaufman, J. (2013). Fundamentals of creativity. *Educational Leadership*, 70(9), 11-15.

Bellanca, J., Fogarty, R., & Pete, B. (2012). *How to teach thinking skills within the Common Core.* Bloomington, IN: Solution Tree Press.

Blythe, H., & Sweet, C. (2013, Summer). "Without contraries": Casting a critical eye on the Common Core. *Kentucky Journal for Excellence in College Teaching and Learning.* Retrieved from http://kjectl.eku.edu/sites/kjectl.eku.edu/files/files/Journal%2013/BlytheSweet_Summer13.pdf

Claude Monet. (2015, January 5). In *Wikipedia, The Free Encyclopedia.* Retrieved from http://en.wikipedia.org/w/index.php?title=Claude_Monet&oldid=641017717http://en.wikipedia.org/wiki/Claude_Monet

Coleman, D., Pimental, S., & Zimba, J. (2012, August). Three core shifts to deliver on the promise of the Common Core State Standards. *The State Education Standard,* 12(2), 9-12.

Combs, L., Cennamo, K., & Newbill, P. (2009, October). Developing critical and creative thinkers: Toward a conceptual model of creative and critical thinking processes. *Educational Technology,* 3-14.

Coyle, D. (2009). *The talent code: Greatness isn't born. It's grown. Here's how.* New York: Bantam Dell.

Coyle, D. The Talent Code. Retrieved from http://thetalentcode.com/

Csikszentmihalyi, M. (1996). *Creativity: Flow and the psychology of discovery and invention.* New York: Harper Collins Publishers.

Csikszentmihalyi, M. (1999). Implications of a systems approach for the study of creativity. In R. Sternberg (Ed.), *The handbook of creativity* (pp. 313-335). Cambridge, United Kingdom: Cambridge University Press.

Dietrich, A. (2004). The cognitive neuroscience of creativity. *Creativity and Neuroscience,* 11(6), 1011-1026.

Drapeau, P. (2014). *Sparking student creativity: Practical ways to promote innovative thinking and problem solving.* Alexandria, VA: ASCD.

Dweck, C. (2006). *Mindset: The new psychology of success.* New York: Ballantine Books.

Edison, T. (1910). Quote Investigator. Retrieved from http://quoteinvestigator.com/2012/07/31/edison-lot-results/

Editorial Projects in Education Research Center. (2013). *Findings from a national survey of teacher perspectives on the Common Core.* Bethesda, Maryland: Editorial Projects In Education, Inc. Retrieved from http://www.edweek.org/media/epe_survey_teacher_perspctives_common_core_2013.pdf

Freedman, R. (1987). *Lincoln: A photobiography.* New York: Clarion Books.

Gladwell, M. (2008). *Outliers: The story of success.* Boston: Little, Brown & Company.

Greene, D. (2013). How Common Core Standards kill creative teaching. Retrieved from http://www.usnews.com/opinion/articles/2014/03/17/how-common-core-standards-kill-creative-teaching

Jeffrey, L. (2013). *Amazing American inventors of the 20th century.* Berkeley Heights, NJ: Enslow Publishers, Inc.

Johann Sebastian Bach. (2015). In *Wikipedia, The Free Encyclopedia*. Retrieved from http://en.wikipedia.org/wiki/Johann_Sebastian_Bach

Jonides, J. (2010, February). Better cognition through training and interaction with the environment. Presentation made at the Conference on Learning and the Brain: Using Brain Research to Raise IQ & Achievement. San Francisco, CA.

Kentucky Department of Education. Retrieved from www.education.ky.gov

McCulley, E.A., (2006). *Marvelous Mattie: How Margaret E. Knight became an inventor.* Hagerstown, Maryland: Phoenix Color Corporation.

Medina, J. (2008). *Brain rules.* Seattle, WA: Pear Press.

Mindset Works, Inc. (2014). Retrieved from http://www.mindsetworks.com/default.aspx

National Basketball Association. (2014). Michael Jordan bio. NBA Encyclopedia. Retrieved from http://www.nba.com/history/players/jordan_bio.html).

NGA Center for Best Practices, & CCSSO. (2015). Common Core State Standards: About the standards. National Governors Association Center for Best Practices, Council of Chief State School Officers: Washington D.C. Retrieved from http://www.corestandards.org/read-the-standards/

NGA Center for Best Practices, & CCSSO. (2010a). *Common Core State Standards for mathematics.* Washington, DC: Authors. Retrieved from http://www.corestandards.org/Math/Practice/

NGA Center for Best Practices, & CCSSO. (2010b). Common Core State Standards: Read the standards. National Governors Association Center for Best Practices, Council of Chief State School Officers: Washington D.C. Retrieved from http://www.corestandards.org/read-the-standards/

O'Toole, G. (2015). I have gotten a lot of results! I know several thousand things that won't work. Retrieved from http://quoteinvestigator.com/2012/07/31/edison-lot-results/

Rothman, R. (September 12, 2014). Does the Common Core limit teaching? Retrieved from http://blogs.edweek.org/edweek/learning_deeply/2014/09/does_the_common_core_limit_teaching.html

NGSS Lead States. (2013). Next Generation Science Standards: For states, by states. Achieve, Inc. on behalf of the twenty-six states and partners that collaborated on the NGSS. Retrieved from http://www.nextgenscience.org/

Pohlen, J. (2012), *Albert Einstein and relativity for kids: His life and ideas with 21 activities and thought experiments.* Chicago, IL: Chicago Review Press, Inc.

Reimer, W., & Reimer, L. (1994). *Mathematicians are people, too.* Upper Saddle River NJ: Dale Seymour Publications.

Robinson, K. (2001). *Out of our minds: Learning to be creative.* Oxford, England: Capstone Publishing Limited.

Root-Berstein, R., & Root-Berstein, M. (2013). The art and craft of science. *Educational Leadership 70*(5), 16-21.

Rutledge, A. (2008). On creativity. Retrieved from http://alistapart.com/article/oncreativity

Scholastic, Inc. (2014). Primary sources update: Teachers' views on Common Core State Standards. Retrieved from http://www.scholastic.com/primarysources/PrimarySources-2014update.pdf

Starko, A. (2013). Creativity on the brink. *Education Leadership, 70*(5), 54-56.

Starko, A. (2014). Creativity and the Common Core (Blog post). Retrieved from http://creativiteach.me/creativity-and-the-curriculum/creativity-and-the-common-core/

Sternberg, R. (2006). Creating a vision of creativity: The first 25 years. *Psychology of Aesthetics Creativity and the Arts, Special Vol.* (1), 2-12.

Sternberg, R., Grigorenko, E., & Singer, J. (2004). *Creativity: From potential to realization.* Washington, DC: American Psychological Association.

Sternberg, R. J., & Lubart, T. I. (1999). The concept of creativity: Prospects and paradigms. In R. J. Sternberg (Ed.), *Handbook of creativity* (pp. 3-15). Cambridge: Cambridge University Press.

The Washington Post. (2012). Tea party groups mobilizing against Common Core education overhaul. Retrieved from http://articles.washingtonpost.com/2013-05-30/politics/39627200_1_tea-party-groups-common-core-state-standards-governors/2

Endnotes

[1] Copyright © 2010 National Governors Association Center for Best Practices and Council of Chief State School Officers. All rights reserved

Chapter 11

What's Next? The Promise for Our Children's Future

Terry Holliday

The Common Core Standards initiative arrived on the scene in 2009. Education standards were not a new topic. Standards had been in place in every state since the No Child Left Behind act of 2001 (NCLB). However, there was a new reality in the nation. Education's mission was now changing. Over time, it shifted from compulsory attendance to an expectation of high school graduation for all children. With the changing economy and new focus on global competitiveness by the mid-2000s, the education mission had once again changed to an expectation that all students reach not only high school graduation, but also reach college and career readiness.

When states started to look at measures tied to college and career readiness (i.e. ACT/SAT scores, NAEP 12th grade preparedness, percentage of students taking remedial courses, number of high school graduates not able to meet standards for the military, and surveys from business community), the gap between the new mission and current reality proved significant. It was apparent that only about 30-40% of high school graduates were ready for the next step of college and/or career.

With this new reality, state education chiefs met in November 2007, to discuss the opportunity to establish a single set of world-class standards for public schools that were benchmarked to college and career readiness. In 2008, a report entitled *Benchmarking for Success: Ensuring U.S. Students Receive a World-Class Education* (National Governor's Association, Council of State School Officers, & Achieve, Inc., 2008) was released by Achieve, Inc. In April 2009, NGA and CCSSO convened Governors and chief state school officers to discuss creation of the Common Core State Standards Initiative (CCSS). States were asked to commit to the process, and 49 states and territories agreed to participate in a state-led effort to develop common standards. Throughout the ensuing months, states convened practitioner committees to provide feedback to a national steering committee that was organizing the final product. In June 2010, the CCSS were presented to states for adoption. Eventually, over forty states adopted the CCSS, and the remaining states revised their state standards to ensure high school graduates would achieve college and career readiness. The promise for our children's future was now in place. The theory of action was that states would adopt more rigorous standards, implement and assess the standards, build accountability systems for districts, schools, and educators based on the standards and in so doing, more students would graduate from high school ready for college and careers. Our national and state economies would be stronger since we would now have a more qualified workforce and individual students would have a brighter future. Our graduates would be able to compete in the global economy since the standards were benchmarked against other nations. What is the current state of that "promise"? What happened and why did it happen? What is the future of that "promise"?

Standards on Trial in the Court of Public Opinion

August 2014 will be documented as a "bad month" for the Common Core State Standards (CCSS) initiative. Abraham Lincoln once said, "Public opinion in this country is everything" (Basler, 1953). And whether you subscribe to that notion or not, the August 2014 release of two national polls on the CCSS would seem, at least on the surface, to be a blow to standards supporters.

The first results came from the *Education Next* (EdNext) poll (2014), a poll taken annually for about 14 years. The results (see Table 11.1) show a decline in support for the Common Core State Standards across all political groups, but more so among the general public, Republicans and teachers.

Table 11.1. Education Next Poll of Support for Common Core State Standards

Percent of "yes" respondents to the questions, "Do you support the use of Common Core State Standards in your state?"		
	2013	2014
Public	65%	53%
Republicans	57%	43%
Democrats	64%	63%
Teachers	76%	46%
Table 11.1 The Education Next Poll of Support for Common Core Standards indicates a general decline in public support from 2013 to 2104, even though some groups support the standards more than other groups.		

In another poll released the same month, we saw similar results. The PDK/Gallup poll (Phi Delta Kappa, 2014), which has been around for more than fifty years and is one of the most highly respected of the polls, indicated 60% of respondents oppose using CCSS in their local schools to guide what teachers teach. Eighteen percent of respondents said the standards were too challenging; 40% said the standards were not challenging enough; and 36% said the standards were just right.

Both polls showed erosion in support for the CCSS from the previous year. In 2012, hardly anyone in the general public had even heard of the CCSS. Why such a steep drop in such a short time, and why such a particularly steep drop in teacher support? What started as a state led initiative to ensure a brighter future for our children now appeared to be losing support.

Historical Perspective on Standards

In order to understand what has happened to public opinion regarding the CCSS initiative, we have to go back a short time in history. Most historians would document the current education reform era as having its beginning with the *Nation at Risk* report in 1983 (United States Commission on Excellence in Education, 1983). Since then, we have seen the following education reform initiatives: Goals 2000: Educate America Act (1994), voluntary national standards and assessments, No Child Left Behind (2001), CCSS, Race to the Top and No Child Left Behind waivers. What happened to previous education reform initiatives centered on standards, and what is the future of the current initiatives?

While the *Nation at Risk* report was issued under the Reagan administration, then Vice-president George H.W. Bush certainly continued to push for education reform when he became president in 1989. President Bush convened governors in September of that year in Charlottesville, Virginia, to focus on education. In his welcoming remarks (Bush, G. H., 1989) President Bush made it clear that the federal government was to play a supporting role and help coordinate efforts of states to reform education. While the summit was intended to be a sharing of best practices, oddly there were no educators present. President Bush indicated that the federal government was going to help states find answers; however, the President stated the best solutions would be found at the state and local levels. The education summit was the first meeting of the President and ,overnors to specifically discuss education since the Great Depression. The summit resulted in national goals for education that President Bush shared with the nation in his 1990 State of the Union address (1990). There were six goals:

1. All children in America will start school ready to learn.
2. The high school graduation rate will increase to at least 90 percent.
3. American students will leave grades four, eight, and twelve having demonstrated competency in challenging subject matter including English, mathematics, science, history, and geography; and every school in America will ensure that all students learn to use their minds well, so they may be prepared for responsible citizenship, further learning, and productive employment in our modern economy.
4. U.S. students will be first in the world in science and mathematics achievement.
5. Every adult American will be literate and possess the knowledge and skills necessary to compete in a global economy and exercise the rights and responsibilities of citizenship.
6. Every school in America will be free of drugs and violence and will offer a safe, disciplined environment conducive to learning.

Congress implemented the goals through The Goals 2000: Educate America Act (P.L. 103-227, 1994) which was signed into law in March 1994 by President Bill Clinton (a participating governor at the 1989 summit). The Act provided resources to states and communities to ensure that all students reach their full potential. The national goals era came to an end just seven years later when Congress passed the No Child Left Behind act in January, 2001, and eliminated all funding for Goals 2000 in December of that year.

The NCLB Act continued the focus on goals with a 13 year goal for the nation's schools that every child would reach proficiency in language arts and math by 2014. The act focused on standards. Every state was required to adopt standards in language arts, math, and science. The act continued a focus on assessments; however, states were required to adopt standards in math and language arts and move from voluntary assessments to assessments of language arts and math in grades 3-8 and once in high school. Additionally, states were required to assess science once in elementary, middle and high school. Accountability for performance reached new heights with the implementation of adequate yearly progress (a new measure to ensure progress of student subgroups in the percentage meeting proficiency in language arts and math). The formula required states to set annual targets toward the goal of 100% proficient by each subgroup of the student population. Finally, the act put in place a number of sanctions for schools not making adequate yearly progress. Sanctions included labels for schools not making adequate yearly progress, school choice, transportation to school of choice, professional development for educators, and supplemental education service providers. Schools and districts were required to set aside funding for transportation, professional development, and supplemental education services.

The original NCLB act was due for reauthorization in 2007. As a new administration came into office in 2008, educators and the public had become disillusioned with the promise of NCLB. There was a major push for reauthorization, and there was a growing concern that standards needed to be more rigorous so that American high school graduates would be more competitive in a global environment.

The push for reauthorization was set aside as the nation endured the worst economic recession since the Great Depression.

Through the federal stimulus appropriations, the Secretary of Education, Arne Duncan, was granted the most discretionary funding appropriation in the history of federal education funding. The following comes from an executive summary describing the Race to the Top (RTT) program that was provided to states and the public in November 2009 (U.S. Department of Education):

> On February 17, 2009, President Obama signed into law the American Recovery and Reinvestment Act of 2009 (ARRA), historic legislation designed to stimulate the economy, support job creation, and invest in critical sectors, including education. The ARRA lays the foundation for education reform by supporting investments in innovative strategies that are most likely to lead to improved results for students, long-term gains in school and school system capacity, and increased productivity and effectiveness.

The ARRA provides $4.35 billion for the Race to the Top Fund, a competitive grant program designed to encourage and reward states that are creating the conditions for education innovation and reform; achieving significant improvement in student outcomes, including making substantial gains in student achievement, closing achievement gaps, improving high school graduation rates, ensuring student preparation for success in college and careers, and implementing ambitious plans in four core education reform areas:

- adopting standards and assessments that prepare students to succeed in college and the workplace and to compete in the global economy;
- building data systems that measure student growth and success and that inform teachers and principals about how they can improve instruction;
- recruiting, developing, rewarding, and retaining effective teachers and principals, especially where they are needed most; and,
- turning around our lowest-achieving schools.

Race to the Top will reward states that have demonstrated success in raising student achievement and have the best plans to accelerate their reforms in the future. These states will offer models for others to follow and will spread the best reform ideas across their states, and across the country.

The first round of awards saw only two states qualify for funding – Delaware and Tennessee. Eventually, eighteen states would receive some level of funding from RTT.

With the looming deadline of 2014 approaching for all students to reach proficiency in language arts and math, educators and the public were becoming more critical of NCLB. Given that Congress had not been able to reach accord on reauthorization of NCLB, President Obama issued an executive order in September 2011, and Secretary Duncan invited states to apply for a NCLB waiver. NCLB waivers required states to develop plans in three areas:
- transitioning to college- and career-ready standards and assessments;
- developing systems of differentiated recognition, accountability, and support; and,
- evaluating teacher and principal effectiveness and supporting improvement.

On February 9, 2012, in a White House ceremony, President Obama and Secretary Duncan announced the first 10 states to gain a NCLB waiver. The ten states approved for flexibility were Colorado, Florida, Georgia, Indiana, Kentucky, Massachusetts, Minnesota, New Jersey, Oklahoma, and Tennessee.

What Went Wrong? Lessons Learned

The foundation for Goals 2000, NCLB, CCSS, Race to the Top, and No Child Left Behind was the same: if we set higher expectations for all students through rigorous standards, assess the students against the standards, build accountability systems based on the standards, recruit, retain, and train highly qualified educators to implement the standards, then we will reach the lofty goals and aspirations we set for students. Students who reach these higher expectations will have a brighter future and our local, state, and national economies will improve. If you look at any measure against international competition you will see that America has made some progress; however, many nations are now surpassing the U.S. in high school graduation, college completion, math, language arts, and science performance. Let's take a brief look at each of the reform efforts and the lessons learned that can help better plan for our children's future.

Goals 2000 was built on six lofty aspirational goals. While the

U.S. high school graduation rate has slightly improved, we are far from reaching 90% graduation rate in most states. While kindergarten readiness has been a focus of many states, it would be fairly accurate to say that fewer than 70% of kindergarten students are prepared cognitively, socially, emotionally, or physically to enter kindergarten. With regard for the academic goals of being first in the world, we currently have a lower ranking in many international assessments than we did in 1990. Also, by many measures, our schools are no safer today than they were in 1990. The lessons learned from Goals 2000 are as follows:

- Aspirational goals without implementation plans are a dream that will not be realized.
- Educator involvement in setting goals and planning implementation of activities to reach goals is critical.
- Federal involvement in education at any level creates polarization of opinions among states, the public, and with educators charged to reach goals.

NCLB was also built on a lofty aspirational goal. Every child was to reach proficiency in language arts and math by 2014. Of course, by 2011, it became apparent that this goal would never be reached. Many educators and the public were very concerned that their local schools were being labeled as failures by a federal law even though the schools were making significant progress. The NCLB Act lost credibility with the general public. NCLB allowed states to set their own standards and develop their own assessments. As results started to come in from the National Assessment of Education Progress (NAEP), it became apparent that many states had set very low standards and their state assessments were not very rigorous. It was not unusual for a state to report 90% proficiency on the state assessment, while NAEP results would show less than 30% of students scoring proficient. The lessons learned from NCLB are similar to lessons learned from Goals 2000:

- Allowing states to set standards and assessments while being held to an unreachable goal leads to a "race to the bottom" where states try to avoid failure and public transparency as long as possible.
- Aspirational goals without implementation plans are a dream that will not be realized.

- Educator involvement in setting goals and planning implementation of activities to reach goals is critical.
- Federal involvement in education at any level creates polarization of opinions among states, the public, and with educators charged to reach goals.

The CCSS initiative was built on a voluntary state led effort to identify those standards that all students should reach in order to achieve college and career readiness upon graduation from high school. However, the work became entangled with the well-intentioned efforts of the Race to the Top competition and No Child Left Behind waivers promoted by Secretary Duncan. The term "Common Core" has become a polarizing and politicized term in the nation. Most education writers have documented three issues that have led to major pushback for the CCSS:

1. There has been a significant increase in media reporting about CCSS. Depending on the media source, the public has been confronted with a barrage of information, some factual, some not, and it has led to a polarization of opinions regarding the Common Core State Standards.
2. With the pressure and rush to implement NCLB waiver requirements for standards, assessments and teacher evaluations, the general public and especially teachers have connected CCSS with federal overreach.
3. With the rush to implement NCLB waiver requirements in some states, teachers feel they have not been provided adequate support in training or resources to implement the standards. With the rush to assess the standards and utilize the results from testing in waiver-required teacher evaluation systems, again, teachers feel they are being held accountable for implementing new standards and assessments without adequate support and time to gain needed knowledge and expertise.

Lessons Learned from Common Core Implementation

At a November 2013 meeting of the CCSSO, former Governor Mike Huckabee suggested that the term "Common Core" needed to be changed (Layton, January, 2014). He predicted a huge pushback on the CCSS. Gov. Huckabee fully supported the standards and said the reasoning behind development of the standards was very sound. But, due to the political forces mobilizing against anything that remotely connected to the Obama administration, he recommended that CCSSO and NGA change the name of the Common Core. Gov. Huckabee's prediction has come to fruition. As mentioned earlier in this chapter, the political push back on the term "Common Core" grew into opposition to the Common Core standards themselves as reported in the recent PDK/Gallup Poll and the EdNext poll (Education Next, 2014). The NGA has pulled away from publicly discussing the Common Core due to the challenges of the current NGA president, Gov. Mary Fallin, in her home state of Oklahoma (CBS News, June 6, 2014).

Over the past year we have seen legislative involvement in either supporting the Common Core or trying to remove the Common Core. Nowhere is the debate more heated than in Louisiana. State school chief John White and the state board of education have been sued by Governor Jindal. The state board has joined with parents and other groups to sue Governor Jindal. Governor Jindal has indicated an interest in suing the federal government. At the core of the debate is what Governor Jindal sees as federal overreach in not only implementation of state education standards but also in the assessment of state standards. Recently, similar lawsuits were filed in Missouri.

Other states have seen similar debates. Indiana recently became the first state to drop the Common Core; however, their state standards being used to replace the Common Core are very similar. Florida has gone through a review process and implemented changes to the Common Core by adding or clarifying math standards for courses such as Algebra II, pre-calculus, and calculus. To date, Oklahoma has been the only state to abandon CCSS and replace the standards with their previous state standards. As a result, Oklahoma lost their NCLB waiver since they were unable to meet the condition that the state adopt college and career ready standards. Kentucky, the first state to adopt the CCSS, recently announced the Kentucky Core Academic Standards Challenge. The Challenge asks the public and educators to review the current state standards (based on the CCSS) and provide feedback on possible edits or changes to the standards (Kentucky Department of Education,

2014). From Michigan to Mississippi, from Georgia to New York, the debate around Common Core has been growing and more states are now looking to edit or replace the standards. There is a growing sense that lawsuits such as the one filed by Gov. Jindal in Louisiana will proliferate as the debate intensifies. The lawsuits will challenge the constitutionality of the RTT grants and the conditional nature of the NCLB waivers. Most experts and even the Congressional Research Office predict (Dilger & Boyd, 2014) that challenges to the RTT grant process will not be successful since the grant process was voluntary; however, many are predicting the lawsuits challenging the NCLB waiver process will be successful. Their reasoning is that the conditional nature of the waivers based on the requirements - standards, assessments, teacher/leader evaluations, and turning around low performing schools - runs counter to the original NCLB waiver language which was intended to be state led requests for waivers that would improve teaching and learning. Also, many experts believe the conditional natures of the NCLB waivers exceeds the intent of the original NCLB legislation in that college and career ready standards and teacher/leader evaluations were not a part of the original legislation (Erpenbach, 2014).

One of the key reasons the debate around Common Core has been growing has to do with assessments. In the RTT competition, Secretary Duncan awarded over $360 million to two assessment consortia, Partnership for Assessment of Readiness for College and Careers (PARCC) and the Smarter Balanced Assessment Consortia (SBAC), to develop high quality assessments tied to the common core standards. What started as an initiative with the involvement of over 35 states has now dwindled significantly. One example is Tennessee. Tennessee was one of the first two states to receive a RTT grant. Tennessee committed to implementing the Common Core standards and the assessments being developed by the PARCC. During the last legislative session, the Tennessee legislature withdrew support of the PARCC assessment and required the Tennessee Department of Education to implement a procurement process to develop and administer a state developed assessment. Tennessee is not alone in this issue. North Carolina, Kansas, Georgia, and a number of other states have withdrawn from the testing consortia and are currently developing state tests.

Additionally, there are two issues driving teacher pushback on

Common Core. Teachers in many states are very concerned about the rushed implementation of the Common Core standards and have made it clear that their needs have not been met. Teachers need time to learn about the standards. They need time to improve their content knowledge and pedagogy in order to implement the standards. They need access to professional development tied to the standards. They need resources and materials to support implementation of the standards. Teachers connect poor implementation to the accelerated timelines included in the RTT competition and the NCLB waivers. Perhaps the final straw for teachers and their unions was the linking of test scores to teacher evaluations. Teachers are very clear that they want to be held accountable for helping students grow each year; however, many teachers feel the current use of test scores in evaluation using methods such as value-add is not an appropriate approach. Teachers and their unions cite the weak research base supporting value-add and the weak correlations between effective teaching and value-add in some of the states using this model (Walker, 2014).

As we reflect back on the past 25 years of education reform efforts, we see much progress but we also see the same mistakes being made. Setting goals without implementation plans leads to frustration at the classroom level and will eventually derail any reform efforts. Any hint of federal involvement or oversight into education reform creates a polarization in communities. Lack of educator involvement at the beginning of any reform effort will lead to failure of the reform.

Where Will We Be in 3-5 Years? What is the Future of the Promise?

If the Common Core standards were the foundation to the future of our children, where will the standards be in five years? What will happen to our children's future? What will happen to state and national economies? While the present picture I have painted does appear to be bleak, the lessons we have learned from the first education summit in 1989 through the current implementation of Common Core Standards can help states lead the work toward college and career readiness for all students.

In my forty-three years of education, I have never seen a vision catch the imagination of educators, students, parents, and business leaders as well as the vision of college and career readiness for all students. In particular, the collaboration between Kentucky's K-12 and higher education systems regarding the implementation of standards and expectations for college and career readiness is unprecedented. When we began the work in 2009, only 30% of Kentucky high school graduates were prepared for college and career. The most recent 2014 results show we now have 62% of graduates ready for college and career (Kentucky Department of Education School Report Card, 2014). An additional 15,000 high school graduates are able to enter college and career programs without taking remediation courses. The savings to parents and students is estimated at $15,000,000 and the likelihood of graduates being successful in postsecondary or career training is greatly increased. The success in Kentucky is evidence that when higher education, business community, legislators, the governor, and K-12 collaborate, then progress in improving student outcomes can happen.

It is time for some predictions. I believe we will see the term "Common Core" dropped from the lexicon of states. Instead, we will see a focus on state standards benchmarked against other states and countries we are competing against. There will be a national database to allow the public to compare standards from their state against standards from other states and countries. We will see the National Assessment of Education Progress continue to be the "gold standard" assessment against which all state assessments are measured. The NAEP assessments will continue to report on percentage of students reaching proficiency, and the percentage for each state will be compared against results from state assessments. How closely the NAEP and state results match will be a good indicator of whether or not states are using rigorous assessments tied to college and career readiness. We will see further development and reporting, with state by state comparisons, on the percentage of students who graduate with college and career readiness. We will see a common definition of college remediation and state by state reporting and comparisons of remediation rates. We will see a blending of college and career readiness through more emphasis on career pathways and more opportunities for work-based learning. Finally, we will see significant changes in assessments. While we will continue to see summative assessments in language arts, math, and science, we will see a move toward grade span testing rather than testing every year. Funds saved by implementing grade span testing will be used to push formative assessment or classroom based assessment that provides more immediate feedback to improve the teaching and learning process. If we are to see the college and career ready "promise" to our children flourish, it will be critical that higher education and business leaders become more vocal and active. When parents and local communities see and hear higher education and business communities support college and career readiness, public support for the efforts will increase.

Our children's future is closely tied to the economic future of our communities and our nation. It is my dream that our nation has truly learned from the mistakes and successes of the past 25 years, and that we will look to expand our horizons to other countries that have passed us in educational attainment. The theory of action that includes standards, assessments, accountability, and educator evaluation has some promise for the future. However, this theory of action alone will not get our nation to where we need to be. As we look at other nations whose education systems are more highly effective than our own, we certainly see national standards and assessments. However, we also see tremendous efforts to professionalize the teaching vocation and provide teachers with salaries and esteem similar to other professions. We also see a major emphasis on students taking responsibility for their learning and parents engaging with educators to support teaching and learning. America has always looked for the silver bullet and the cheap and easy fix. What we have learned from our past 25 years and in looking at other nations is that there is no silver bullet. Education reform is, by its very nature, a messy and complex effort. As we work together, we must stay focused on our children's future rather than on the mistakes of our past. To paraphrase John Dewey – "if we teach the children of today as we did the children of yesterday, then we will rob our children of tomorrow."

References

Basler, R.P. (Ed.). (1952). Speech at Columbus, Ohio, September 16, 1859. *The Collected Works of Abraham Lincoln* (Vol. 3), 400-425. Retrieved from http://www.mrlincolnandfreedom.org/inside.asp?ID=82&subjectID=2

Bush, G.H. (1989). Speech to the Governor's National Education Summit. Charlottesville, VA. Retrieved from http://www.archives.nysed.gov/edpolicy/research/res_essay_bush_ghw_edsummit.shtml

Bush, G.H. (1990). State of the Union Address. Washington, D.C. Retrieved from http://millercenter.org/president/bush/speeches/speech-3423

CBS News. (June 6, 2014). Common Core Standards repealed in Oklahoma. Retrieved from http://www.cbsnews.com/news/common-core-repeal-in-oklahoma-signed-by-governor-mary-fallin/

Dilger, J., & Boyd, E. (July 15, 2014). Block grants: Perspectives and controversies. Congressional Research Service. Retrieved from http://fas.org/sgp/crs/misc/R40486.pdf

Education Next. (2014). No common opinion on the Common Core. Retrieved from http://educationnext.org/2014-ednext-poll-no-common-opinion-on-the-common-core/

Erpenbach, W. (2014). A study of states' requests for waivers from the requirements of the No Child Left Behind Act of 2001: New developments in 2013-2014. Council of Chief State School Officers. Retrieved from http://www.ccsso.org/Documents/2014/ASR_SCASS_ESEA%20Flex%20Addendum.pdf

Goals 2000: Educate America Act of 1994. Pub. L. 103-227. H.R. 1804. (1994). Retrieved from https://www.govtrack.us/congress/bills/103/hr1804

Kentucky Department of Education. (2014). Kentucky Core Academic Standards challenge. Retrieved from http://www.education.ky.gov

Kentucky Department of Education. (2014). State School Report Card College and Career Readiness. Retrieved from http://applications.education.ky.gov/SRC/DeliveryTargetByState.aspx

Layton, L. (January 30, 2014). Some states rebrand Common Core education standards. *The Washington Post.* Retrieved from http://www.washingtonpost.com/local/education/some-states-rebrand-controversial-common-core-education-standards/2014/01/30/a235843e-7ef7-11e3-9556-4a4bf7bcbd84_story.html?hpid=z2

National Governor's Association, Council for Chief State School Officers, & Achieve, Inc. (2008). Benchmarking for Success: Ensuring U.S. Students Receive a World-Class Education. National Governor's Association: Washington, D.C. Retrieved from http://www.achieve.org/BenchmarkingforSuccess

No Child Left Behind Act of 2001, P.L. 107-110, 20 U.S.C. § 6319 (2002).

Phi Delta Kappa. (2014). 46th annual PDK/Gallup poll of the public's attitudes toward the public schools. Retrieved from http://pdkintl.org/programs-resources/poll/

United States. National Commission on Excellence in Education. (1983). *A nation at risk: The imperative for educational reform: A report to the nation and the Secretary of Education, United States Department of Education.* Washington, D.C.: The Commission.

United States Department of Education. (2009). *Race to the top: Executive summary.* Retrieved from https://www2.ed.gov/programs/racetothetop/executive-summary.pdf

Walker, T. (May 30, 2014). New student strikes blow against value-added teacher evaluation. NEAToday. Retrieved from http://neatoday.org/2014/05/30/new-study-strikes-latest-blow-against-value-added-teacher-evaluation/

About the Authors

Dr. **Krista Althauser** is an associate professor in the College of Education at Eastern Kentucky University where she teaches undergraduate and graduate courses in elementary math instruction and teacher leadership. She received her bachelor's, master's, educational specialist, and doctorate degrees from Eastern Kentucky University. She has 20 years experience working in the elementary school setting as a classroom teacher, elementary curriculum specialist, and gifted and talented program coordinator. She has provided professional development and workshops as well as presentations at international, national, and state conferences on math instruction, instructional practices for struggling learners, curriculum design, formative assessment strategies, and standards based learning. She resides in Richmond, Kentucky, with her husband, Scott, and children, Meghan and Bradley.

Dr. **Dorie Combs** is a Professor in the Department of Curriculum and Instruction at Eastern Kentucky University and teaches undergraduate and graduate courses in curriculum planning and reading / language arts. She earned Bachelor's and Master's Degrees in Secondary English Education from the University of South Carolina and a Ph.D. in Educational Psychology from the University of Kentucky. Dorie has 15 years of teaching experience at the middle school level in Columbia, SC and Lexington, KY. She served on the Kentucky Board of Education for 8 years and participated in several national study groups related to school reform and college / career readiness. Dorie has recently collaborated on several publications and presentations related to implementation of the Common Core Standards.

Dr. **J. Cody Davidson** has been an educational administrator in college admissions, financial aid, and adult basic/secondary education, a research and policy analyst and a postsecondary instructor for two- and four-year institutions. He has presented at nationally recognized conferences such as the Association for Institutional Research (AIR) and the Association for the Study of Higher Education (ASHE) and serves on the Editorial Board of the *Journal of Student Financial Aid* and *College Student Affairs Journal*. He has published in *Higher Education Policy, Journal of College Student Retention: Research, Theory, and Practice, Community College Journal of Research and Practice, Journal of Student Financial Aid, Journal of Continuing Higher Education* and the *Kentucky Journal of Higher Education Policy and Practice*. Cody is married to Carrie Davidson and they have two daughters, Evangeline and Noelle.

Dr. **Martha M. Day** is Associate Professor of Science Education at Western Kentucky University. She serves as executive director of GSKyTeach and co-director of SKyTeach, programs that are part of a national initiative led by the National Mathematics and Science Initiative to improve teacher quality in the STEM disciplines. Dr. Day is President Elect of the UTeach STEM Educator's Association, a national organization committed to developing STEM literacy for all students through innovation and excellence in university-based teacher education. Dr. Day is a frequent presenter at national conferences on topics related to inquiry-based instruction, project based learning, increasing cognitive complexity in assessments, and content area literacy. She also trains school leaders and teachers in mentoring and coaching beginning teachers. Dr. Day has 15 years of K-12 teaching and administrative experience in urban school settings. Her current research and writing focuses on 5E inquiry science activities for the science classroom.

Dr. **Richard E. Day** is an Associate Professor of Educational Foundations at Eastern Kentucky University. He joined the Curriculum & Instruction faculty in 2007 as a visiting lecturer following a 31-year career in Kentucky public schools. He has published in the *Register of the Kentucky Historical Society*, the *American Educational History Journal*, and the *Journal of Negro Education*. Along with Dr. Jo Ann Ewalt, Dr. Day contributed a chapter titled, "Education Reform in Kentucky: Just What the Court Ordered," to *Kentucky: Government, Politics, and Public Policy* which received the Thomas D. Clark Medallion. His 2003 Dissertation, "Each Child, Every Child: The Story of the Council for Better Education, Equity, and Adequacy in Kentucky Schools" received the "Dissertation of the Year" award from the Education Law Association.

Dr. **Sam Evans** is Dean, College of Education and Behavioral Sciences at Western Kentucky University. He has been actively involved in educator preparation at the state and national level and he is currently serving on the Board of Directors of the Green River Regional Educational Cooperative and the Susan Vitale Clinical Education Complex, a member of the WKU Campus Child Care Governing Body Committee, the Board of Governors of The Renaissance Group, and is a regional representative on the Teacher Education Council for State Colleges and Universities Executive Committee. His scholarly interests relate to affective characteristics of effective teachers, documenting teacher candidate impact on P-12 student performance, and the transformation of educator preparation. He has served as the author and co-author of numerous publications including manuscripts in the following journals: *Theory and Research in Social Studies, The Social Studies, The International Journal of Social Education, Teacher Education and Practice, Southern Social Studies Journal,* and *Action in Teacher Education.*

Dr. **Ginni Fair** earned her Ed.D. in Curriculum and Supervision from the University of Kentucky and is an Associate Professor in Curriculum and Instruction at Eastern Kentucky University. She primarily teaches methods and literacy development courses. She previously spent 10 years in the middle school language arts classroom, concluding her tenure in the P-12 realm by being recognized as a Foundation Teacher at Model Lab School. Dr. Fair was a university partner who assisted in training Kentucky teachers through Kentucky Leadership Networks during the roll-out phase of the Common Core standards in the state. She was also one of the coordinators for EKU's campus initiative to integrate the Common Core standards across general education and teacher preparation courses and has presented on the topic locally, regionally, and nationally. At one point, an audience member said at the conclusion of a session, "You really should write a book! So many others could benefit from the process you've used and the lessons you've learned." So that's exactly what she and Dr. Combs have done! Dr.

Fair has also collaborated multiple times with her husband, a middle school science teacher, publishing and presenting on issues related to content area literacy. She and her husband, Jason; four children, Chase, Kalli, Kenedee, and Jenna; and two dogs, Moses and Rizzoli, reside in Richmond, Kentucky.

Shannon W. Gilkey has worked in education as a high school teacher, university administrator, and as a state postsecondary policy staff. Shannon has presented nationally on issues surrounding P-20 alignment, teacher preparation, and developmental and remedial education reform. Shannon is married to Dr. Meghan Riddle and they have one son, Jack.

Saundra Hamon is the Assistant Director of Program Standards in the Office of Next Generation Learners at the Kentucky Department of Education in Frankfort, Kentucky. She received her master's degree in Supervision: Curriculum and Instruction from Marshall University and has done post-secondary work at the University of Kentucky. After teaching thirteen years in West Virginia, she and her family moved to Lexington, KY where she taught elementary students and served as a Professional Staff Assistant to administrators in Lexington's public school system before accepting a position as an Elementary Writing Consultant at KDE in 1999 and later serving as manager for Early Literacy. She currently resides in Winchester, KY with her husband, Richard, their dog Brody and their many fruit trees.

Terry Holliday, Ph.D., was selected as Kentucky's fifth commissioner of education in July 2009. Holliday served as superintendent of the more than 20,000-student Iredell-Statesville school district from 2002 until 2009. Under his leadership, the Iredell-Statesville school district received the 2008 Malcolm Baldrige National Quality Award. Dr. Holliday is currently serving on the National Assessment Governing Board (NAGB), and on the Malcom Baldrige Board of Overseers. He has served on the board of directors of the Council of Chief State School Officers (CCSSO) since December 2010, and as board president in 2014. Holliday is the co-author of Running All the Red Lights: A Journey of System-Wide Educational Reform. He earned a bachelor's degree from Furman University; a master's degree and education specialist degree from Winthrop University; and a doctorate from the University of South Carolina.

Gill Hunter is an Associate Professor in the Department of English and Theatre at Eastern Kentucky University. He is co-Director of the EKU Writing Project and teaches and researches in English Teaching pedagogy and Irish literature. He lives in Berea, Kentucky with his wife, a middle school principal, and their two girls and two dogs.

Karen Kidwell is the Director of the Division of Program Standards in the Office of Next Generation Learners at the Kentucky Department of Education. The Division of Program Standards houses 3 branches: School Readiness, Academic Core, and Coordinated School Health. Karen is also Project Manager for Kentucky's system of Leadership Networks, a comprehensive professional learning system designed to build district capacity around the implementation of academic standards (specifically, the Common Core Standards in ELA and Mathematics and the Next Generation Science Standards) within the context of highly effective teaching, learning, and assessment practices in response to Kentucky's college and career readiness agenda-*Unbridled Learning*. The Leadership Network approach has been recognized nationally as a model for how state education agencies can support standards implementation through effective professional learning. Karen earned her BS in Elementary Education and Mathematics from the University of Louisville (1986) and her MA in Education from Georgetown College (1993). Between 2006 and 2008 she completed *The Executive Leadership Program for Educators* at Harvard University as a member of the Kentucky Department of Education team.

Rico Tyler is a Master Teacher with the SkyTeach program at Western Kentucky University and is a faculty member with the WKU School of Teacher Education and Department of Physics and Astronomy. Before coming to WKU in 2001 he spent 19 years as a high school physics, astronomy and history teacher. During this time he received the Presidential Award for excellence in Science Teaching. He is also has 33 years of experience teaching with the Kentucky Governor's Scholars Program. Mr. Tyler is a well-known presenter on topics related to science instructional design. His recent international experience includes working with teachers and instructional specialists from Italy and Saudi Arabia. For the past several years his creative and outreach interests have focused on the Next Generation Science Standards. Mr. Tyler was a partner with the University of Kentucky Partnership Institute for Math and Science Reform's Science leadership Support Network. Currently he is heavily involved with the Kentucky Department of Education Science Teacher leadership Network. He also advises several school districts on implementing the Next Generation Science Standards.

www.ingramcontent.com/pod-product-compliance
Lightning Source LLC
Chambersburg PA
CBHW071432150426
43191CB00008B/1106